$ 19.95

• THE •
JUNIOR VISUAL
DICTIONARY

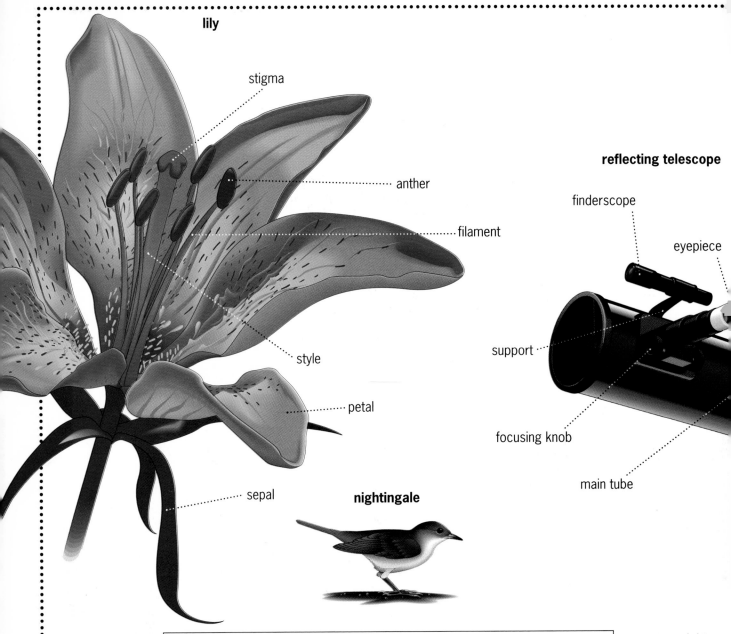

lily

stigma

anther

filament

style

petal

sepal

reflecting telescope

finderscope

eyepiece

support

focusing knob

main tube

nightingale

counterweight

Canadian Cataloguing in Publication Data

Corbeil, Jean-Claude

The junior visual dictionary

Includes index,

ISBN: 2-89037-759-8

1. Picture dictionaries, English - Juvenile literature.
2. English language - Dictionaries - Juvenile literature.
I. Archambault, Ariane. II. Title.

PE1629.C67 1994   j423' .1   C94-940907-3

Created and produced by Québec/Amérique International
a division of Éditions Québec/Amérique Inc.
425, rue St-Jean-Baptiste, Montréal, Québec, Canada, H2Y 2Z7.
Tel. : 514-393-1450 Fax : 514-866-2430

Printed and bound in Canada.

JEAN-CLAUDE CORBEIL • ARIANE ARCHAMBAULT

THE JUNIOR VISUAL DICTIONARY

Authors
Jean-Claude Corbeil
Ariane Archambault

Director of Computer Graphics
François Fortin

Art Directors
Jean-Louis Martin
François Fortin

Graphic Designer
Anne Tremblay

Computer Graphics Designers
Marc Lalumière
Jean-Yves Ahern
Rielle Lévesque
Anne Tremblay

Jacques Perrault
Jocelyn Gardner
Christiane Beauregard
Michel Blais
Stéphane Roy
Alice Comtois
Benoît Bourdeau

Computer Programming
Yves Ferland

Data Capture
Serge D'Amico

Page Make-up
Lucie Mc Brearty
Pascal Goyette

Technical Support
Gilles Archambault

Production
Tony O'Riley

ÉDITIONS QUÉBEC/AMÉRIQUE

SKY

EARTH

4

VEGETABLE KINGDOM

FRUITS AND VEGETABLES

GARDENING

ANIMAL KINGDOM

HUMAN BODY

ARCHITECTURE

HOUSE

DO-IT-YOURSELF

CLOTHING

PERSONAL ARTICLES

COMMUNICATIONS

ROAD TRANSPORT

RAIL TRANSPORT

MARITIME TRANSPORT

AIR TRANSPORT

SPACE TRANSPORT

SCHOOL

MUSIC

TEAM GAMES

WATER SPORTS

WINTER SPORTS

ATHLETICS

CAMPING

INDOOR GAMES

MEASURING DEVICES

5

ENERGY

HEAVY MACHINERY

SYMBOLS

SKY

SOLAR SYSTEM

planets and moons

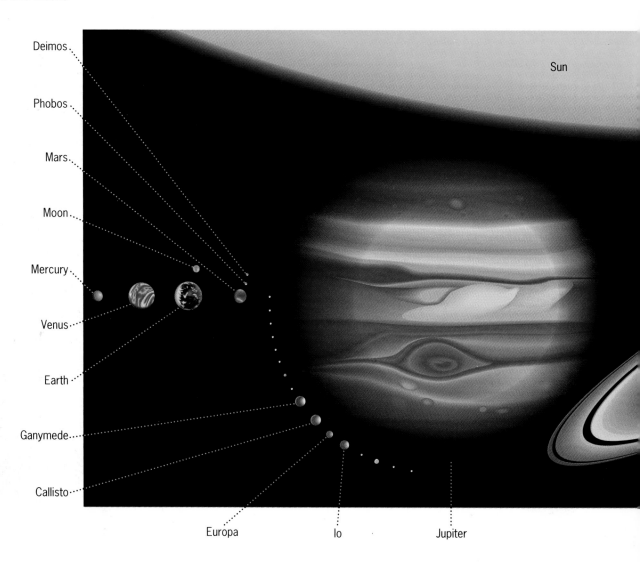

Deimos
Phobos
Mars
Moon
Mercury
Venus
Earth
Ganymede
Callisto

Europa
Io
Jupiter

Sun

orbits of the planets

asteroid belt

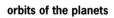

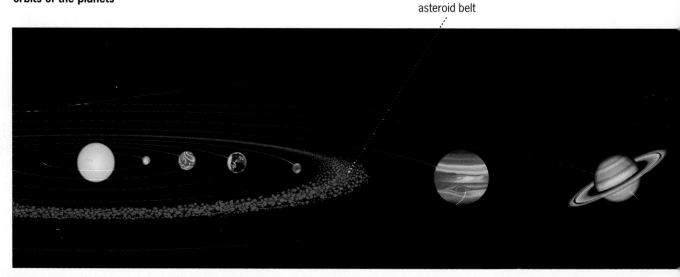

6

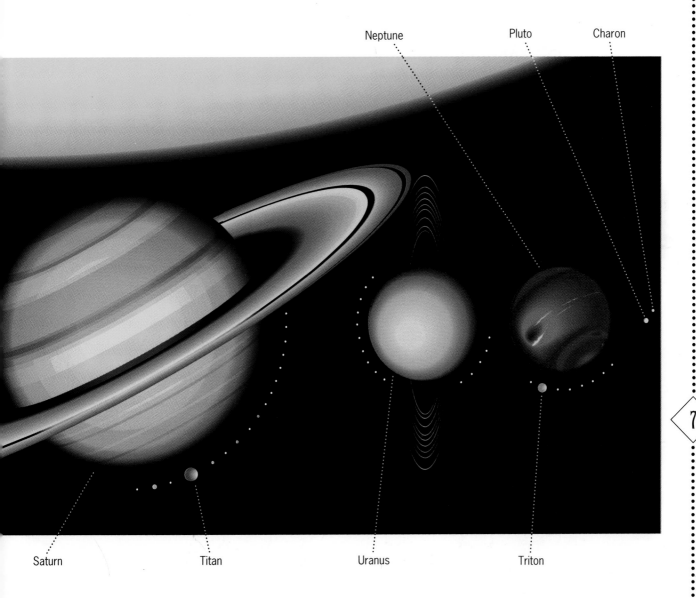

Neptune

Pluto

Charon

Saturn

Titan

Uranus

Triton

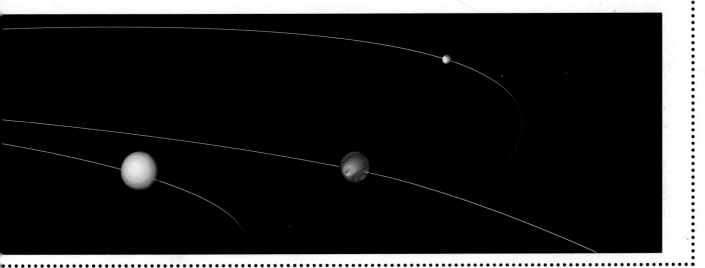

SKY ···

SUN

structure of the Sun

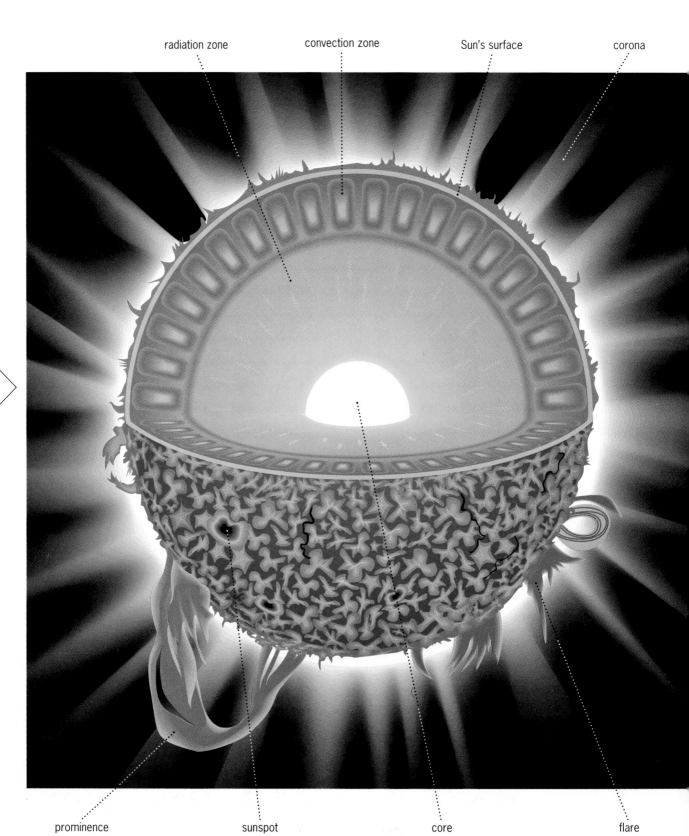

radiation zone   convection zone   Sun's surface   corona

prominence   sunspot   core   flare

8

MOON

bay

cliff

ocean

lake

sea

mountain range

crater

wall

cirque

PHASES OF THE MOON

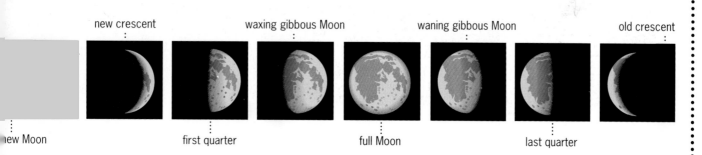

new crescent

waxing gibbous Moon

waning gibbous Moon

old crescent

new Moon

first quarter

full Moon

last quarter

COMET

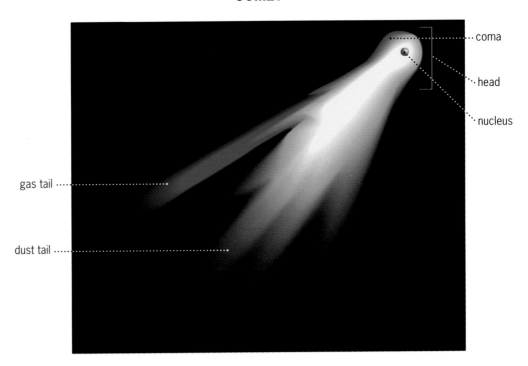

coma

head

nucleus

gas tail

dust tail

SOLAR ECLIPSE

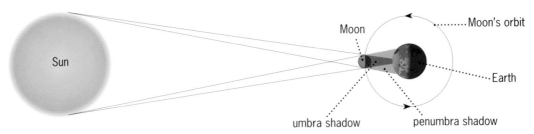

Moon

Moon's orbit

Sun

Earth

umbra shadow

penumbra shadow

TYPES OF SOLAR ECLIPSES

 total eclipse

 annular eclipse

 partial eclipse

LUNAR ECLIPSE

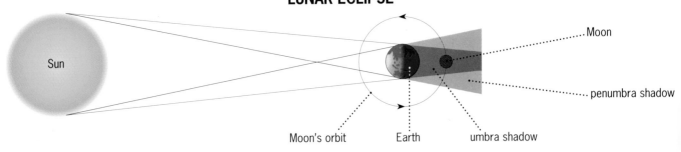

Sun

Moon

penumbra shadow

Moon's orbit

Earth

umbra shadow

TYPES OF LUNAR ECLIPSES

partial eclipse

 total eclipse

REFLECTING TELESCOPE

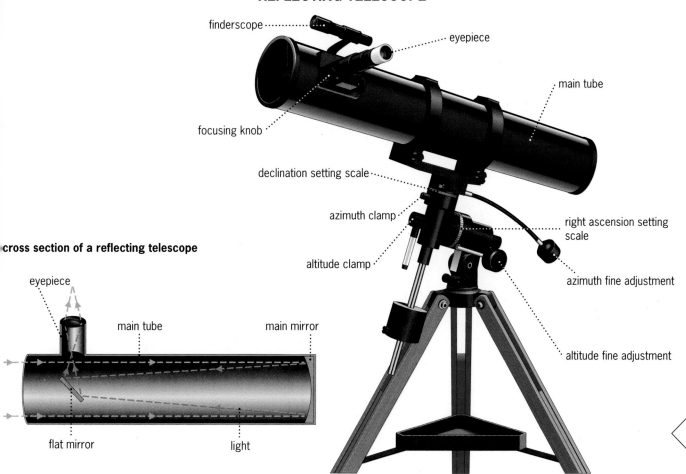

finderscope

eyepiece

main tube

focusing knob

declination setting scale

azimuth clamp

right ascension setting scale

altitude clamp

azimuth fine adjustment

altitude fine adjustment

cross section of a reflecting telescope

eyepiece

main tube

main mirror

flat mirror

light

REFRACTING TELESCOPE

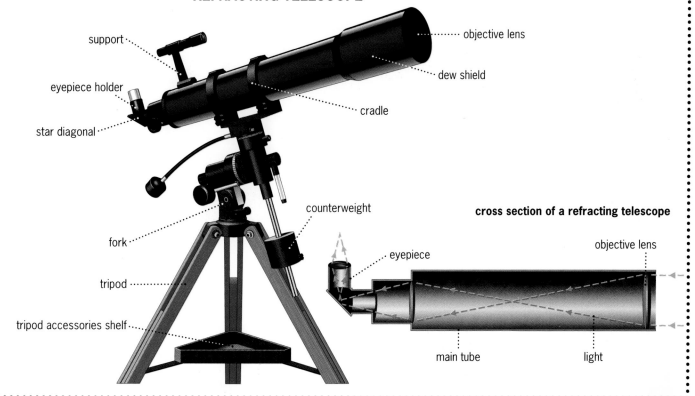

support

objective lens

eyepiece holder

dew shield

star diagonal

cradle

counterweight

fork

cross section of a refracting telescope

tripod

objective lens

eyepiece

tripod accessories shelf

main tube

light

EARTH COORDINATE SYSTEM

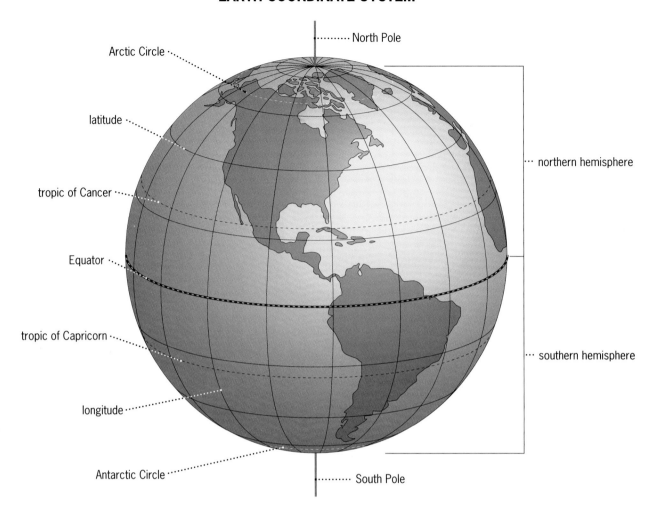

North Pole
Arctic Circle
latitude
tropic of Cancer
Equator
tropic of Capricorn
longitude
Antarctic Circle
South Pole
northern hemisphere
southern hemisphere

STRUCTURE OF THE EARTH

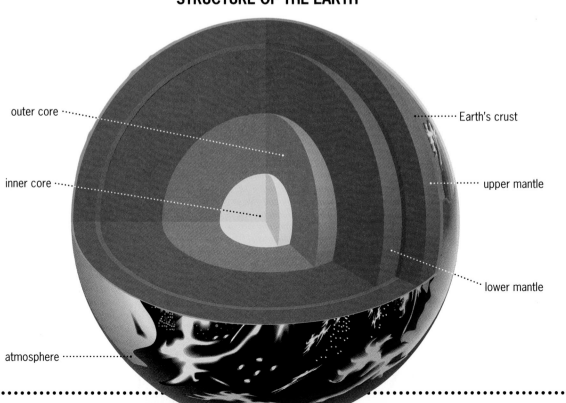

outer core
inner core
atmosphere
Earth's crust
upper mantle
lower mantle

EARTHQUAKE

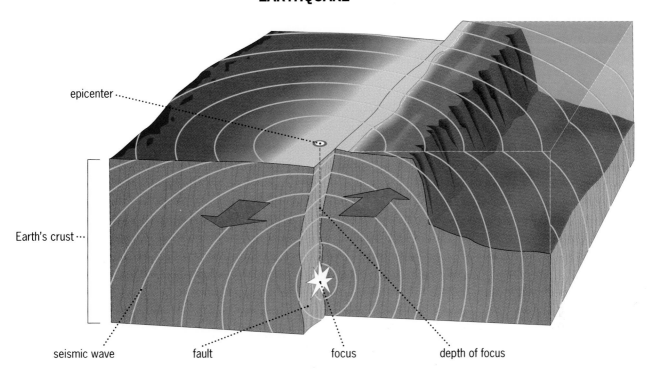

epicenter

Earth's crust

seismic wave

fault

focus

depth of focus

CAVE

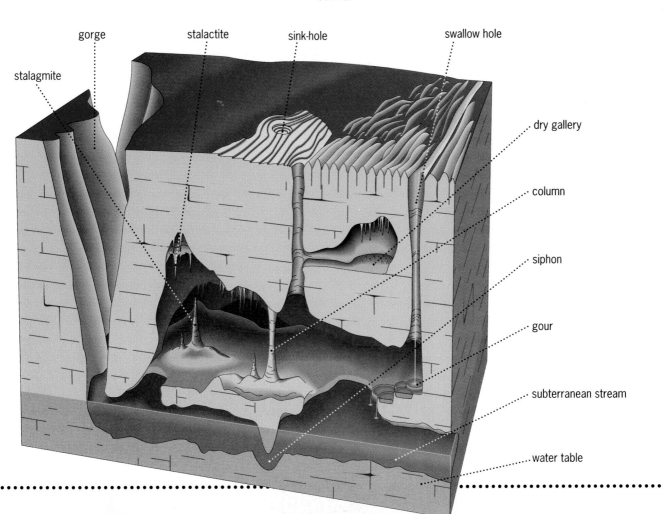

gorge

stalactite

sink-hole

swallow hole

stalagmite

dry gallery

column

siphon

gour

subterranean stream

water table

COASTAL FEATURES

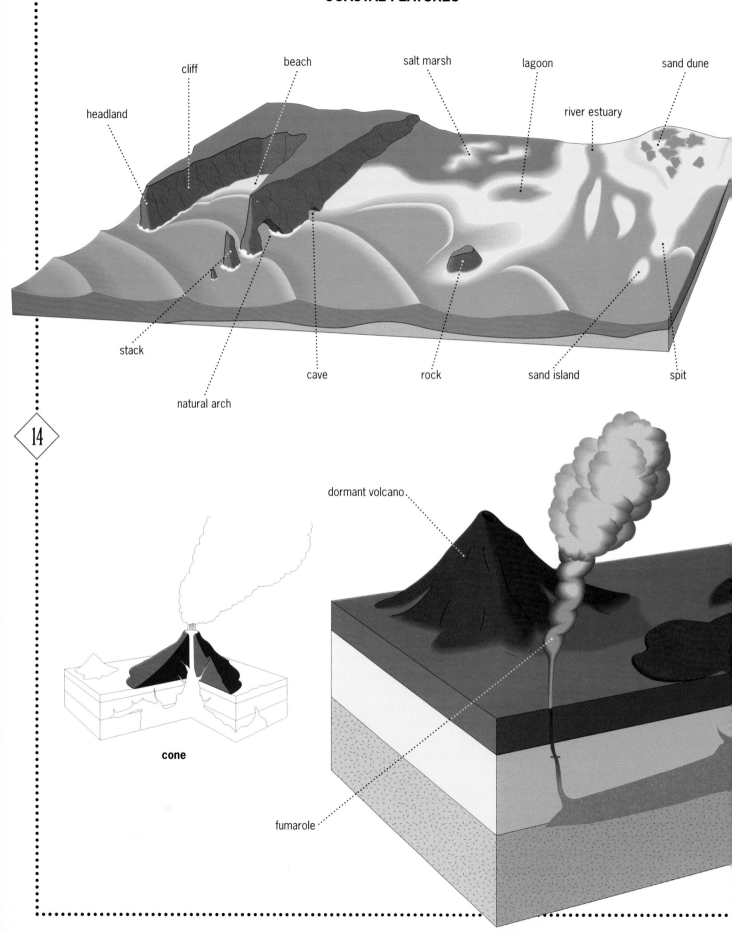

headland

cliff

beach

salt marsh

lagoon

sand dune

river estuary

stack

cave

rock

sand island

spit

natural arch

14

dormant volcano

cone

fumarole

VOLCANO

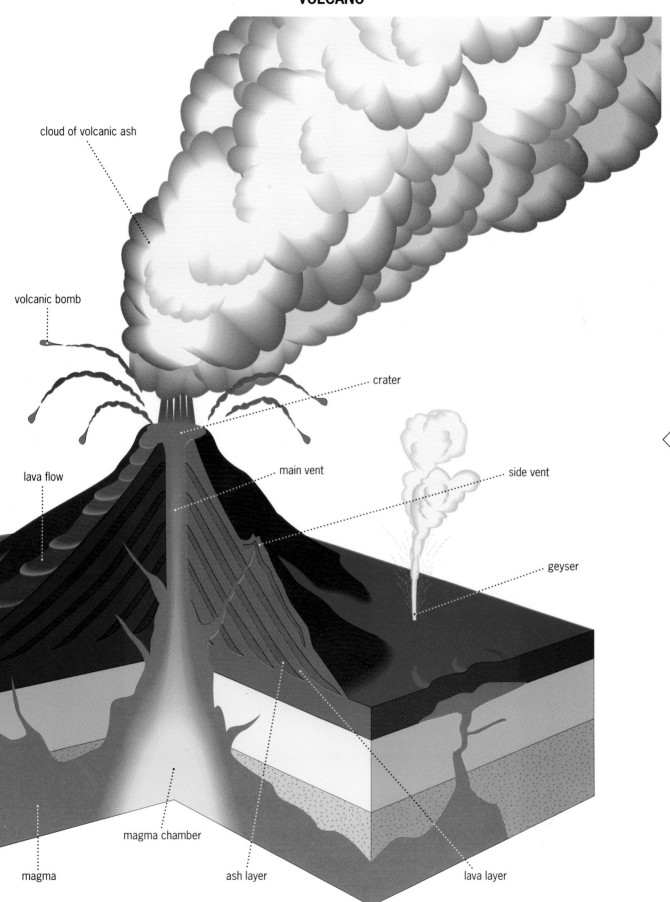

cloud of volcanic ash

volcanic bomb

crater

lava flow

main vent

side vent

geyser

magma

magma chamber

ash layer

lava layer

GLACIER

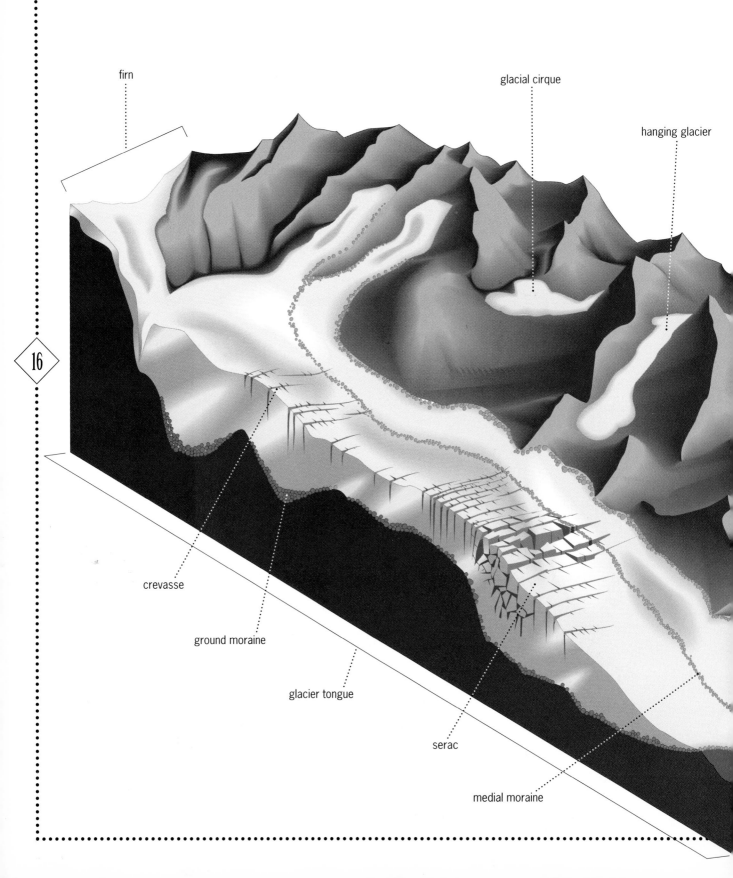

firn

glacial cirque

hanging glacier

crevasse

ground moraine

glacier tongue

serac

medial moraine

MOUNTAIN

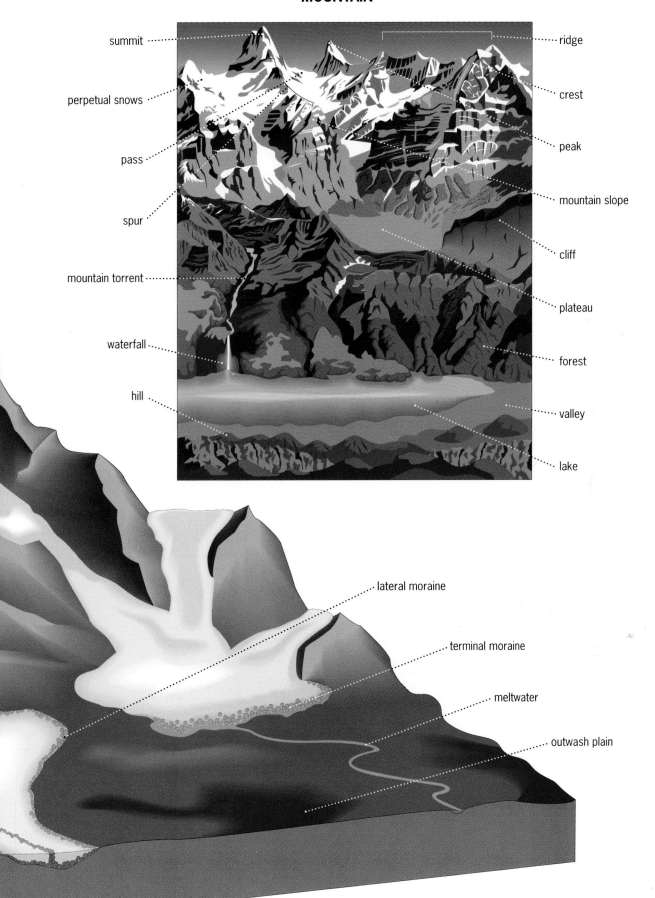

summit

perpetual snows

pass

spur

mountain torrent

waterfall

hill

ridge

crest

peak

mountain slope

cliff

plateau

forest

valley

lake

lateral moraine

terminal moraine

meltwater

outwash plain

THE CONTINENTS

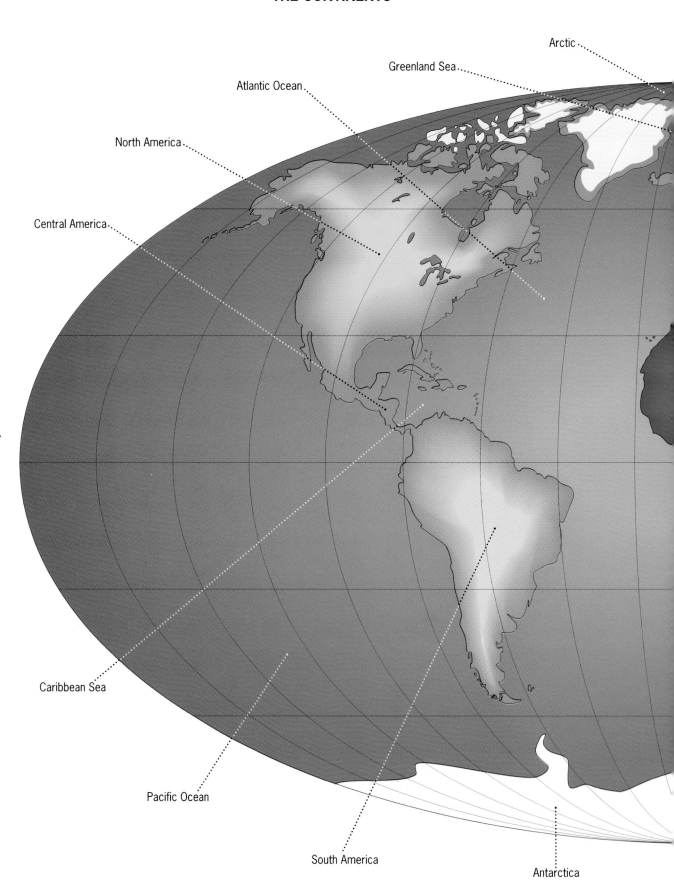

Arctic

Greenland Sea

Atlantic Ocean

North America

Central America

Caribbean Sea

Pacific Ocean

South America

Antarctica

18

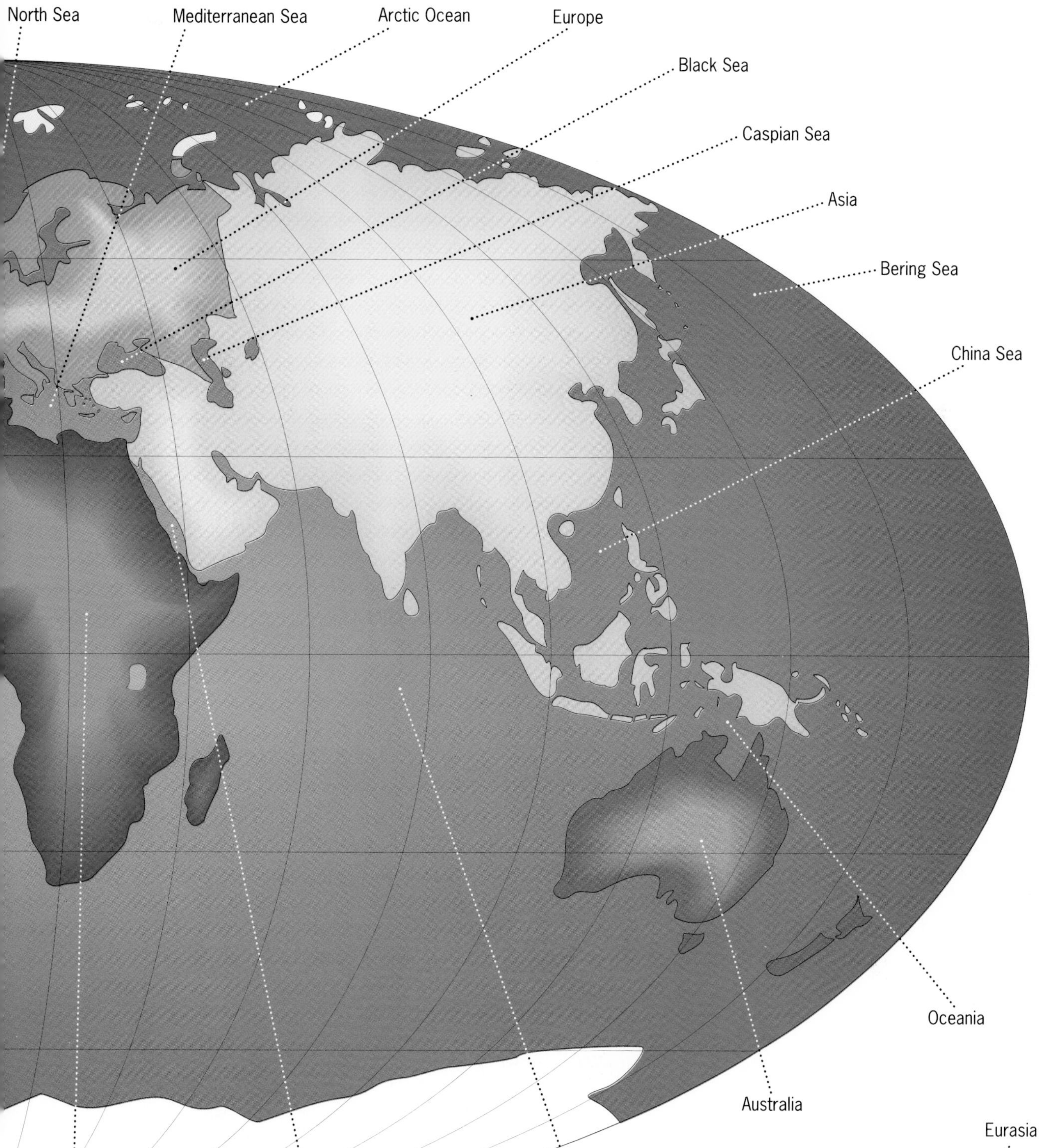

North Sea

Mediterranean Sea

Arctic Ocean

Europe

Black Sea

Caspian Sea

Asia

Bering Sea

China Sea

Oceania

Australia

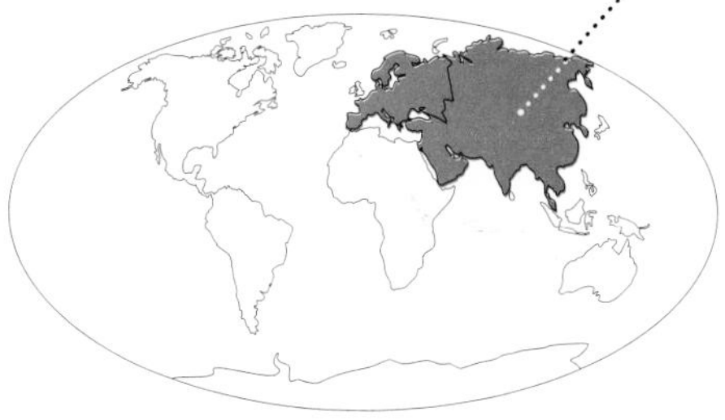

Eurasia

Indian Ocean

Red Sea

Africa

SEASONS OF THE YEAR

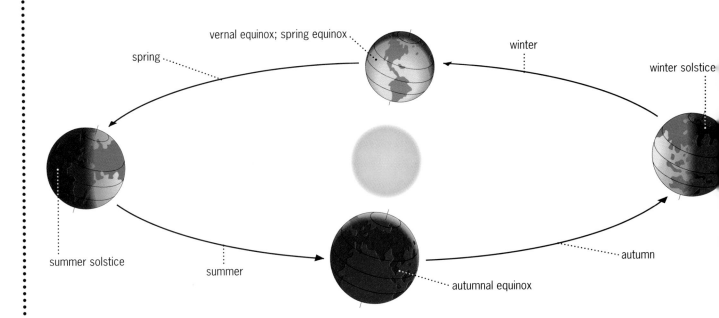

vernal equinox; spring equinox

spring

winter

winter solstice

summer solstice

summer

autumn

autumnal equinox

20

STRUCTURE OF THE BIOSPHERE

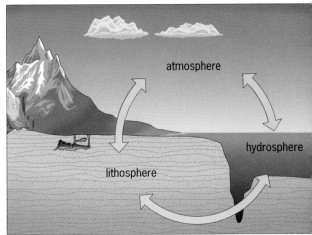

atmosphere

hydrosphere

lithosphere

ELEVATION ZONES AND VEGETATION

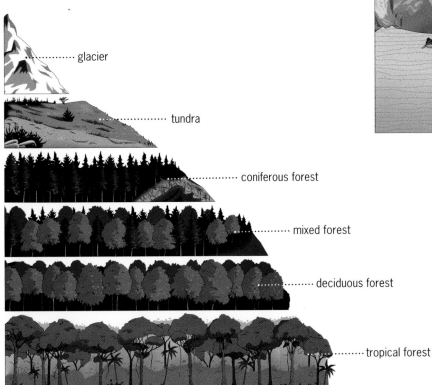

glacier

tundra

coniferous forest

mixed forest

deciduous forest

tropical forest

CLIMATES OF THE WORLD

tropical climates

tropical rain forest

tropical savanna

steppe

desert

temperate climates

humid - long summer

humid - short summer

marine

polar climates

polar tundra

polar ice cap

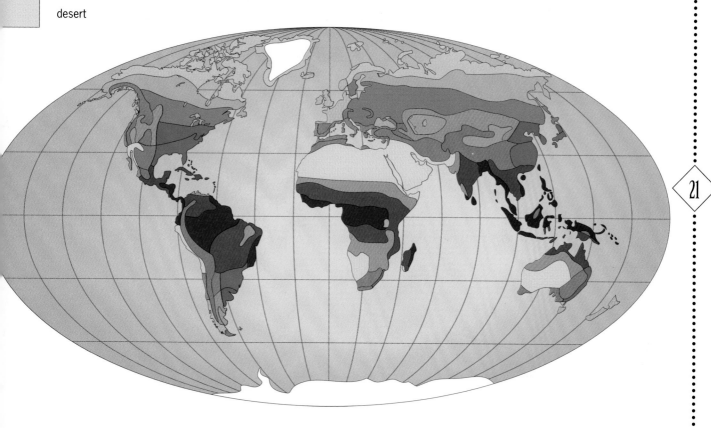

subtropical climates

Mediterranean subtropical

humid subtropical

dry subtropical

continental climates

dry continental - arid

dry continental - semiarid

highland climates

highland climates

subarctic climates

subarctic climates

WEATHER

 mist

 fog

 dew

 glazed frost

stormy sky

22

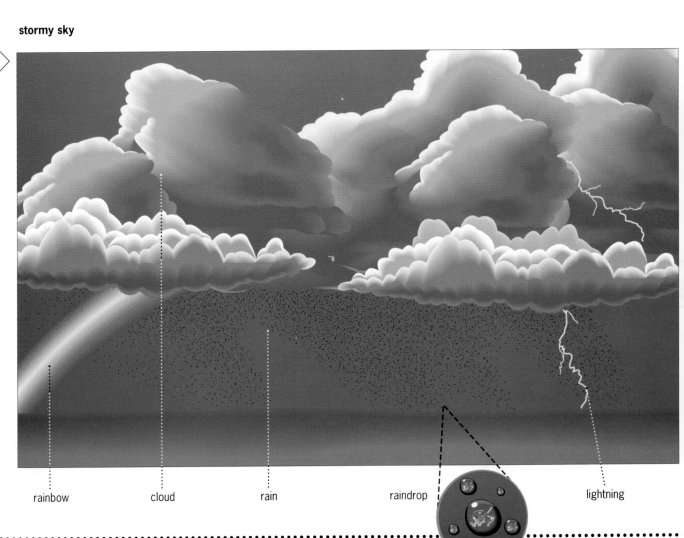

rainbow   cloud   rain   raindrop   lightning

METEOROLOGICAL MEASURING INSTRUMENTS

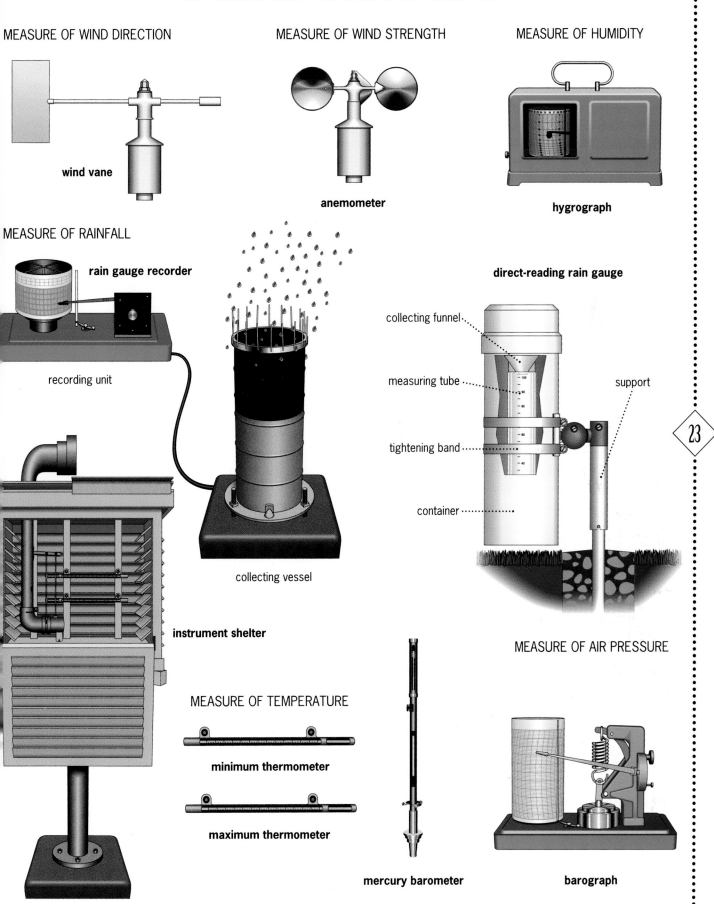

MEASURE OF WIND DIRECTION

wind vane

MEASURE OF WIND STRENGTH

anemometer

MEASURE OF HUMIDITY

hygrograph

MEASURE OF RAINFALL

rain gauge recorder

recording unit

collecting vessel

instrument shelter

direct-reading rain gauge

collecting funnel

measuring tube

tightening band

container

support

MEASURE OF TEMPERATURE

minimum thermometer

maximum thermometer

mercury barometer

MEASURE OF AIR PRESSURE

barograph

23

CARTOGRAPHY

hemispheres

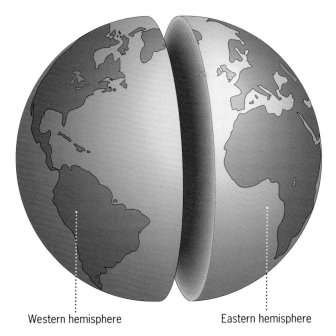

Western hemisphere   Eastern hemisphere

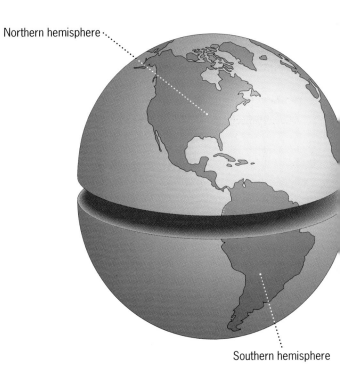

Northern hemisphere

Southern hemisphere

GRID SYSTEM

lines of latitude

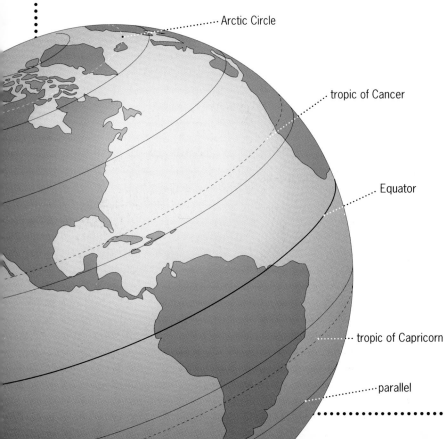

Arctic Circle

tropic of Cancer

Equator

tropic of Capricorn

parallel

lines of longitude

Western meridian   Eastern meridian

prime meridian

MAP PROJECTIONS

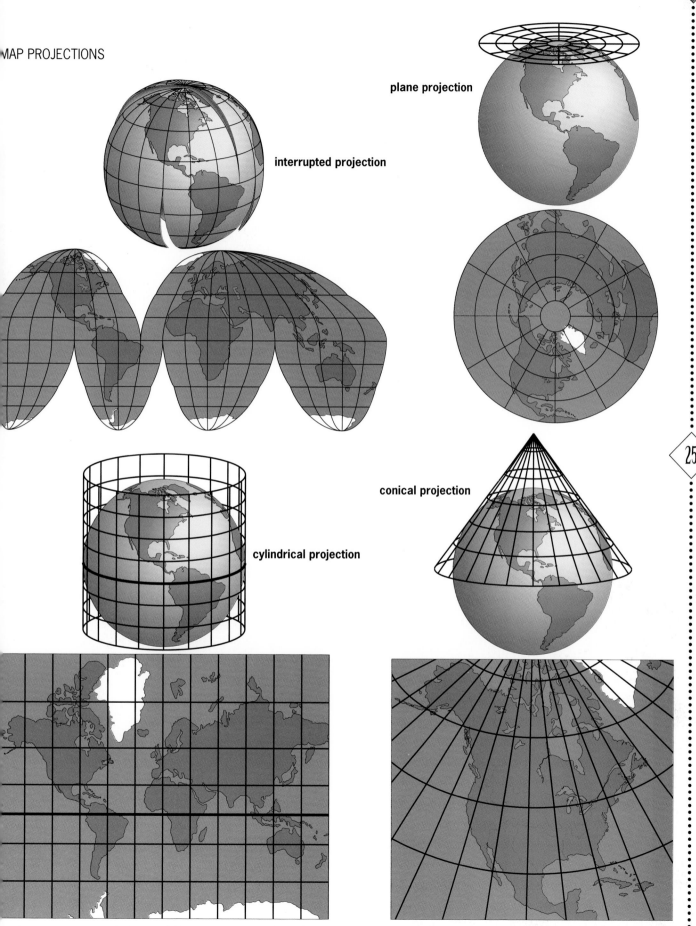

interrupted projection

plane projection

conical projection

cylindrical projection

CARTOGRAPHY

political map

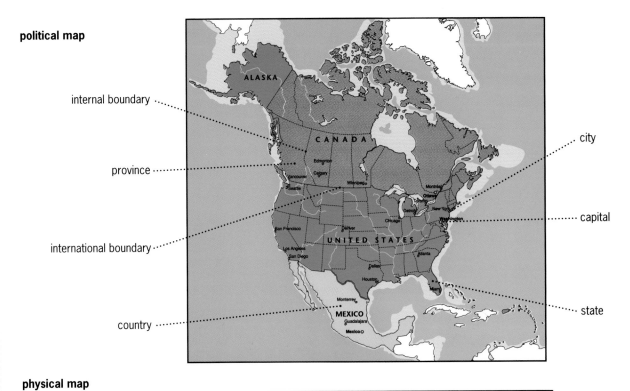

internal boundary

province

international boundary

country

city

capital

state

ALASKA

CANADA

Edmonton
Vancouver
Calgary
Seattle
Winnipeg
San Francisco
Denver
Los Angeles
San Diego
Dallas
Houston
Montreal
Ottawa
Toronto
Detroit
New York
Washington
Chicago
Atlanta
Miami

UNITED STATES

Monterrey
MEXICO
Guadalajara
Mexico ⊙

physical map

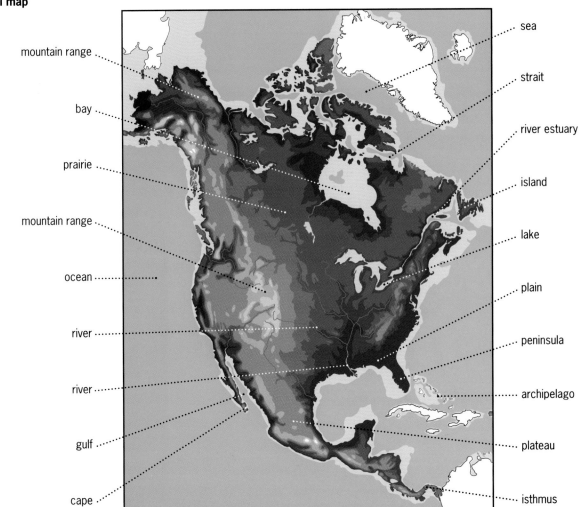

mountain range

bay

prairie

mountain range

ocean

river

river

gulf

cape

sea

strait

river estuary

island

lake

plain

peninsula

archipelago

plateau

isthmus

road map

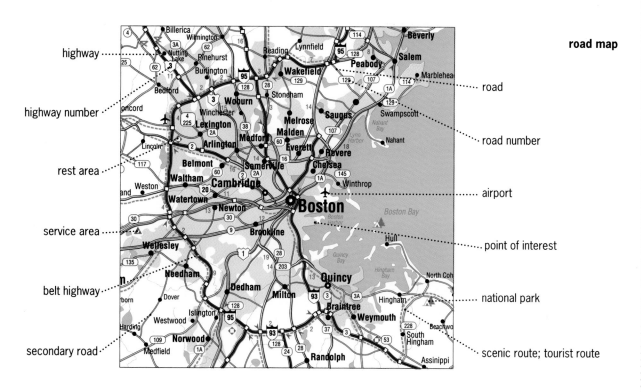

highway

highway number

rest area

service area

belt highway

secondary road

road

road number

airport

point of interest

national park

scenic route; tourist route

COMPASS CARD

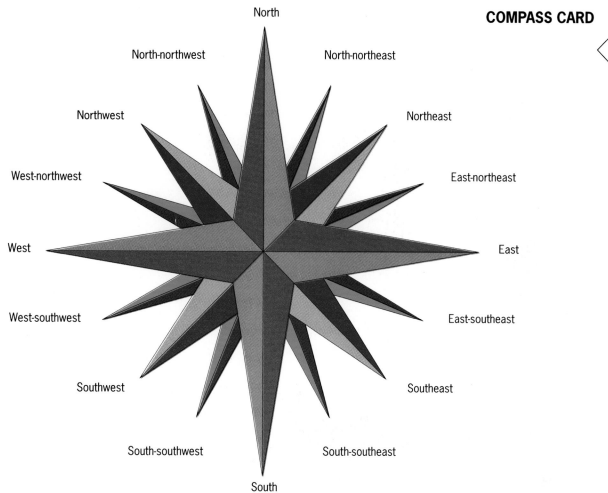

North

North-northwest

North-northeast

Northwest

Northeast

West-northwest

East-northeast

West

East

West-southwest

East-southeast

Southwest

Southeast

South-southwest

South-southeast

South

ECOLOGY

greenhouse effect

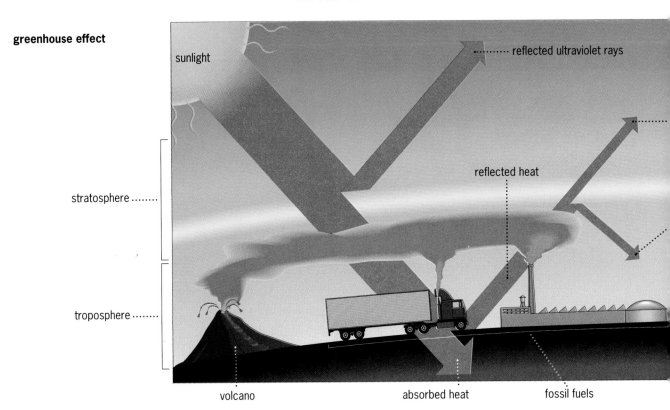

sunlight

········ reflected ultraviolet rays

reflected heat

stratosphere ········

troposphere ········

volcano

absorbed heat

fossil fuels

28

food chain

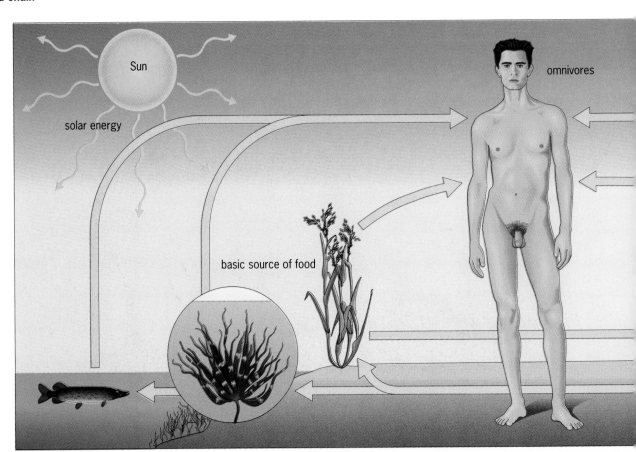

Sun

solar energy

omnivores

basic source of food

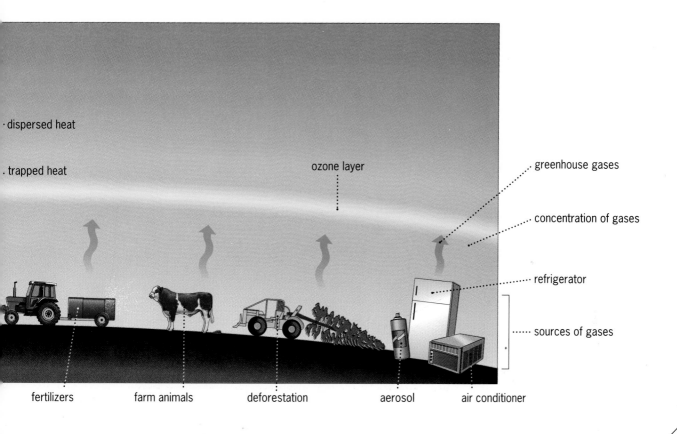

· dispersed heat

. trapped heat

ozone layer

greenhouse gases

concentration of gases

refrigerator

sources of gases

fertilizers

farm animals

deforestation

aerosol

air conditioner

29

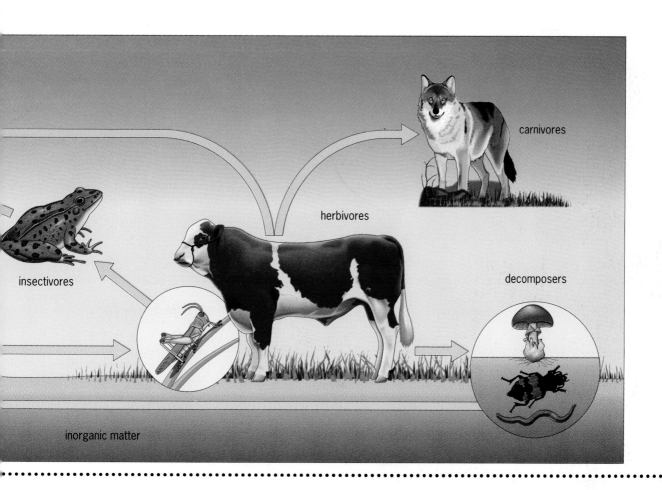

carnivores

herbivores

insectivores

decomposers

inorganic matter

ECOLOGY

atmospheric pollution

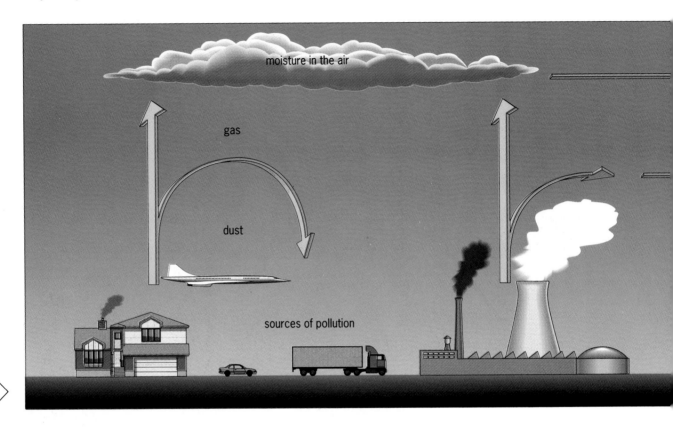

moisture in the air

gas

dust

sources of pollution

water cycle

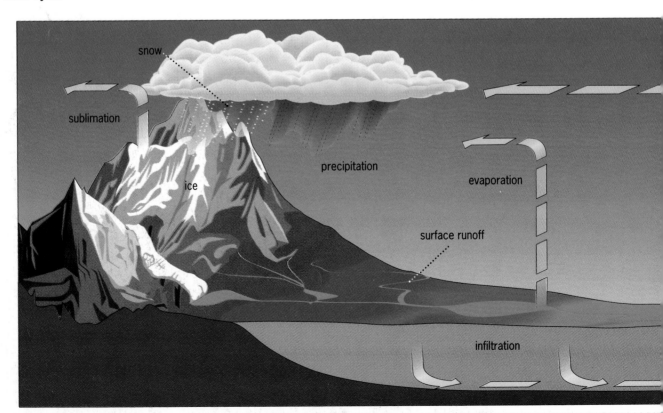

snow

sublimation

precipitation

ice

evaporation

surface runoff

infiltration

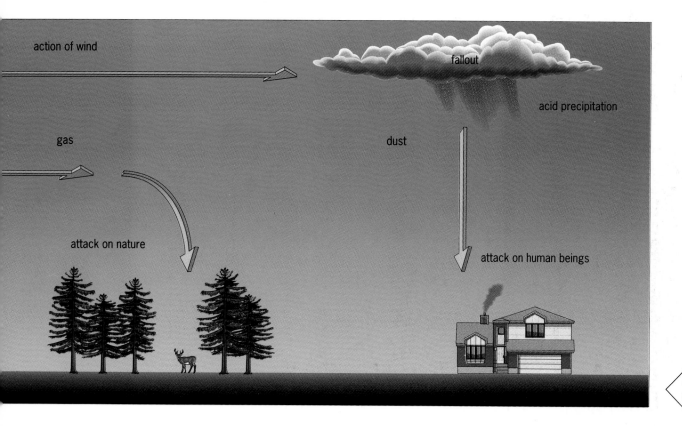

action of wind

fallout

gas

acid precipitation

dust

attack on nature

attack on human beings

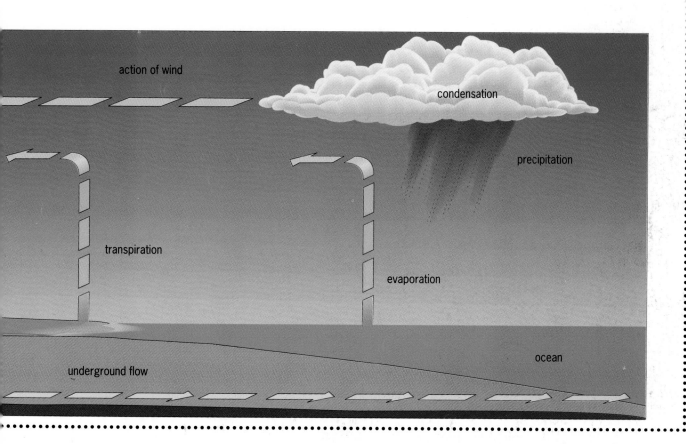

action of wind

condensation

precipitation

transpiration

evaporation

ocean

underground flow

ECOLOGY

food pollution on ground

acid rain

farm pollution

industrial pollution

food pollution in water

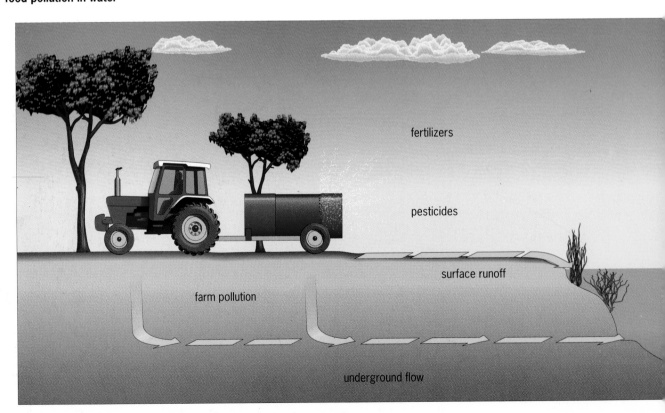

fertilizers

pesticides

surface runoff

farm pollution

underground flow

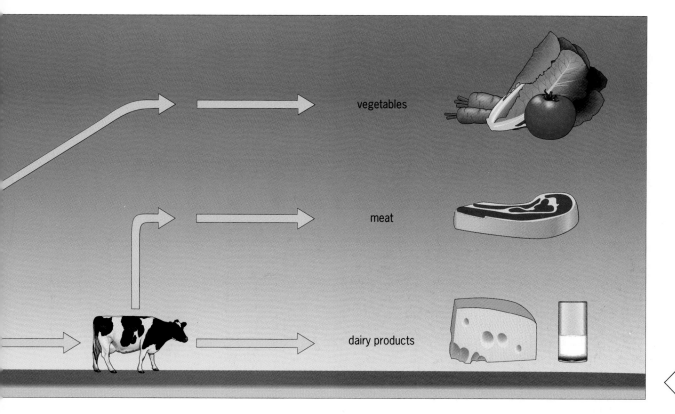

vegetables

meat

dairy products

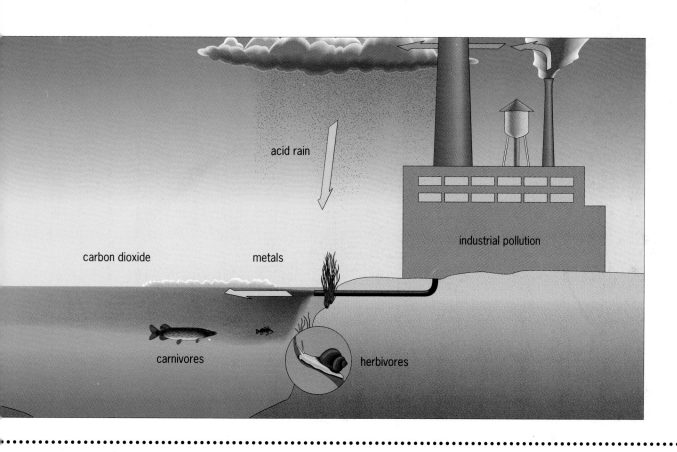

acid rain

industrial pollution

carbon dioxide

metals

carnivores

herbivores

PLANT AND SOIL

SOIL PROFILE

GERMINATION

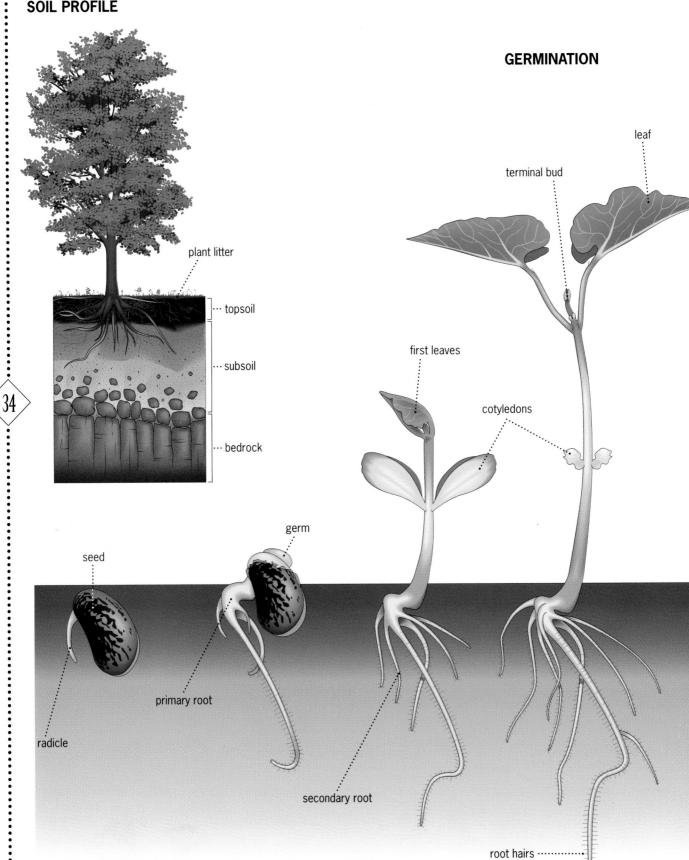

plant litter

topsoil

subsoil

bedrock

34

leaf

terminal bud

first leaves

cotyledons

germ

seed

primary root

radicle

secondary root

root hairs

MUSHROOM

structure of a mushroom

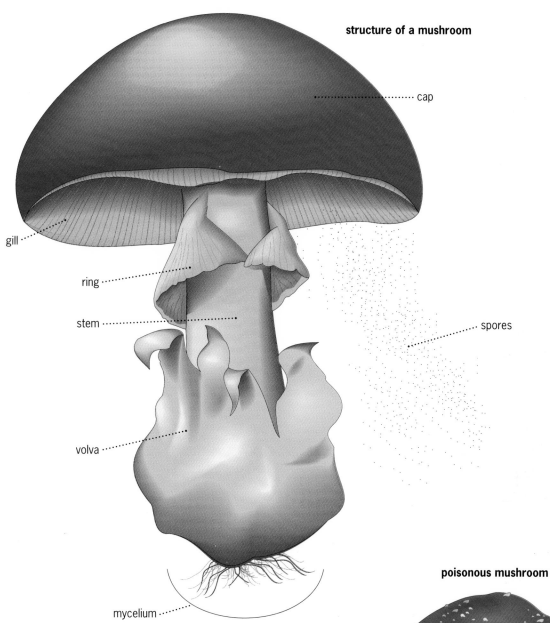

cap

gill

ring

stem

spores

volva

mycelium

poisonous mushroom

edible mushroom

deadly mushroom

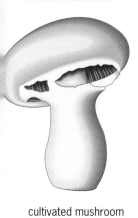

cultivated mushroom

destroying angel

fly agaric

STRUCTURE OF A PLANT

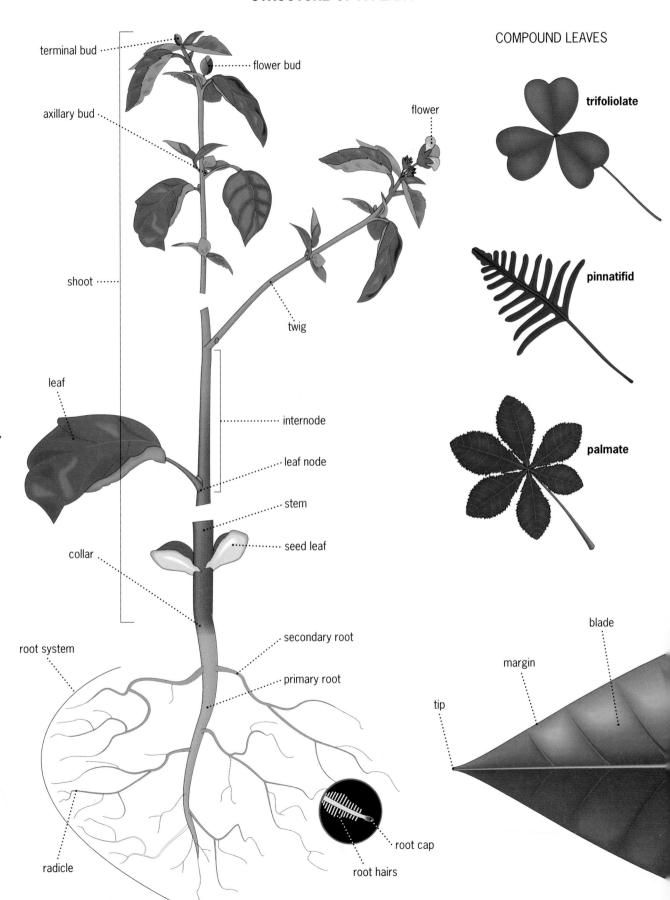

terminal bud

flower bud

COMPOUND LEAVES

axillary bud

flower

trifoliolate

shoot

twig

pinnatifid

leaf

internode

leaf node

palmate

stem

seed leaf

collar

blade

secondary root

margin

root system

primary root

tip

root cap

radicle

root hairs

SIMPLE LEAVES

LEAF MARGINS

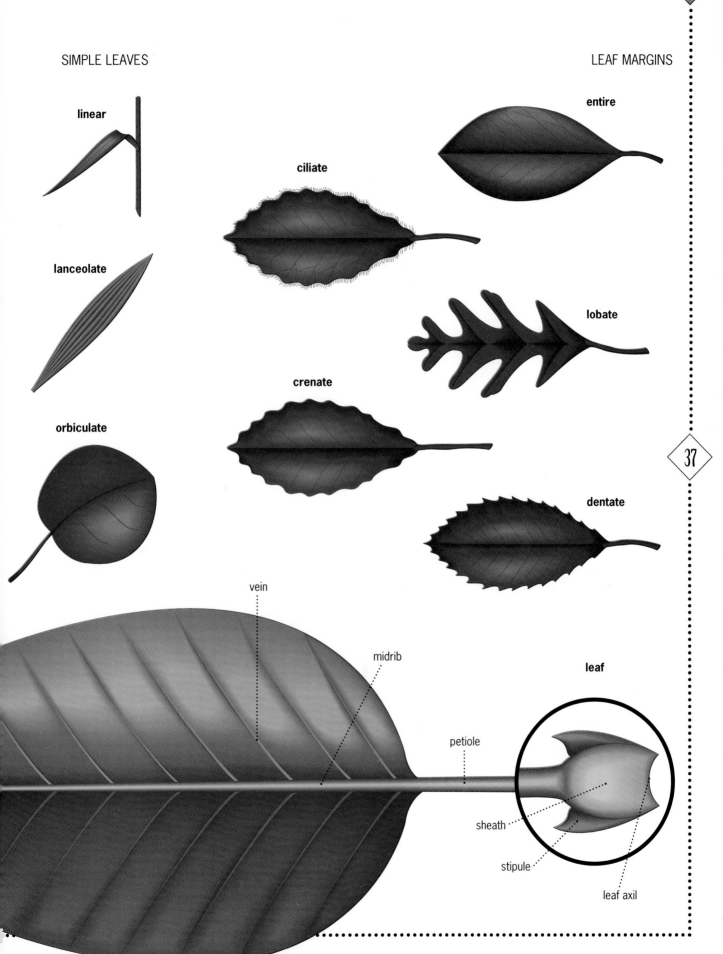

linear

ciliate

entire

lanceolate

lobate

crenate

orbiculate

dentate

vein

midrib

leaf

petiole

sheath

stipule

leaf axil

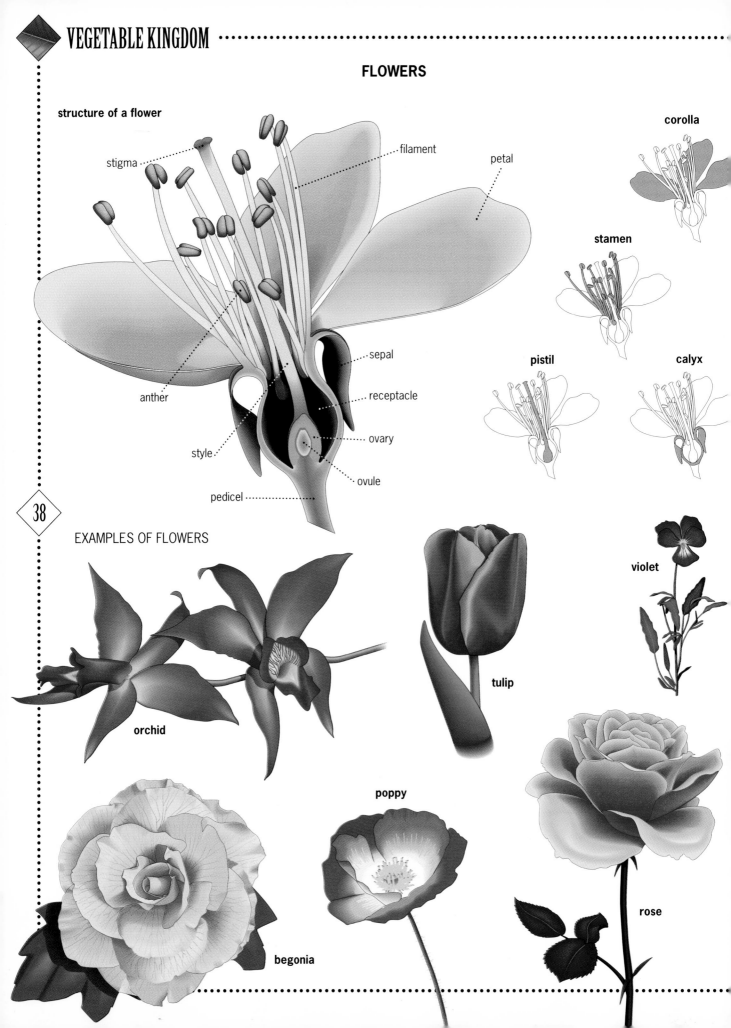

FLOWERS

structure of a flower

stigma

filament

petal

corolla

anther

sepal

receptacle

stamen

style

ovary

pistil

calyx

ovule

pedicel

38

EXAMPLES OF FLOWERS

violet

tulip

orchid

poppy

rose

begonia

lily

sunflower

lily of the valley

crocus

39

arnation

daffodil

TREE

structure of a tree

branches

foliage

top

branch

twig

limb

crown

taproot

trunk

shallow root

radicle

root-hair zone

stump

shoot

cross section of a trunk

annual ring

pith

outer bark

inner bark

heartwood

cambium

sapwood

EXAMPLES OF TREES

poplar

oak

maple

palm tree

weeping willow

birch

42

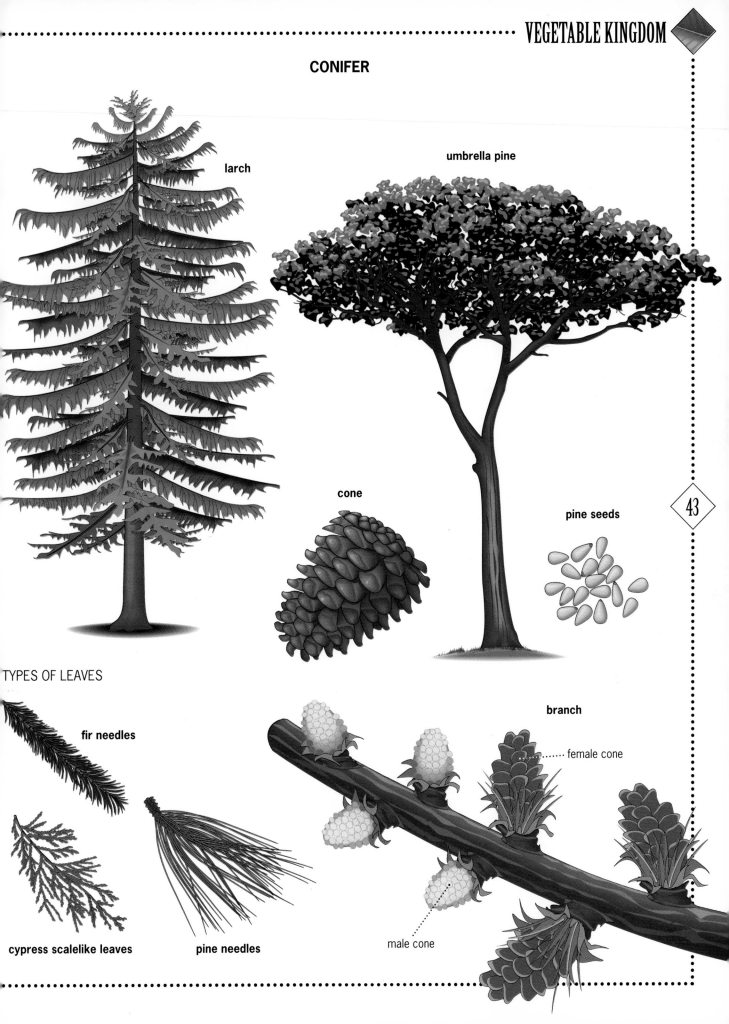

CONIFER

larch

umbrella pine

cone

pine seeds

TYPES OF LEAVES

fir needles

branch

female cone

male cone

cypress scalelike leaves

pine needles

FLESHY FRUITS: BERRY FRUITS

section of a berry

MAJOR TYPES OF BERRIE

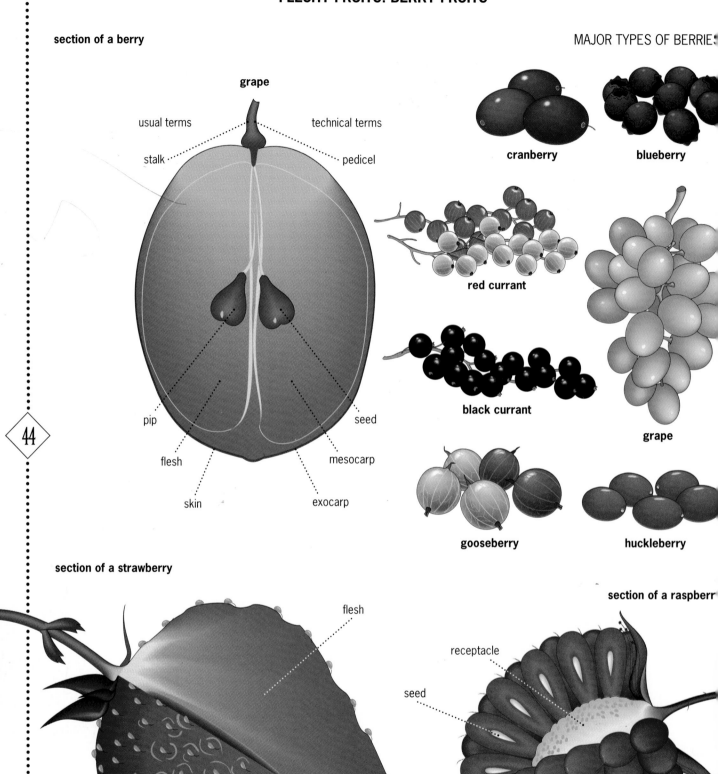

grape

usual terms

technical terms

stalk

pedicel

pip

seed

flesh

mesocarp

skin

exocarp

cranberry

blueberry

red currant

black currant

grape

gooseberry

huckleberry

section of a strawberry

flesh

achene

section of a raspberr

receptacle

seed

drupelet

sepa

44

FLESHY STONE FRUITS

section of a stone fruit

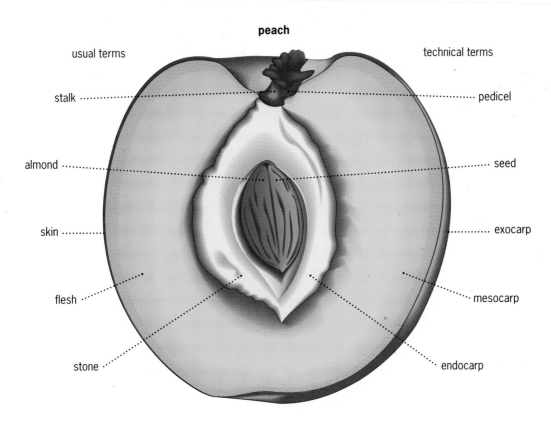

peach

usual terms   technical terms

stalk ···················· pedicel

almond ···················· seed

skin ···················· exocarp

flesh ···················· mesocarp

stone ···················· endocarp

45

MAJOR TYPES OF STONE FRUITS

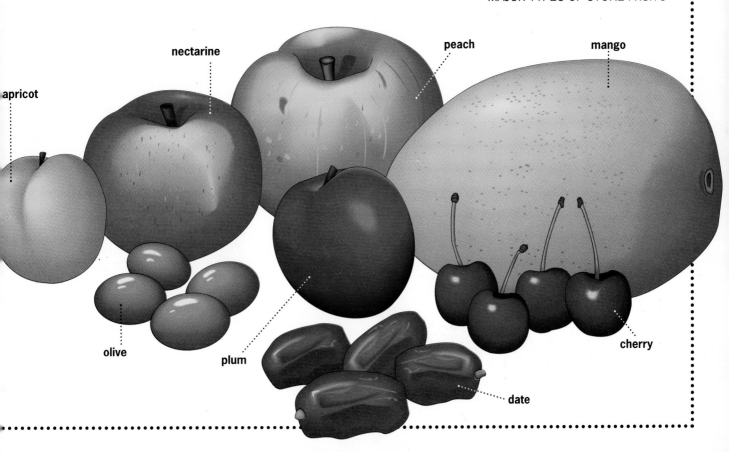

apricot

nectarine

peach

mango

olive

plum

cherry

date

FLESHY POME FRUITS

section of a pome fruit

apple

usual terms   technical terms

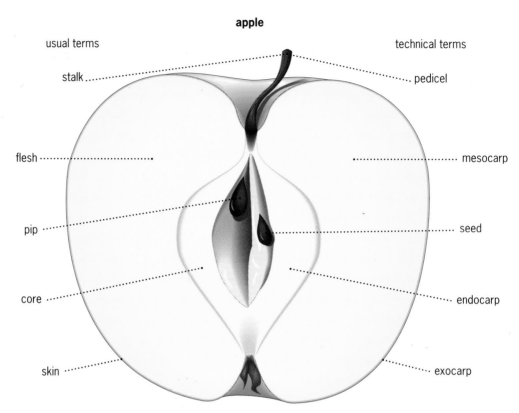

stalk .... pedicel

flesh .... mesocarp

pip .... seed

core .... endocarp

skin .... exocarp

MAJOR TYPES OF POME FRUITS

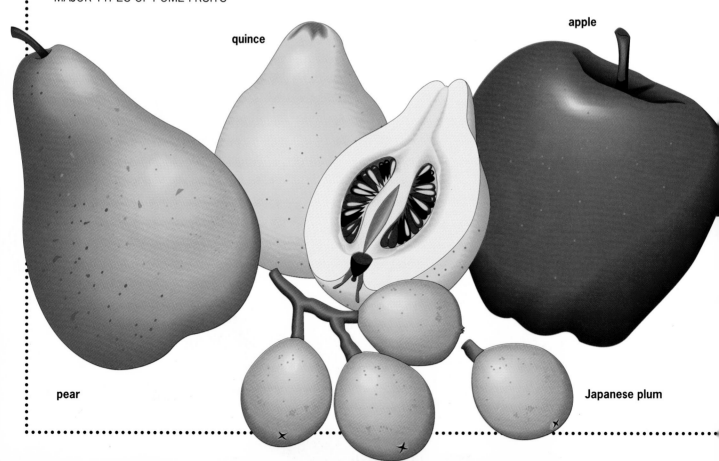

quince

apple

pear

Japanese plum

FLESHY FRUITS: CITRUS FRUITS

section of a citrus fruit

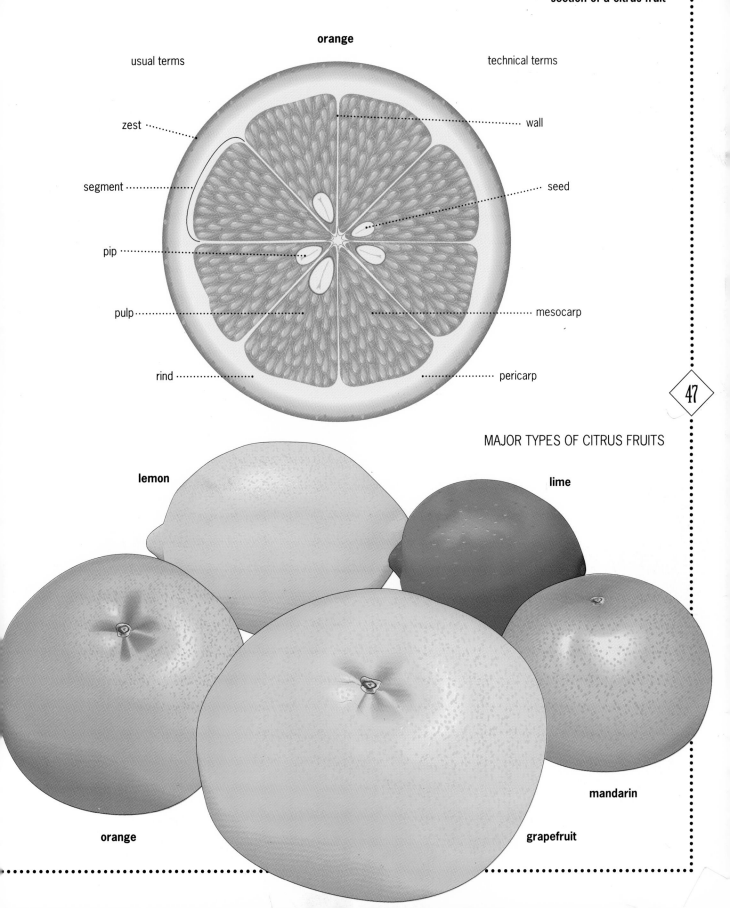

orange

usual terms

technical terms

zest

wall

segment

seed

pip

pulp

mesocarp

rind

pericarp

MAJOR TYPES OF CITRUS FRUITS

lemon

lime

mandarin

orange

grapefruit

TROPICAL FRUITS

MAJOR TYPES OF TROPICAL FRUITS

litchi

kiwi

guava

Japanese persimmon

Indian fig

cherimoya

fig

48

papaya

pomegranate

banana

avocado

pineapple

VEGETABLES

INFLORESCENT VEGETABLES

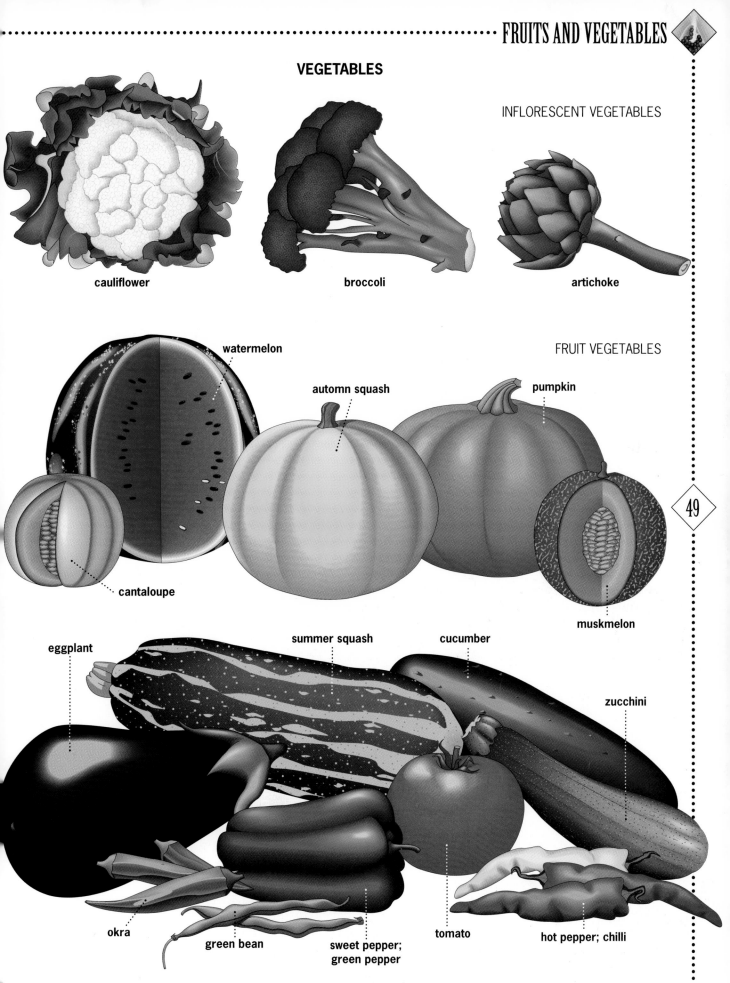

cauliflower

broccoli

artichoke

FRUIT VEGETABLES

watermelon

automn squash

pumpkin

cantaloupe

muskmelon

eggplant

summer squash

cucumber

zucchini

okra

green bean

sweet pepper;
green pepper

tomato

hot pepper; chilli

49

VEGETABLES

section of a bulb

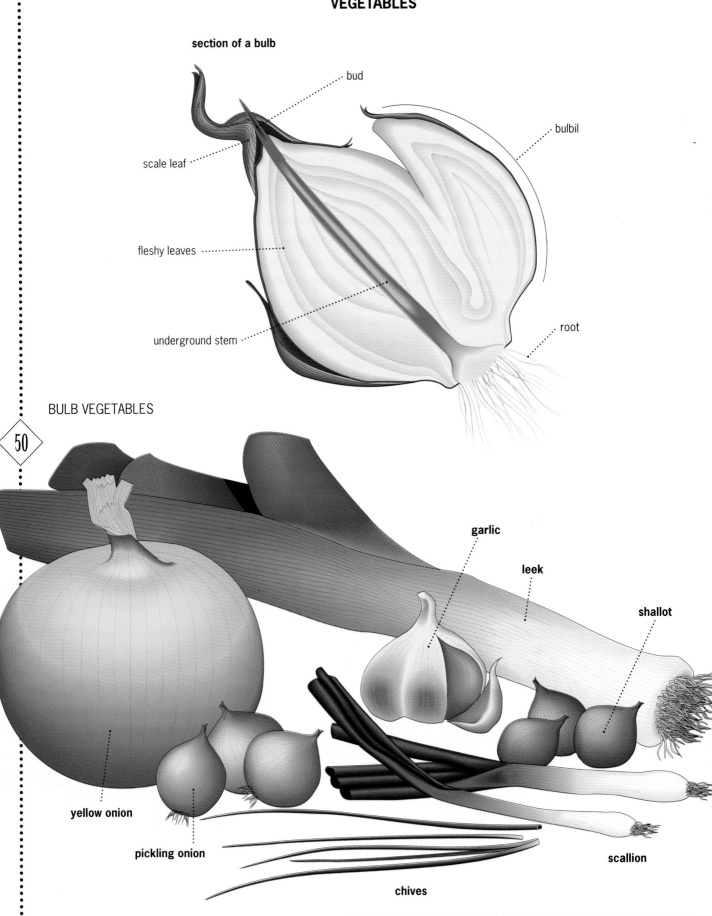

bud

bulbil

scale leaf

fleshy leaves

underground stem

root

BULB VEGETABLES

garlic

leek

shallot

yellow onion

pickling onion

scallion

chives

TUBER VEGETABLES

Jerusalem
artichoke

potato

sweet potato

ROOT VEGETABLES

kohlrabi

swede

turnip

celeriac

beet

horseradish

parsnip

carrot

radish

salsify

VEGETABLES

STALK VEGETABLES

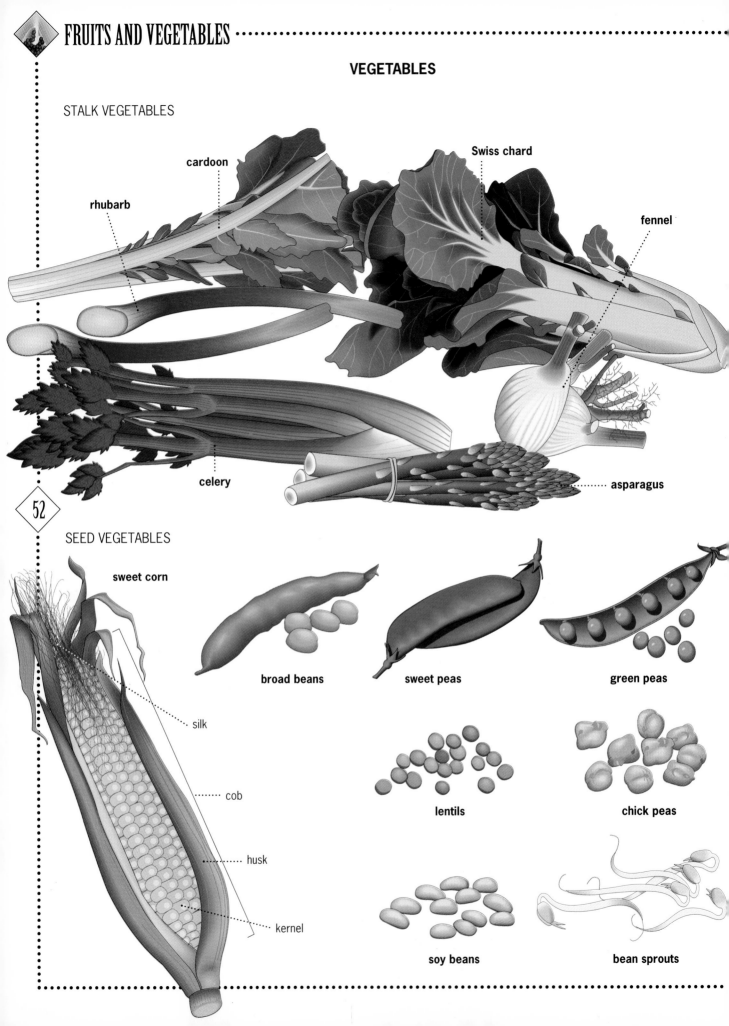

cardoon

rhubarb

Swiss chard

fennel

celery

asparagus

SEED VEGETABLES

sweet corn

silk

cob

husk

kernel

broad beans

sweet peas

green peas

lentils

chick peas

soy beans

bean sprouts

LEAF VEGETABLES

green cabbage

cabbage lettuce

curly endive

spinach

white cabbage

romaine lettuce

chicory

broad-leaved endive

Chinese cabbage

dandelion

curly kale

Brussels sprouts

garden sorrel

watercress

corn salad

vine leaf

53

GARDENING

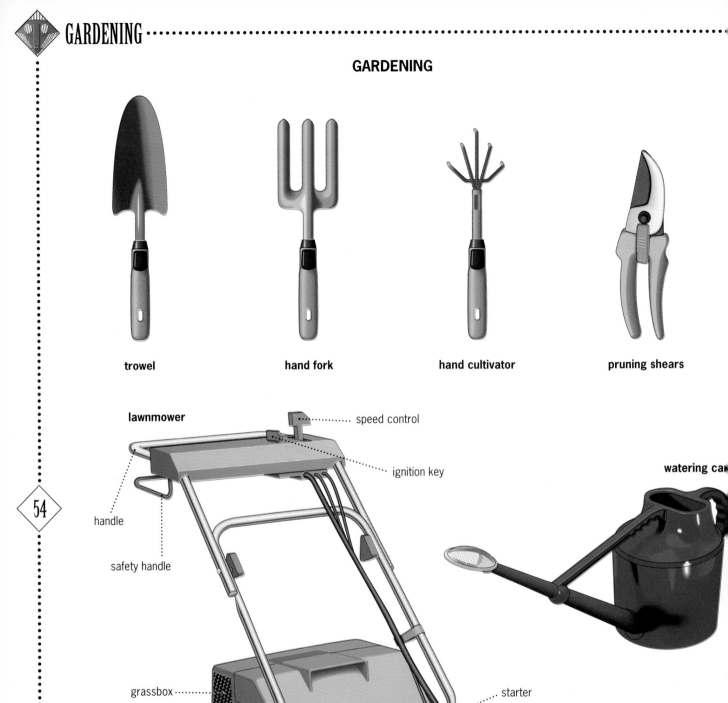

trowel **hand fork** **hand cultivator** **pruning shears**

lawnmower

speed control

ignition key

handle

safety handle

watering ca▶

grassbox ········

starter

motor

deflector ····

casing ····

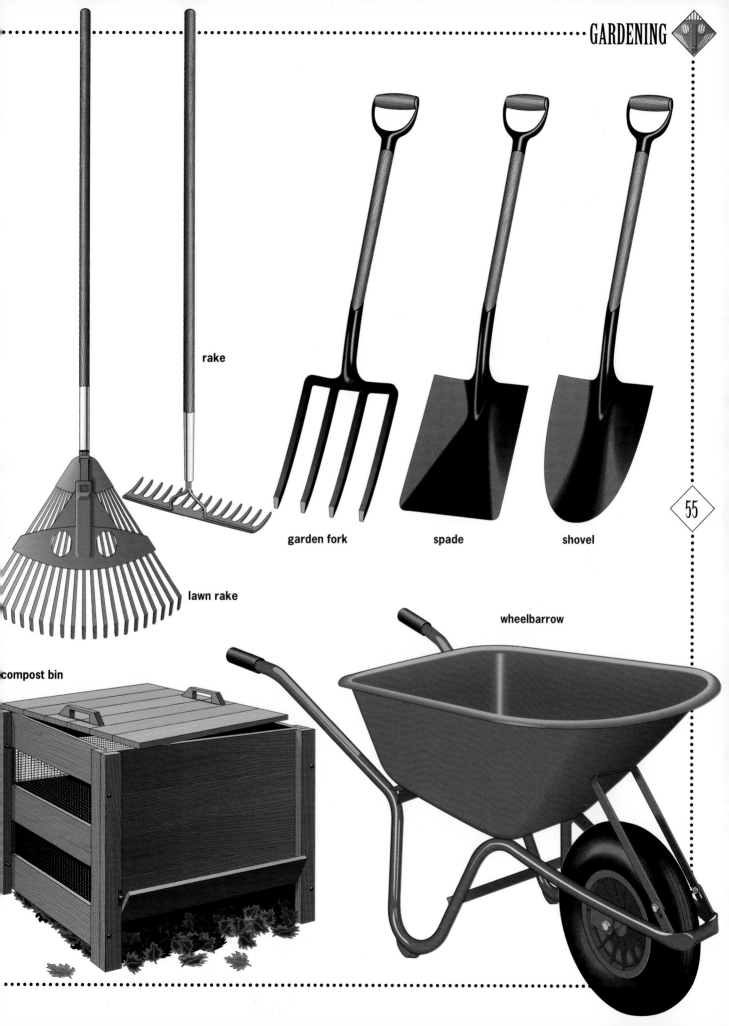

rake

garden fork

spade

shovel

lawn rake

compost bin

wheelbarrow

INSECTS AND SPIDER

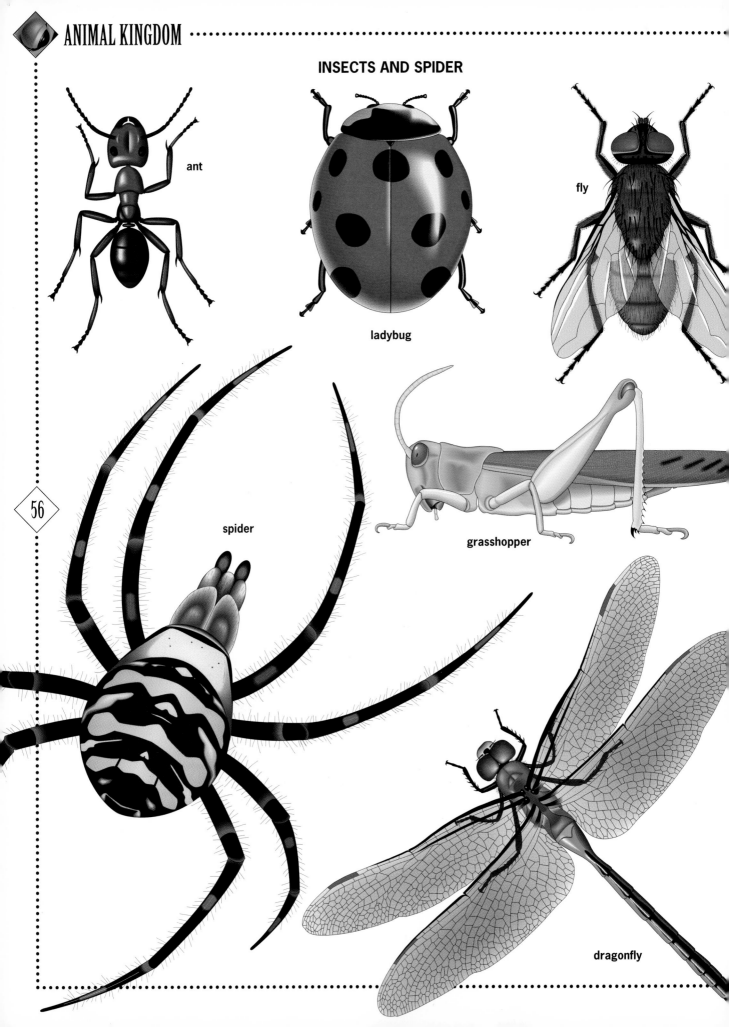

ant

ladybug

fly

spider

grasshopper

56

dragonfly

BUTTERFLY

caterpillar

chrysalis

head

simple eye

mandible

walking leg

proleg

forewing

wing vein

cell

thorax

head

antenna

labial palp

compound eye

proboscis

foreleg

middle leg

claw

hind wing

abdomen

hind leg

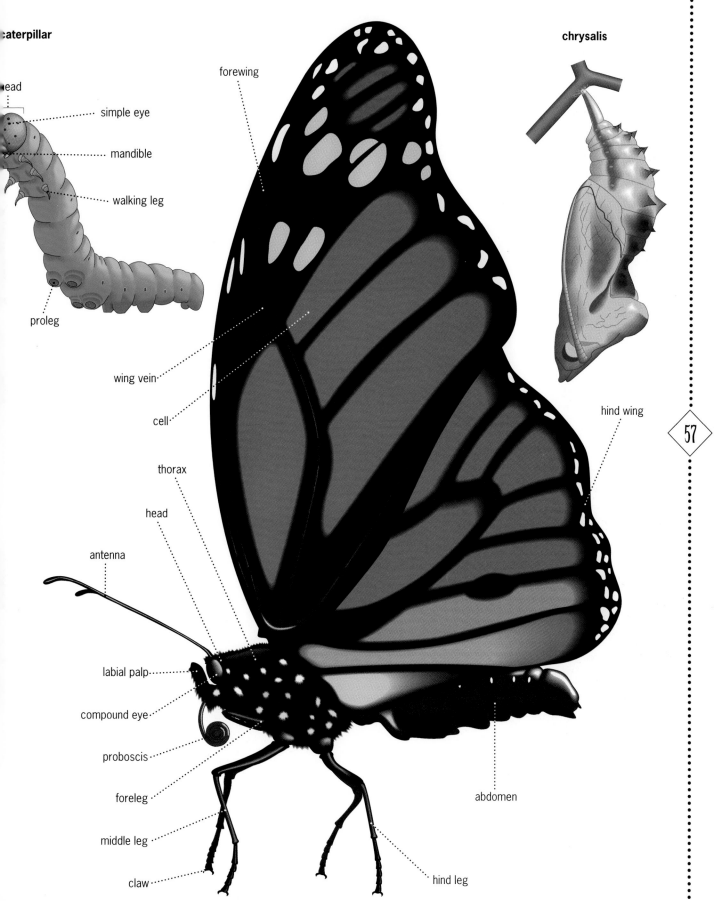

BUTTERFLY

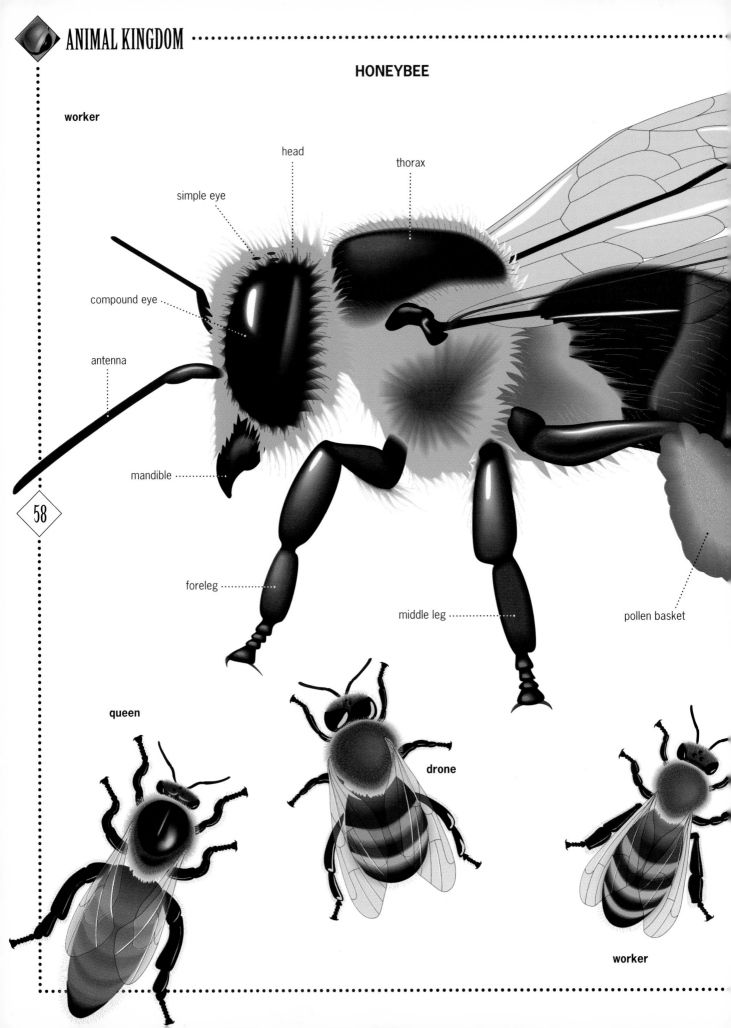

HONEYBEE

worker

simple eye

head

thorax

compound eye

antenna

58

mandible

foreleg

middle leg

pollen basket

queen

drone

worker

HONEYBEE

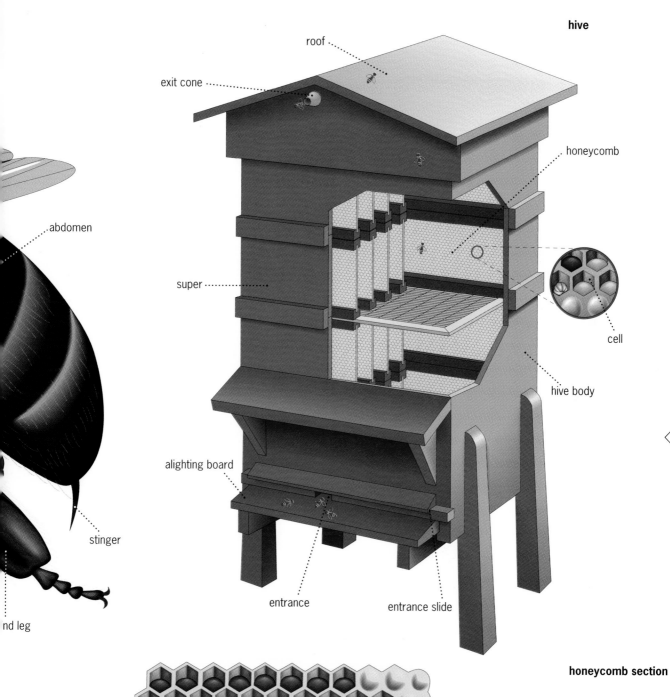

hive

roof

exit cone

honeycomb

abdomen

super

cell

hive body

stinger

alighting board

nd leg

entrance

entrance slide

honeycomb section

honey cell

chrysalis

pollen cell

egg

sealed cell

queen cell

AMPHIBIANS

frog

upper eyelid

snout

eyeball

nostril

mouth

skin

lower eyelid

eardrum

forelimb

digit

webbed foot

web

hind limb

60

LIFE CYCLE OF THE FROG

eggs

tadpole

operculum

forelimb

external gills

hind limb

MAJOR AMPHIBIANS

salamander

tree frog

toad

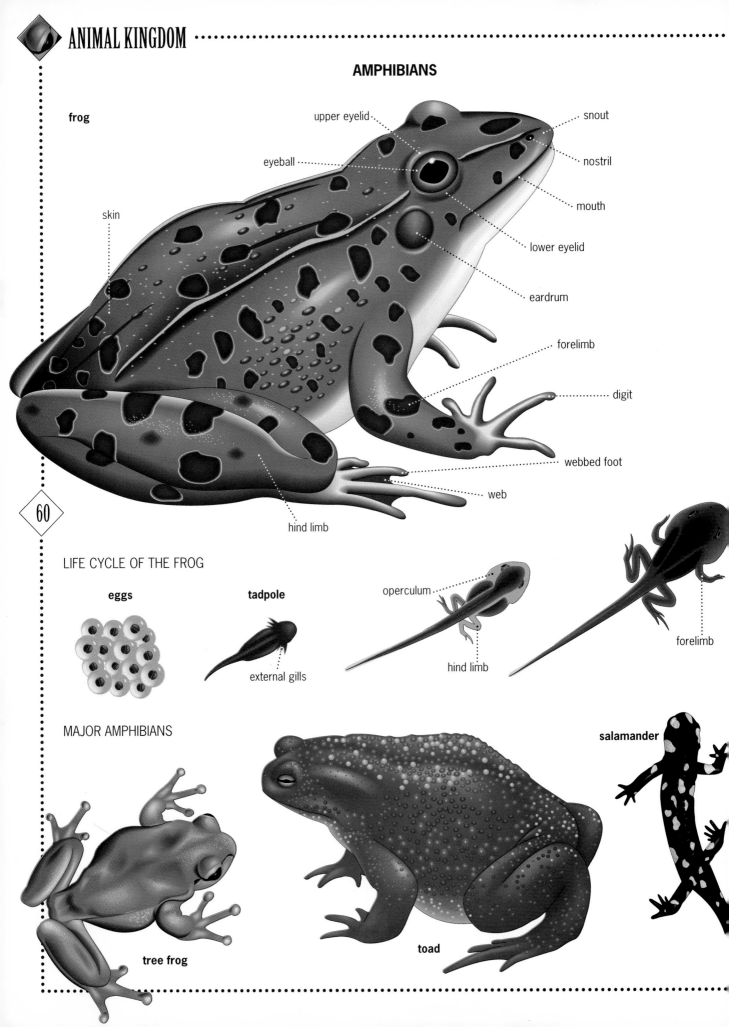

CRUSTACEANS

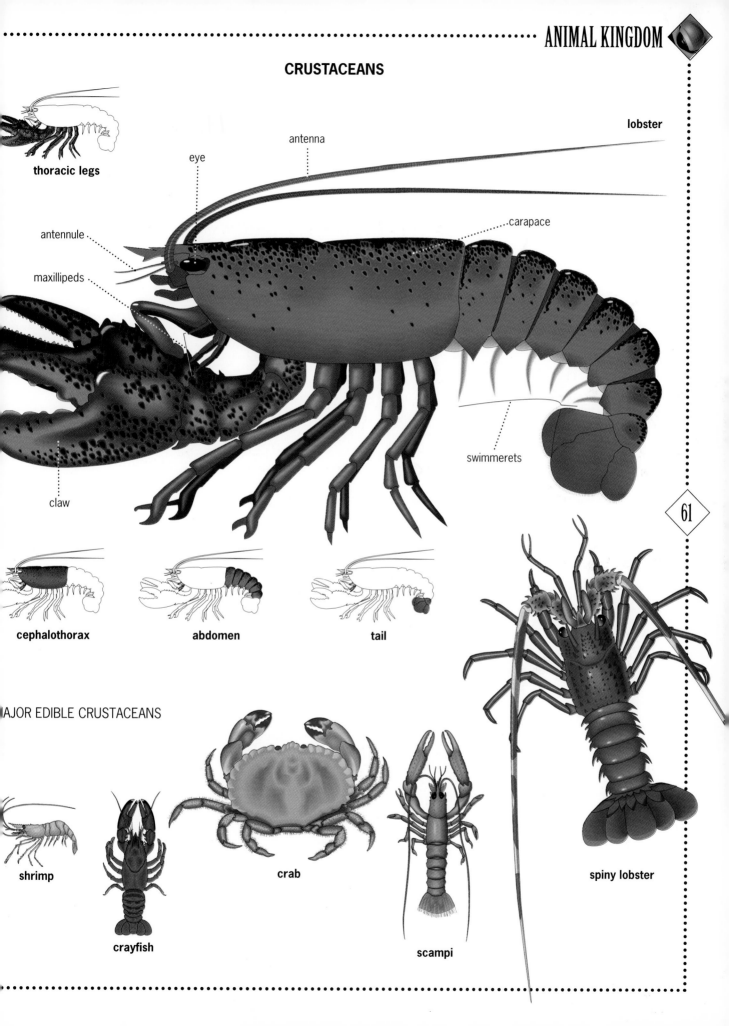

thoracic legs

eye

antenna

lobster

antennule

carapace

maxillipeds

claw

swimmerets

61

cephalothorax

abdomen

tail

AJOR EDIBLE CRUSTACEANS

shrimp

crayfish

crab

scampi

spiny lobster

FISHES

MORPHOLOGY

gills

sea horse

trout

first dorsal fin ··········

nostril

mandible ·····

maxilla

pectoral fin

pelvic fin

swordfish

tuna

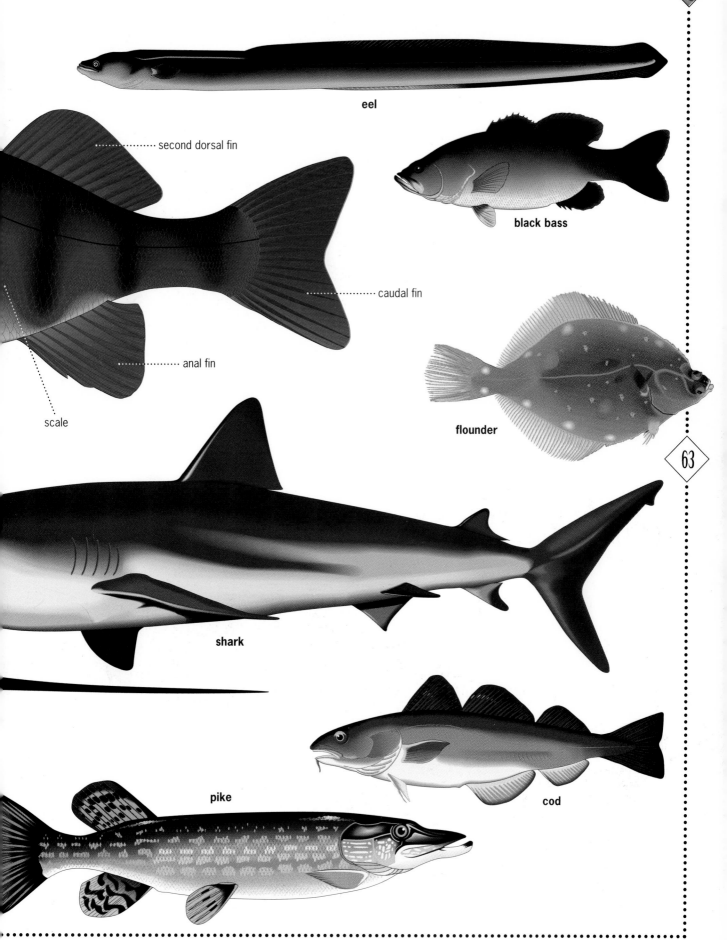

eel

second dorsal fin

black bass

caudal fin

flounder

anal fin

scale

shark

pike

cod

REPTILES

turtle

eardrum

neck

eyelid

eye

horny beak

scale

shell

carapace

plastron

leg

claw

64

cobra

venomous snake's head

movable maxillary

venom-conducting tube

venom canal

fang

venom gland

glottis

tooth

venom gland

tongue sheath

forked tongue

crocodile

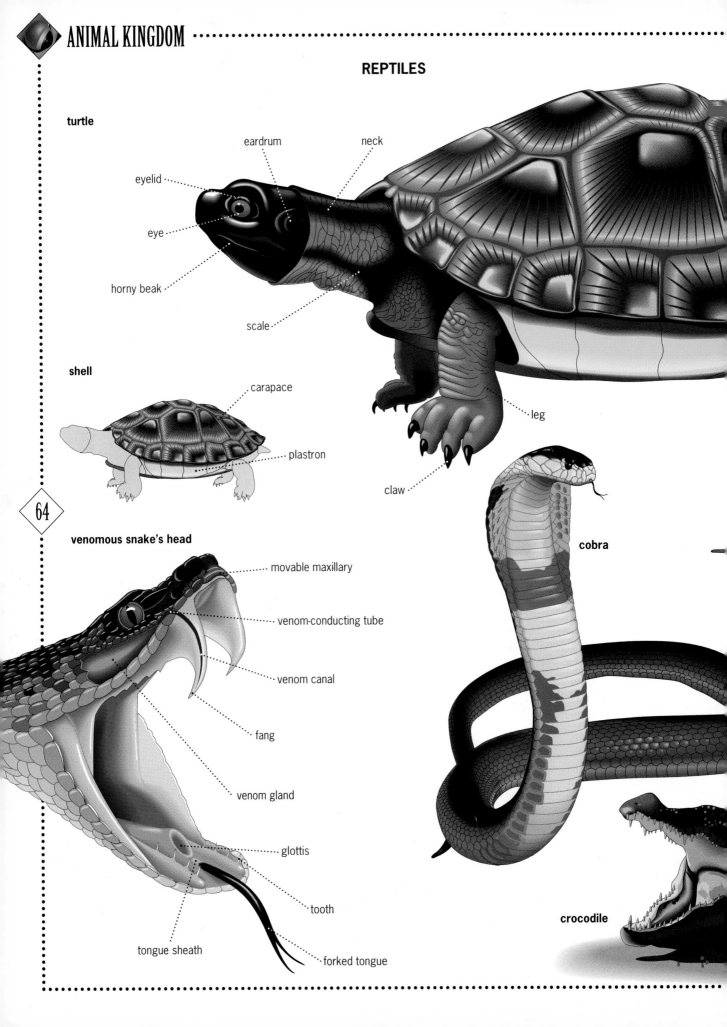

shield

tail

chameleon

lizard

rattlesnake

CAT

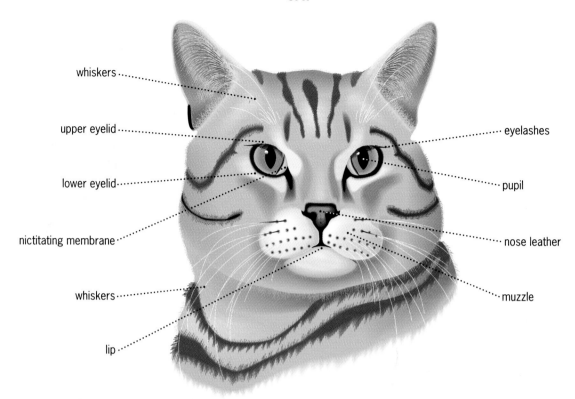

whiskers

upper eyelid

lower eyelid

nictitating membrane

whiskers

lip

eyelashes

pupil

nose leather

muzzle

DOG

MORPHOLOGY

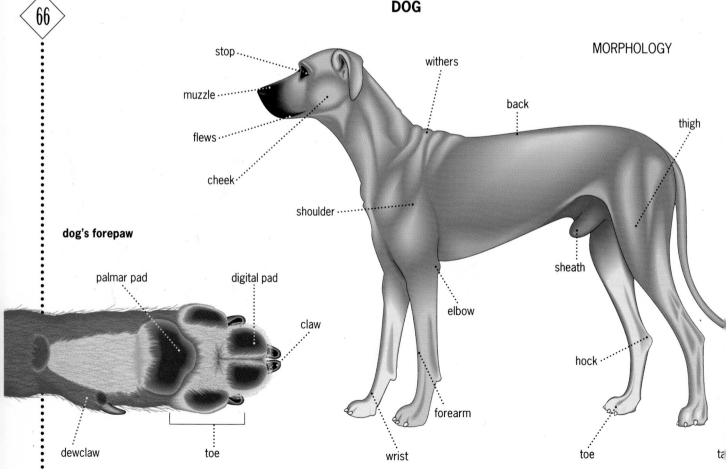

stop

muzzle

flews

cheek

withers

back

thigh

shoulder

sheath

dog's forepaw

palmar pad

digital pad

claw

elbow

hock

dewclaw

toe

wrist

forearm

toe

ta

HORSE

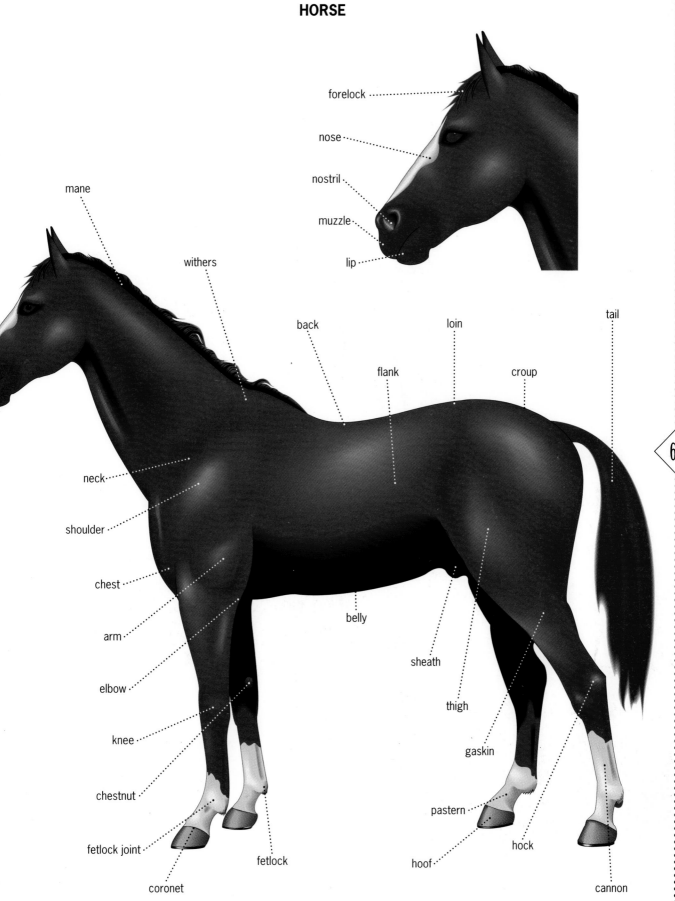

forelock

nose

nostril

muzzle

lip

mane

withers

back

loin

tail

flank

croup

neck

shoulder

chest

arm

belly

elbow

sheath

thigh

knee

gaskin

chestnut

pastern

hock

fetlock joint

fetlock

hoof

coronet

cannon

FARM ANIMALS

hen

chick

rooster; cock

duck

goose

turkey

68

cow

calf

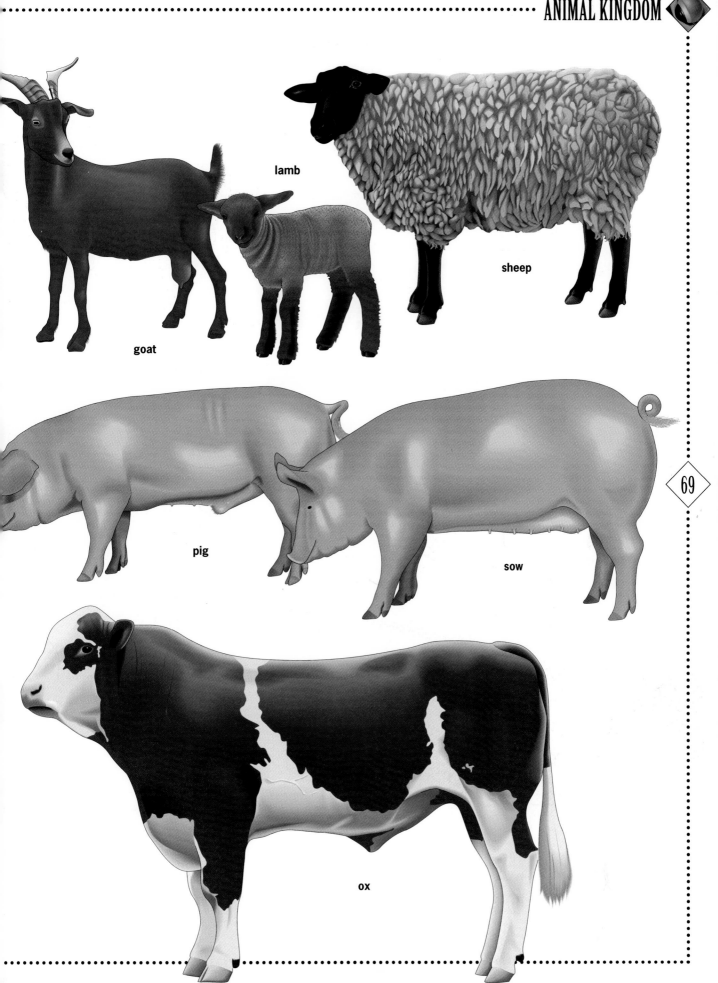

lamb

sheep

goat

pig

sow

ox

TYPES OF JAWS

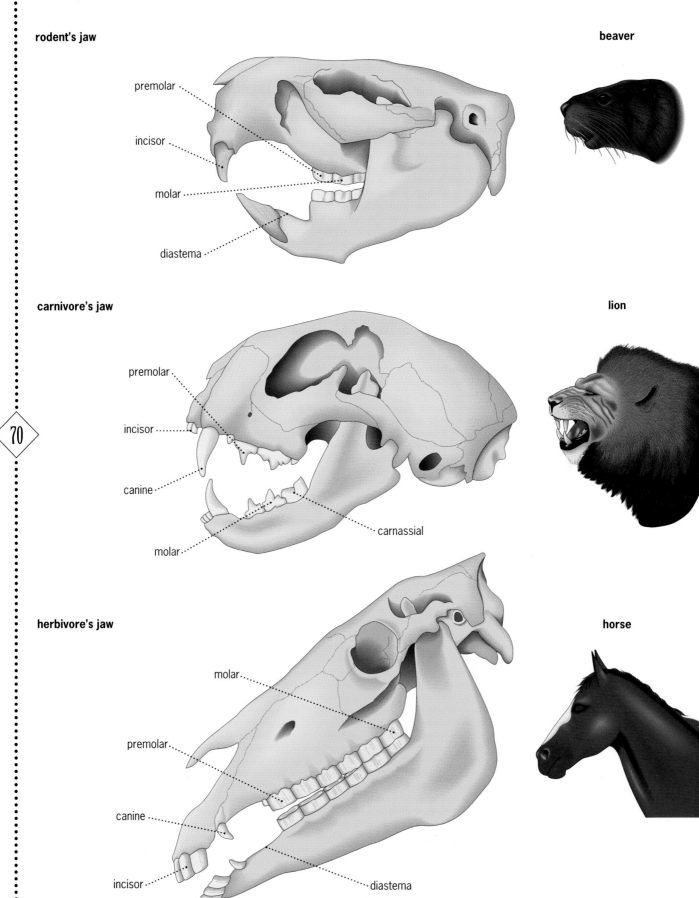

rodent's jaw

beaver

premolar

incisor

molar

diastema

carnivore's jaw

lion

premolar

incisor

canine

carnassial

molar

herbivore's jaw

horse

molar

premolar

canine

incisor

diastema

MAJOR TYPES OF HORNS

horns of mouflon

horns of giraffe

horns of rhinoceros

MAJOR TYPES OF TUSKS

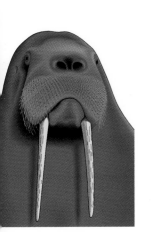
tusks of walrus

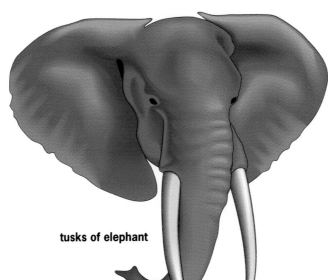
tusks of elephant

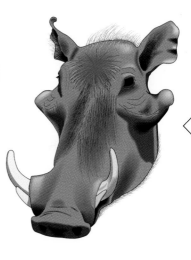
tusks of wart hog

TYPES OF HOOFS

one-toe hoof

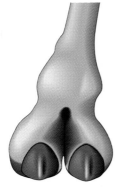
two-toed hoof

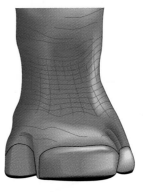
three-toed hoof

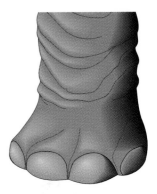
four-toed hoof

WILD ANIMALS

giraffe

polar bear

monkey

lion

dolphin

whale

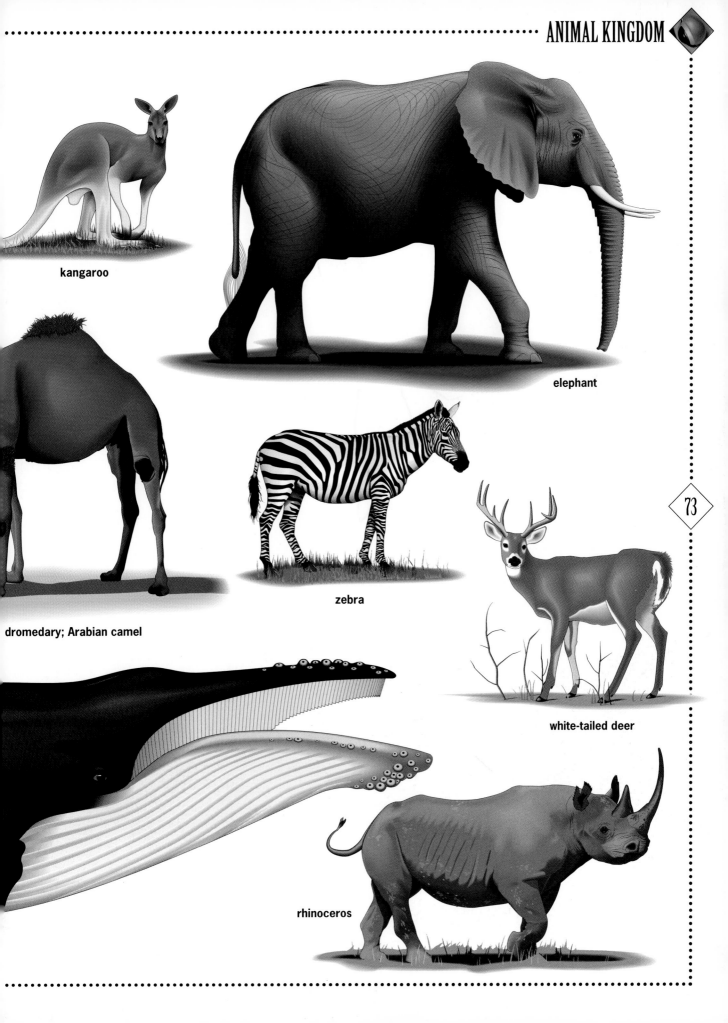

kangaroo

elephant

dromedary; Arabian camel

zebra

white-tailed deer

rhinoceros

BIRD

PRINCIPAL TYPES OF BILLS

MORPHOLOG

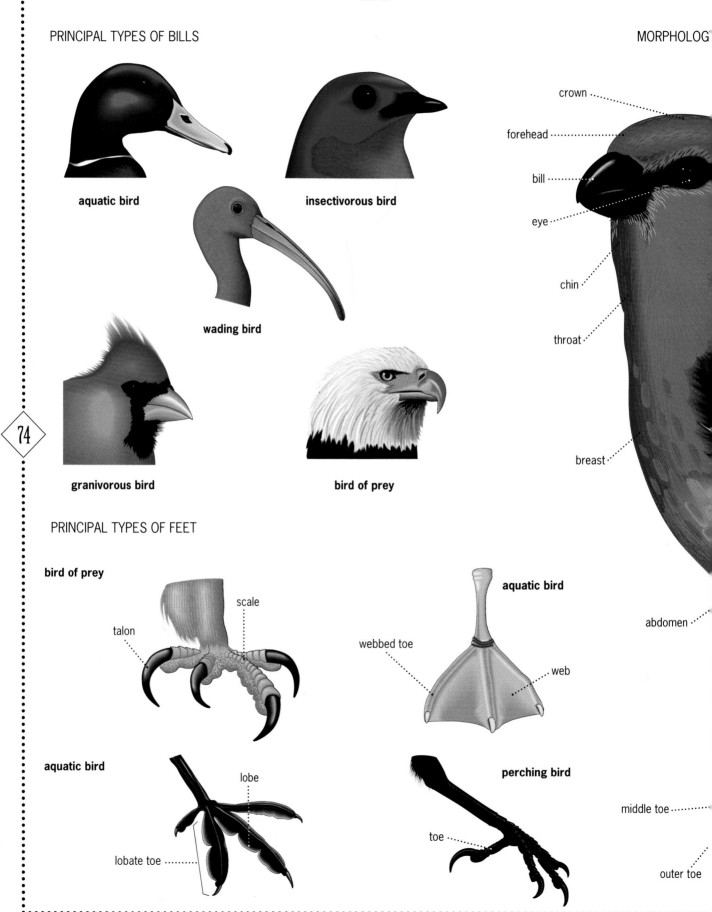

aquatic bird

insectivorous bird

wading bird

granivorous bird

bird of prey

crown

forehead

bill

eye

chin

throat

breast

74

PRINCIPAL TYPES OF FEET

bird of prey

scale

talon

aquatic bird

webbed toe

web

abdomen

aquatic bird

lobe

perching bird

toe

middle toe

lobate toe

outer toe

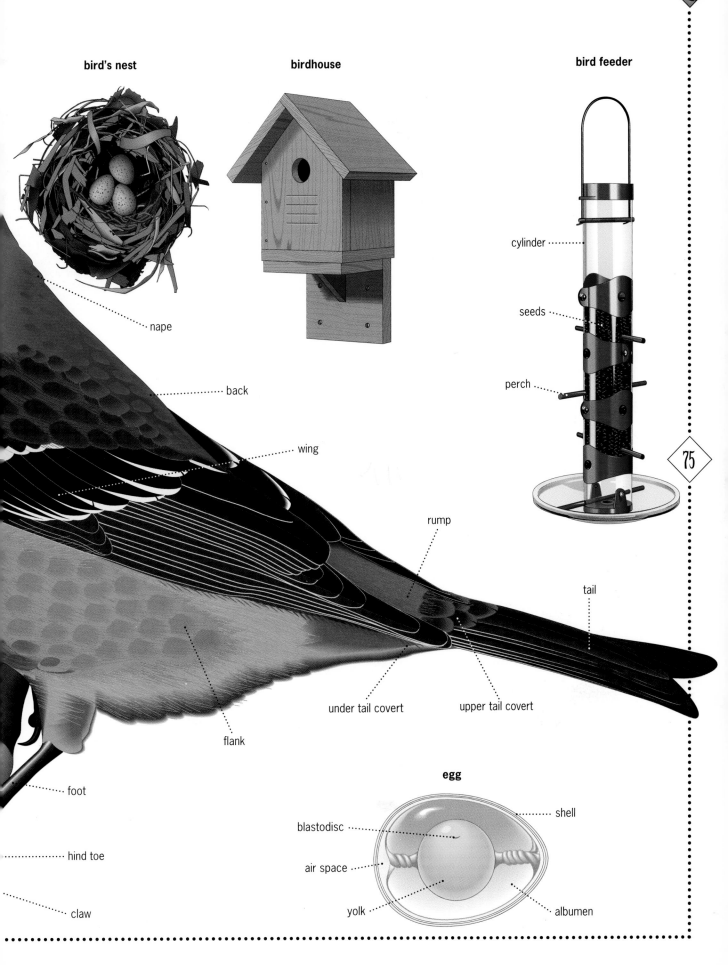

bird's nest

birdhouse

bird feeder

cylinder

seeds

perch

nape

back

wing

rump

tail

under tail covert

upper tail covert

flank

foot

hind toe

claw

egg

blastodisc

shell

air space

yolk

albumen

EXAMPLES OF BIRDS

crow

parrot

stork

swallow

flamingo

ostrich

robin

blue jay

owl

nightingale

hummingbird

peacock

HUMAN BODY, ANTERIOR VIEW

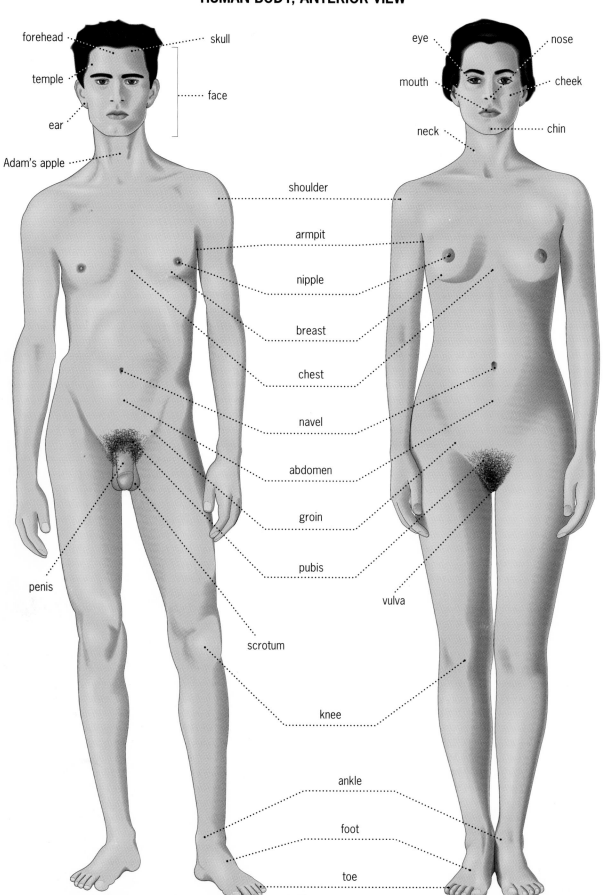

forehead

skull

temple

face

ear

Adam's apple

eye

nose

mouth

cheek

neck

chin

shoulder

armpit

nipple

breast

chest

navel

abdomen

groin

pubis

penis

vulva

scrotum

knee

ankle

foot

toe

78

HUMAN BODY, POSTERIOR VIEW

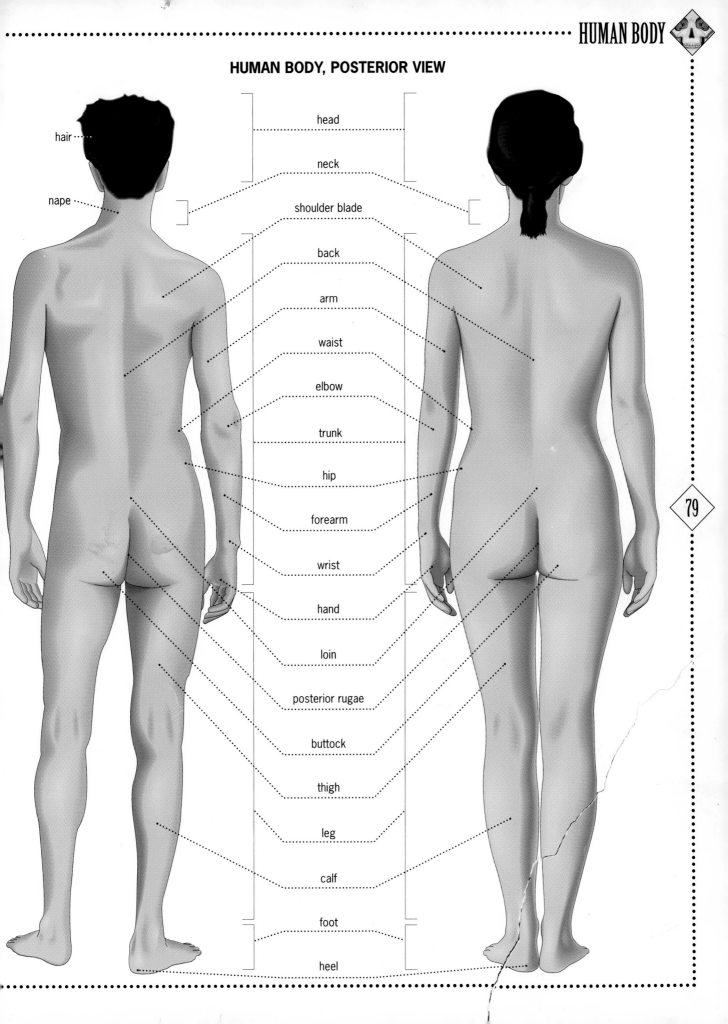

hair

nape

head

neck

shoulder blade

back

arm

waist

elbow

trunk

hip

forearm

wrist

hand

loin

posterior rugae

buttock

thigh

leg

calf

foot

heel

HUMAN BODY, POSTERIOR VIEW

SKELETON

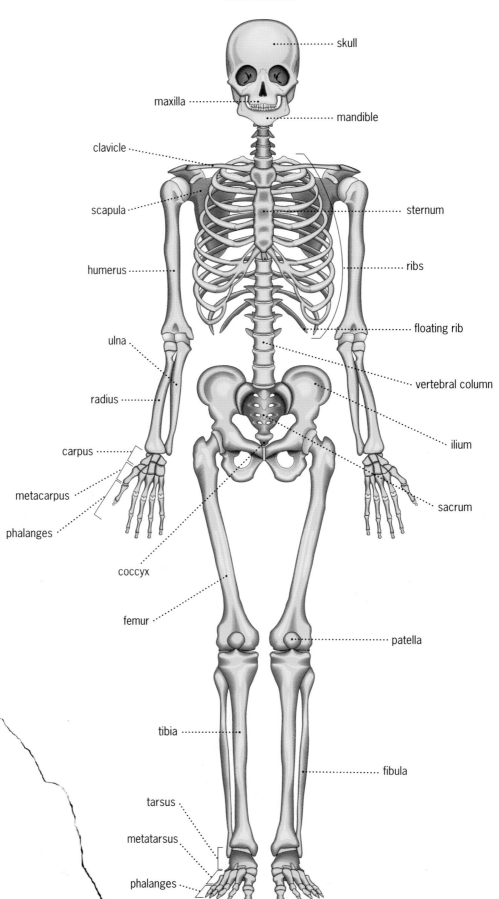

skull

maxilla

mandible

clavicle

scapula

sternum

humerus

ribs

floating rib

ulna

radius

vertebral column

carpus

ilium

metacarpus

phalanges

sacrum

coccyx

femur

patella

tibia

fibula

tarsus

metatarsus

phalanges

HUMAN ANATOMY

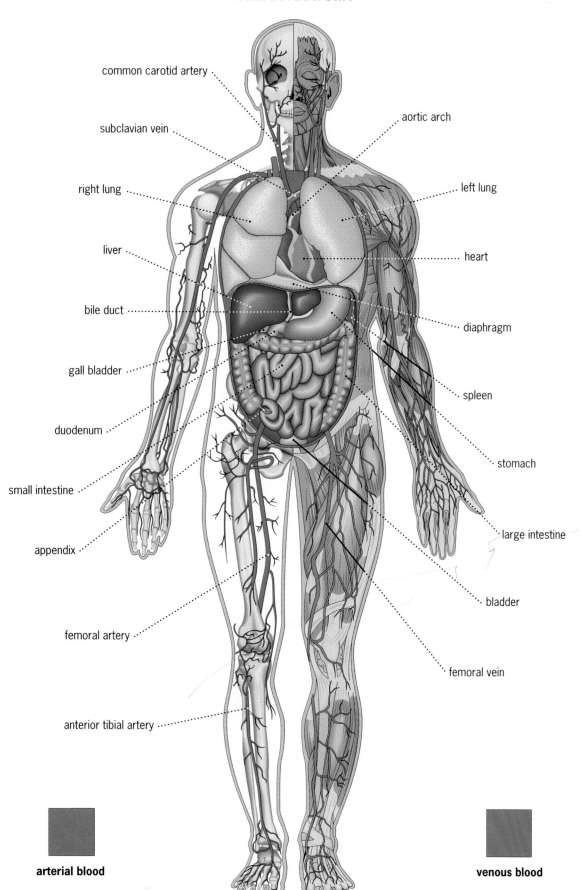

common carotid artery

aortic arch

subclavian vein

right lung

left lung

liver

heart

bile duct

diaphragm

gall bladder

spleen

duodenum

stomach

small intestine

large intestine

appendix

bladder

femoral artery

femoral vein

anterior tibial artery

arterial blood

venous blood

EYE: THE ORGAN OF SIGHT

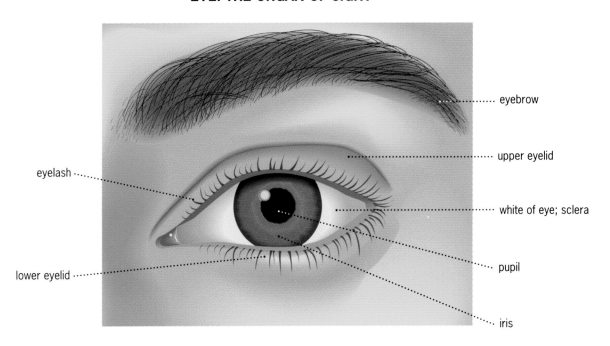

eyebrow

upper eyelid

eyelash

white of eye; sclera

pupil

lower eyelid

iris

HAND: THE ORGAN OF TOUCH

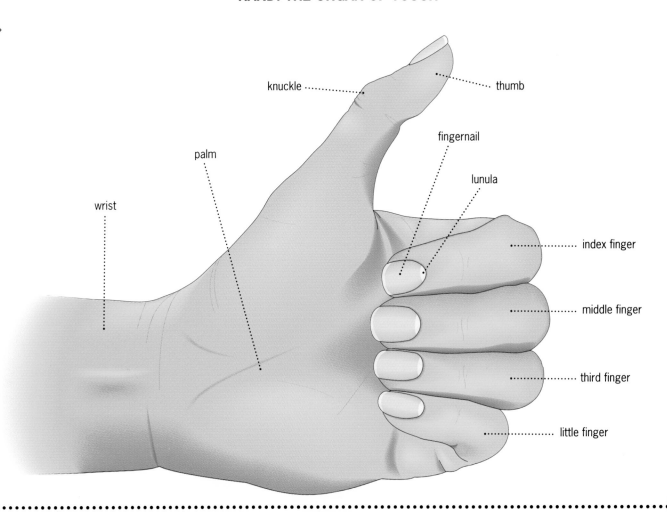

knuckle

thumb

fingernail

lunula

palm

wrist

index finger

middle finger

third finger

little finger

EAR: THE ORGAN OF HEARING

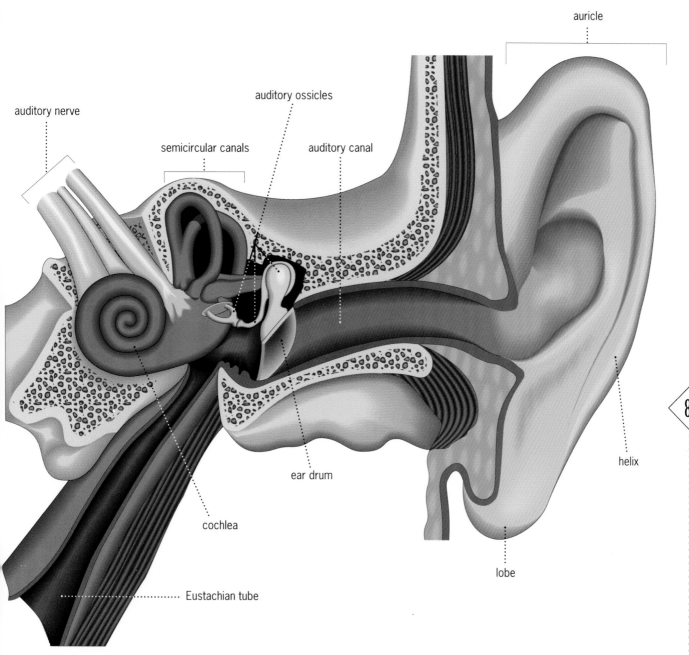

auricle

auditory ossicles

auditory nerve

semicircular canals

auditory canal

helix

ear drum

cochlea

lobe

Eustachian tube

PARTS OF THE EAR

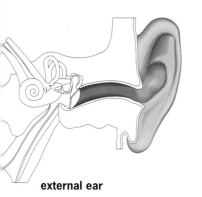

external ear

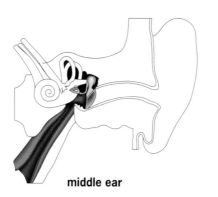

middle ear

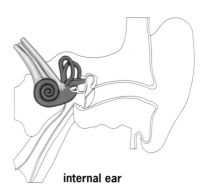

internal ear

NOSE: THE ORGAN OF SMELL

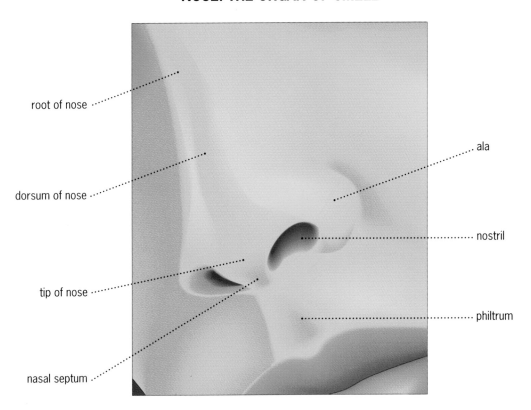

root of nose

dorsum of nose

tip of nose

nasal septum

ala

nostril

philtrum

84

MOUTH: THE ORGAN OF TASTE

taste sensations

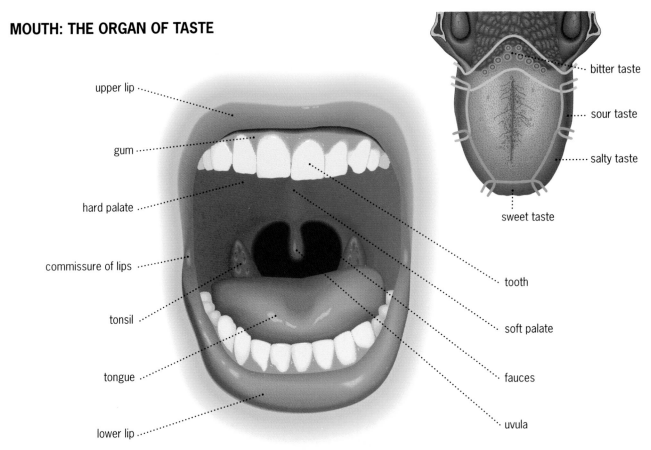

bitter taste

sour taste

salty taste

sweet taste

upper lip

gum

hard palate

commissure of lips

tonsil

tongue

lower lip

tooth

soft palate

fauces

uvula

HUMAN DENTURE

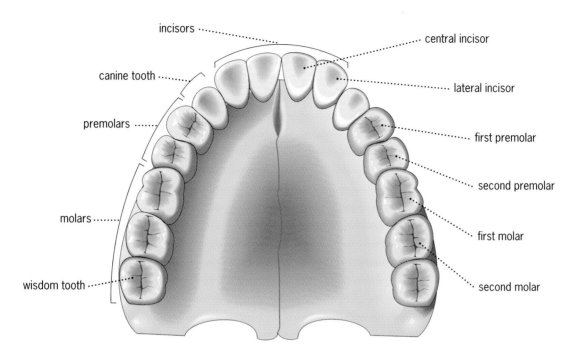

incisors

central incisor

canine tooth

lateral incisor

premolars

first premolar

second premolar

molars

first molar

wisdom tooth

second molar

cross section of a molar

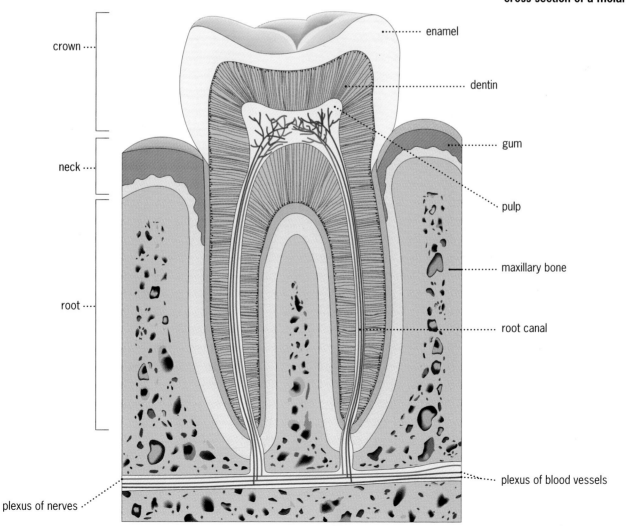

crown

enamel

dentin

neck

gum

pulp

root

maxillary bone

root canal

plexus of blood vessels

plexus of nerves

TRADITIONAL HOUSES

igloo

wigwam

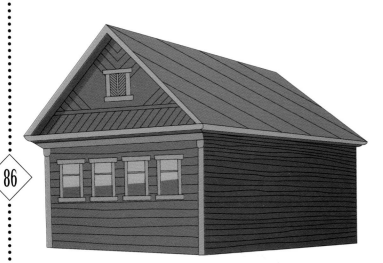

log cabin

mud hut

house on stilts

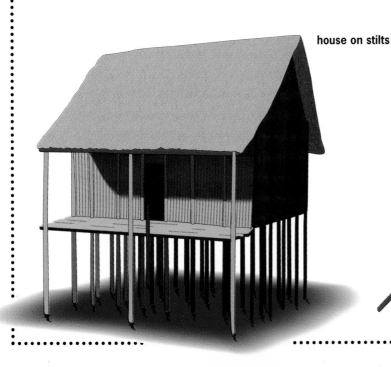

tepee

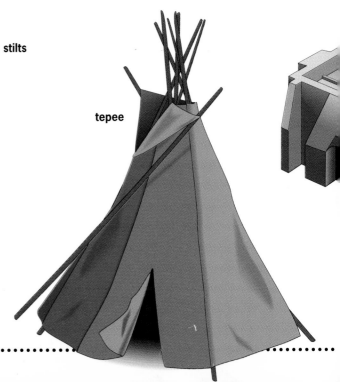

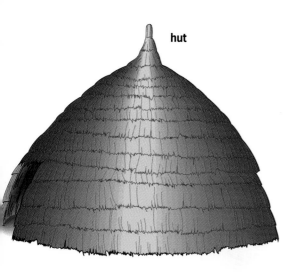

hut

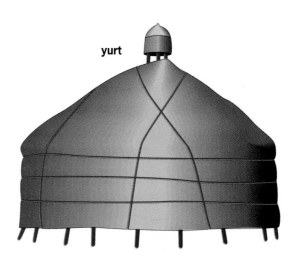

yurt

MOSQUE

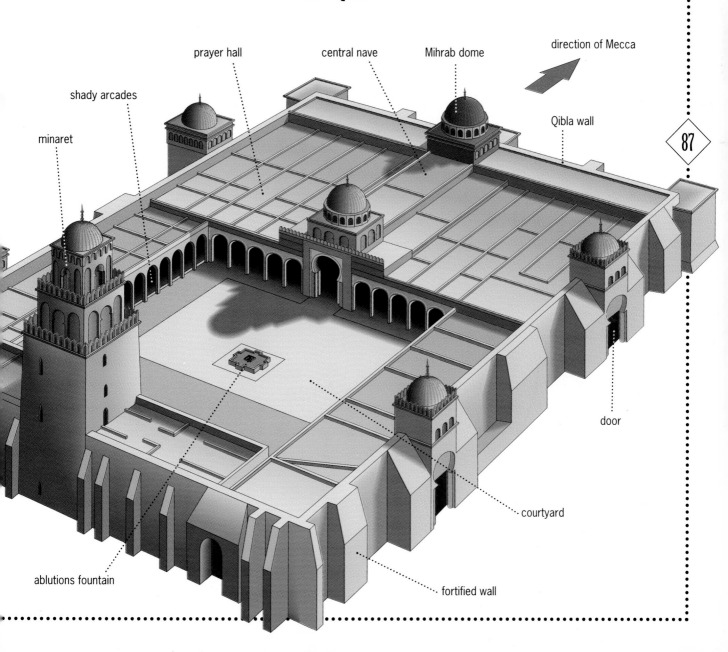

prayer hall

central nave

Mihrab dome

direction of Mecca

shady arcades

Qibla wall

minaret

courtyard

door

ablutions fountain

fortified wall

CASTLE

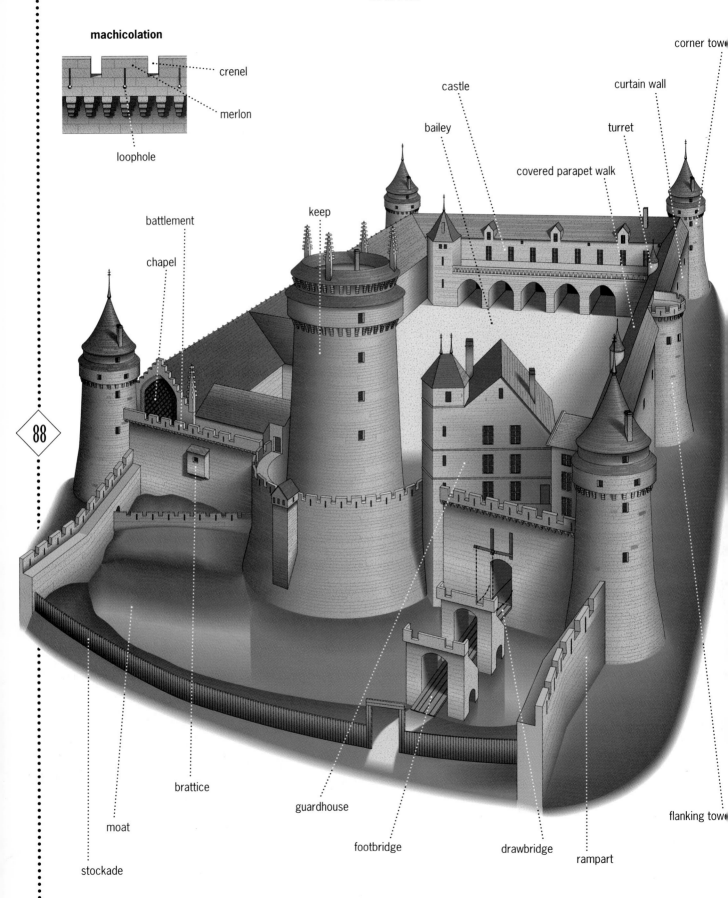

machicolation

crenel

merlon

loophole

castle

bailey

corner tower

curtain wall

turret

covered parapet walk

keep

battlement

chapel

brattice

guardhouse

moat

footbridge

drawbridge

rampart

stockade

flanking tower

GOTHIC CATHEDRAL

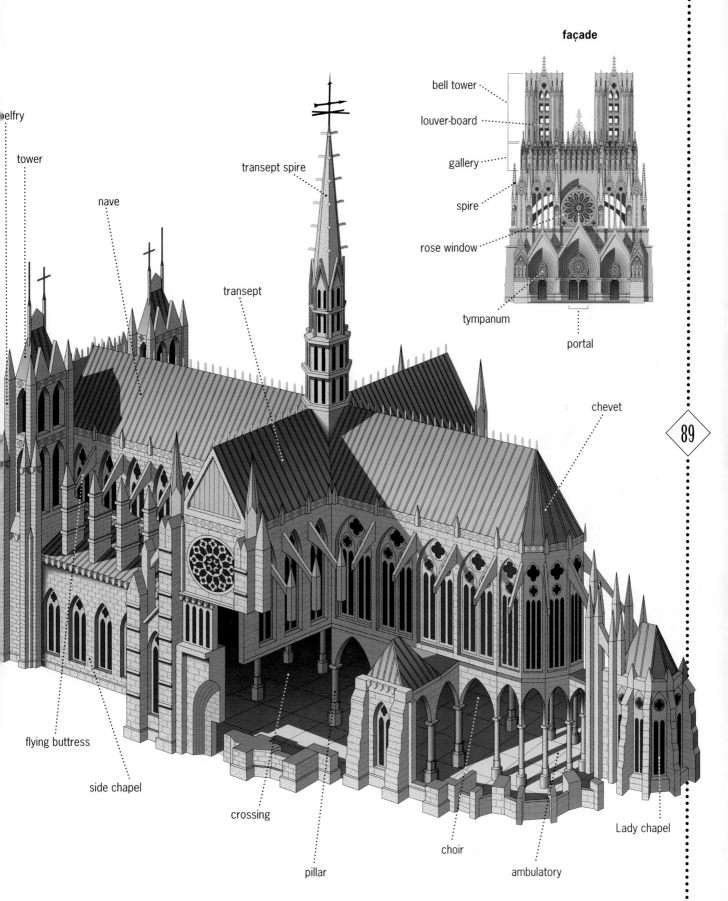

façade

bell tower

louver-board

gallery

spire

rose window

tympanum

portal

belfry

tower

nave

transept spire

transept

chevet

flying buttress

side chapel

crossing

pillar

choir

ambulatory

Lady chapel

DOWNTOWN

square
park
cathedral
convention center
railroad station
office tower
median strip

planetarium
street
railroad
delivery ramp
traffic island
freeway
boulevard

DOWNTOWN

90

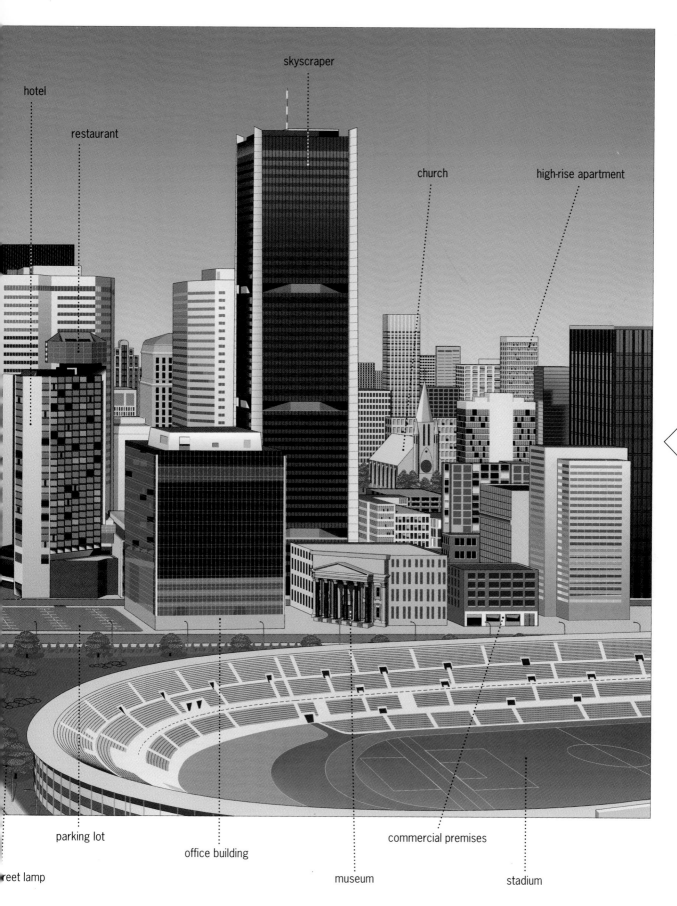

skyscraper

hotel

restaurant

church

high-rise apartment

parking lot

commercial premises

office building

reet lamp

museum

stadium

HOUSE

exterior of a house

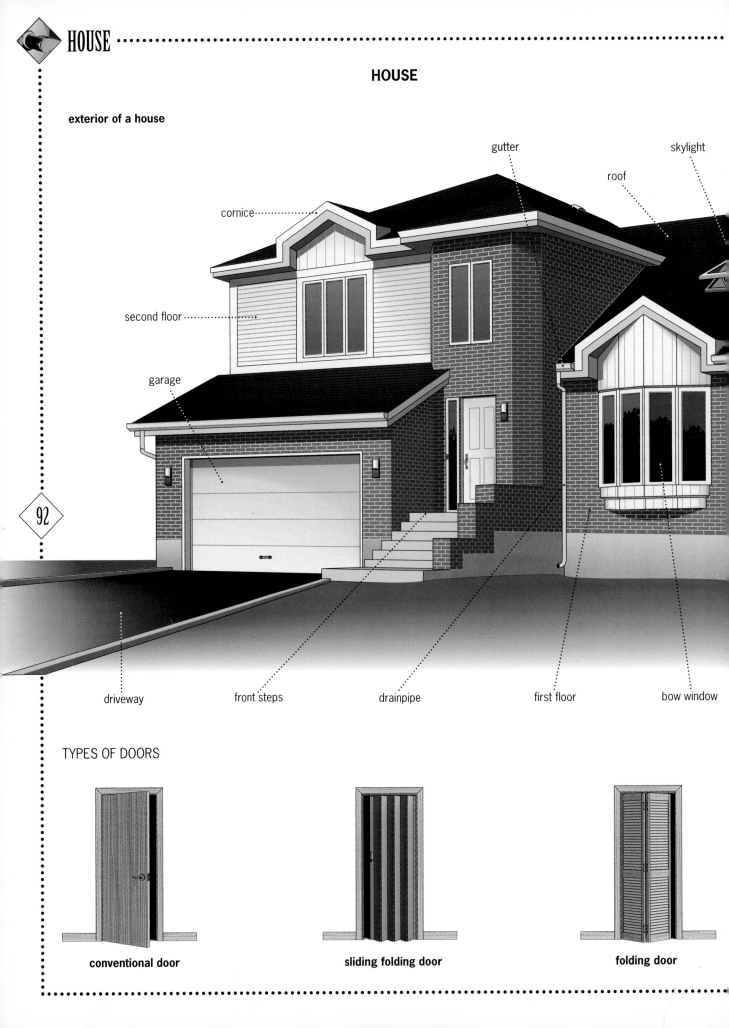

gutter

skylight

roof

cornice

second floor

garage

driveway

front steps

drainpipe

first floor

bow window

TYPES OF DOORS

conventional door

sliding folding door

folding door

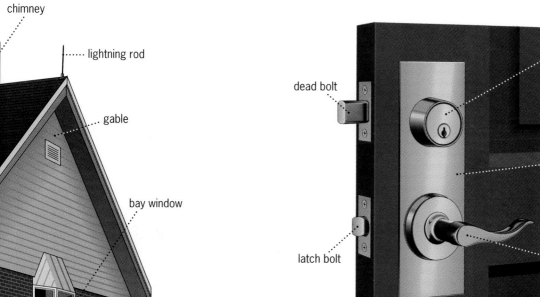

chimney

lightning rod

gable

bay window

basement window

basement

lock

dead bolt

lock

escutcheon

latch bolt

door handle

door

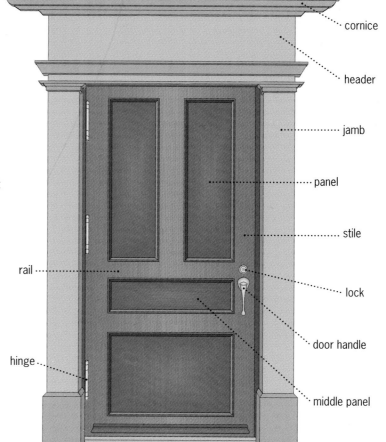

cornice

header

jamb

panel

stile

rail

lock

door handle

hinge

middle panel

threshold

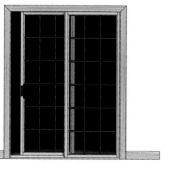

sliding door

WINDOW

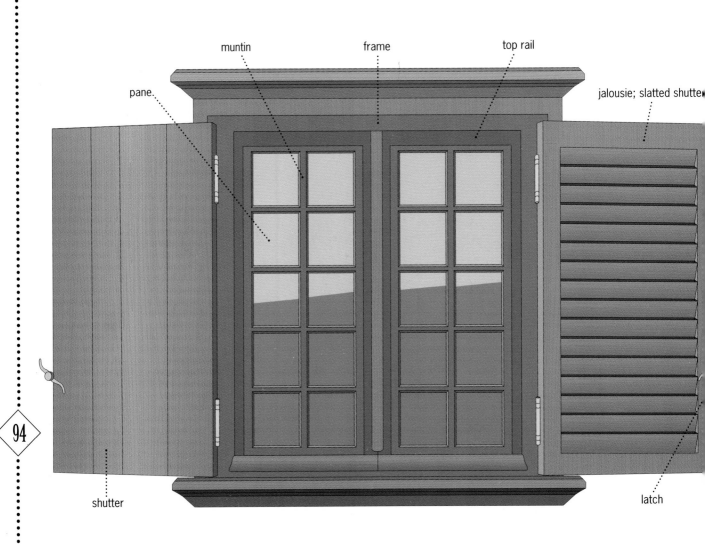

pane

muntin

frame

top rail

jalousie; slatted shutter

shutter

latch

TYPES OF WINDOWS

casement window (inward opening)

casement window (outward opening)

horizontal pivoting window

sliding window

sliding folding window

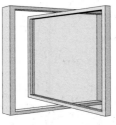

vertical pivoting window

sash window

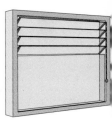

louvred window

BED

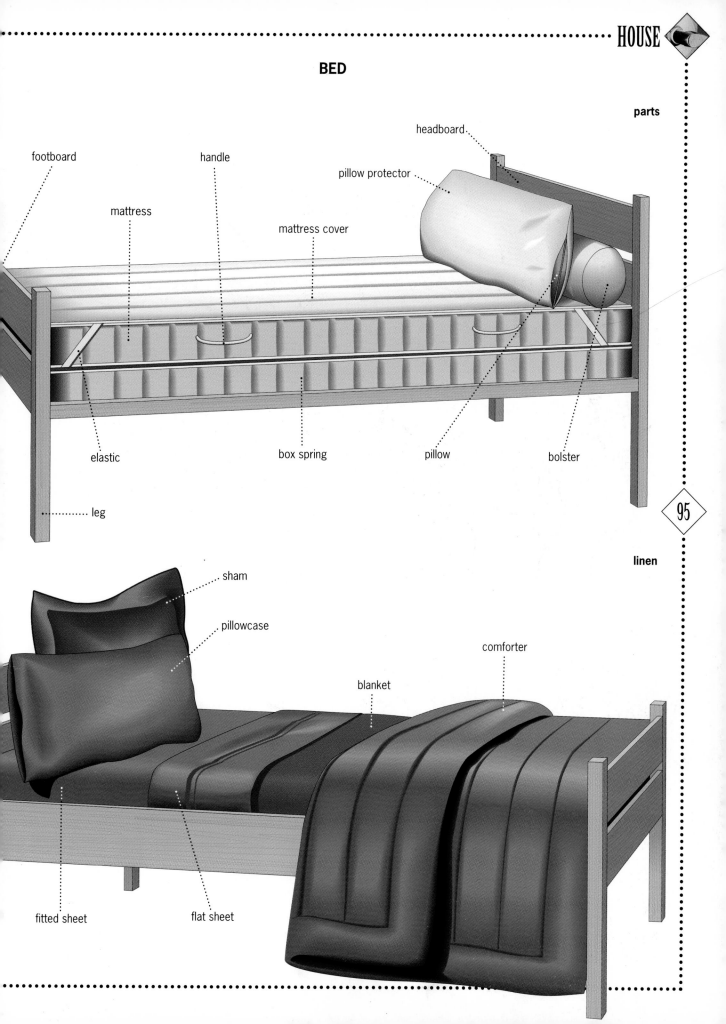

footboard

handle

headboard

pillow protector

mattress

mattress cover

elastic

box spring

pillow

bolster

leg

sham

pillowcase

comforter

blanket

fitted sheet

flat sheet

SEATS

sofa

loveseat

armchair

footstool

bench

bar stool

stool

chaise longue

stacking chairs

folding chair

rocking chair

TABLE AND CHAIRS

side chair

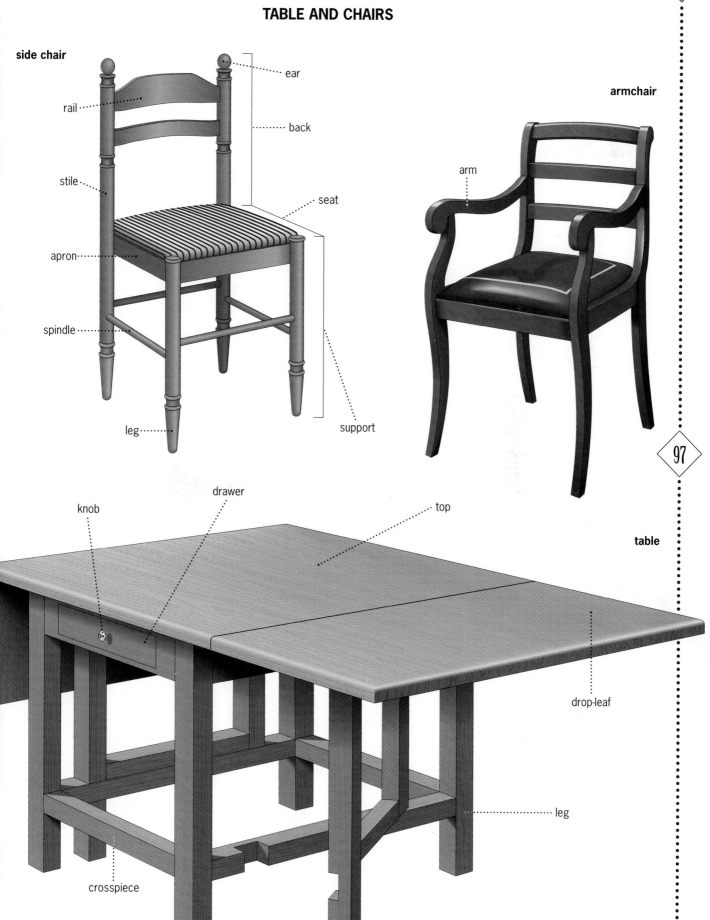

ear

rail

back

stile

seat

apron

spindle

support

leg

armchair

arm

table

knob

drawer

top

drop-leaf

leg

crosspiece

LIGHTS

track lighting

track

transformer

floor lamp

ceiling fixture

table lamp

shade

stand

hanging pendant

wall fixture

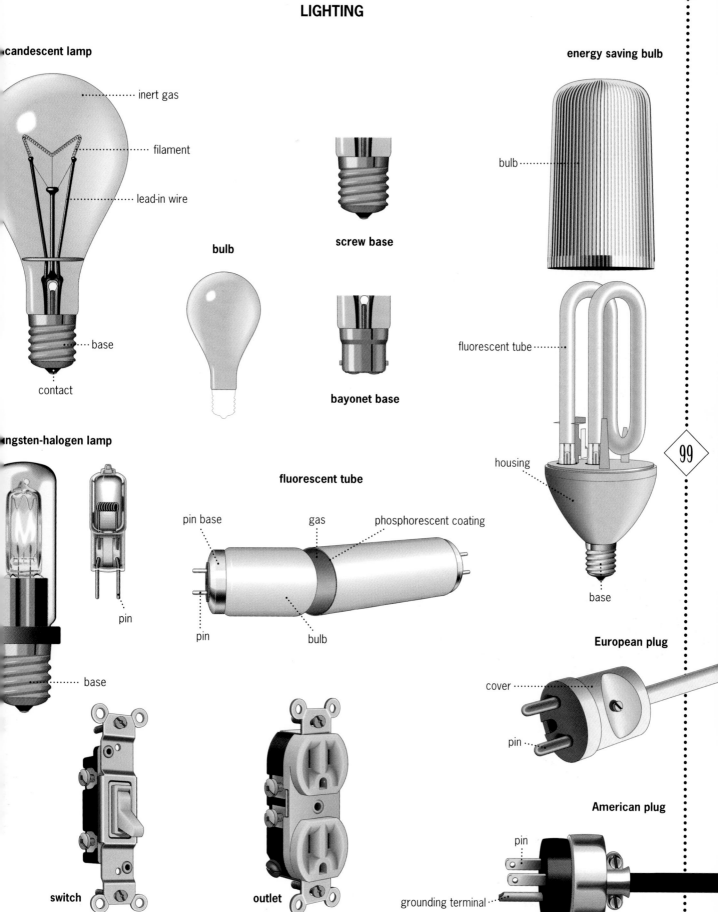

LIGHTING

candescent lamp

- inert gas
- filament
- lead-in wire
- base
- contact

bulb

screw base

bayonet base

ngsten-halogen lamp

- pin
- base

fluorescent tube

- pin base
- gas
- phosphorescent coating
- pin
- bulb

energy saving bulb

- bulb
- fluorescent tube
- housing
- base

European plug

- cover
- pin

American plug

- pin
- grounding terminal

switch

outlet

99

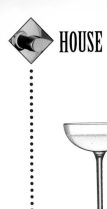
GLASSWARE

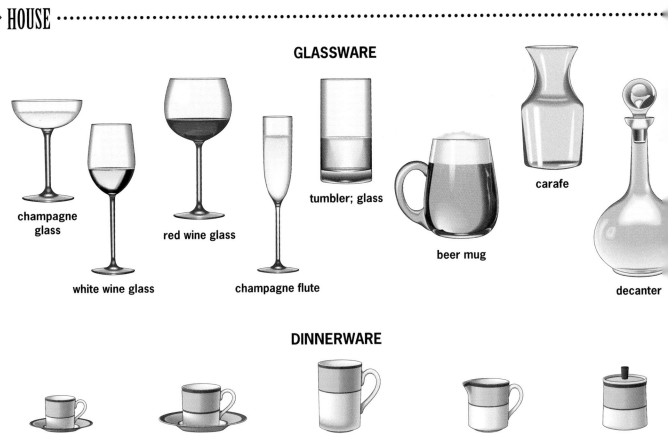

champagne glass

white wine glass

red wine glass

champagne flute

tumbler; glass

beer mug

carafe

decanter

DINNERWARE

coffee cup

cup

mug

creamer

sugar bowl

pepper shaker

salt shaker

butter dish

cereal bowl

soup bowl

salad dish

dinner plate

salad plate

bread and butter plate;
side plate

salad bowl

teapot

coffee plunger

soup tureen

water pitcher

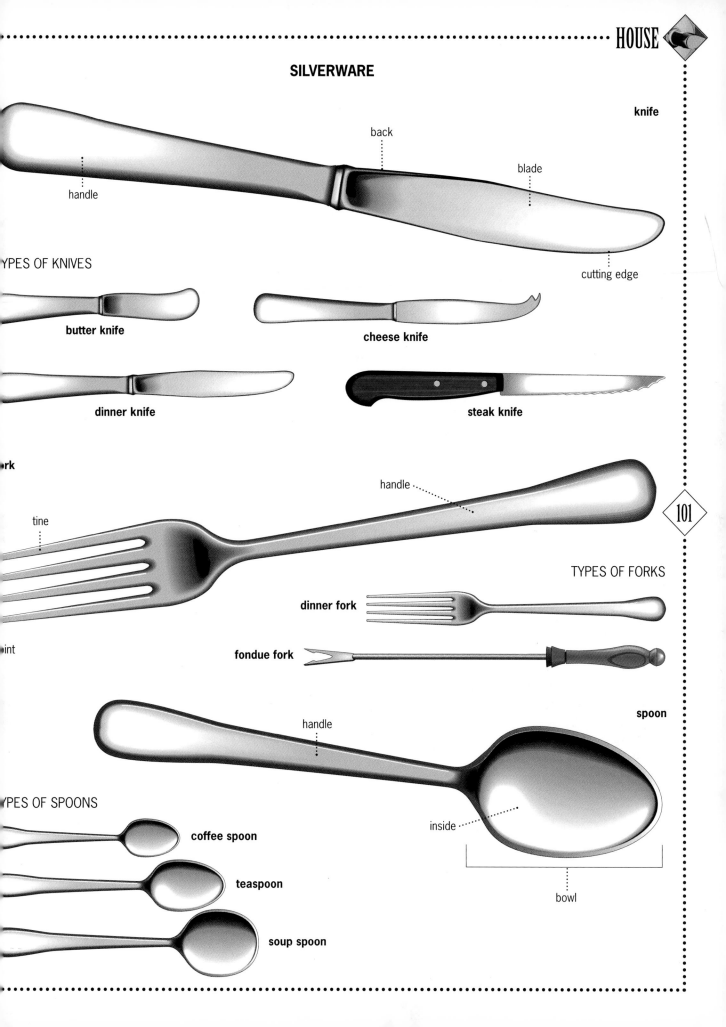

SILVERWARE

knife

back

blade

handle

cutting edge

YPES OF KNIVES

butter knife

cheese knife

dinner knife

steak knife

rk

handle

tine

TYPES OF FORKS

dinner fork

int

fondue fork

spoon

handle

YPES OF SPOONS

coffee spoon

inside

teaspoon

bowl

soup spoon

KITCHEN UTENSILS

ladle

potato masher

spatula

whisk

egg beater

measuring spoons

nutcracker

bottle opener

peeler

lever corkscrew

rolling pin

can opener

paghetti tongs

funnel

ice–cream scoop

colander

lemon squeezer

salad spinner

strainer

grater

COOKING UTENSILS

stockpot; casserole

frying pan

sauté pan

fondue set

wok

fondue pot

burner

double boiler

saucepan

vegetable steamer

roasting pans

pressure cooker

pressure regulator

safety valve

KITCHEN APPLIANCES

automatic drip coffee maker

reservoir

basket

carafe

warming plate

on-off switch

kettle

hand mixer

beater ejector · · · speed control

blender

container

cutting blade

push button

hand blender

beater

toaster

slot

lever

temperature control

REFRIGERATOR

ice cube tray

egg tray

dairy compartment

freezer compartment

thermostat control

butter compartment

106

crisper

refrigerator compartment

guard rail

meat tray

glass cover

shelf

storage door

COOKING APPLIANCES

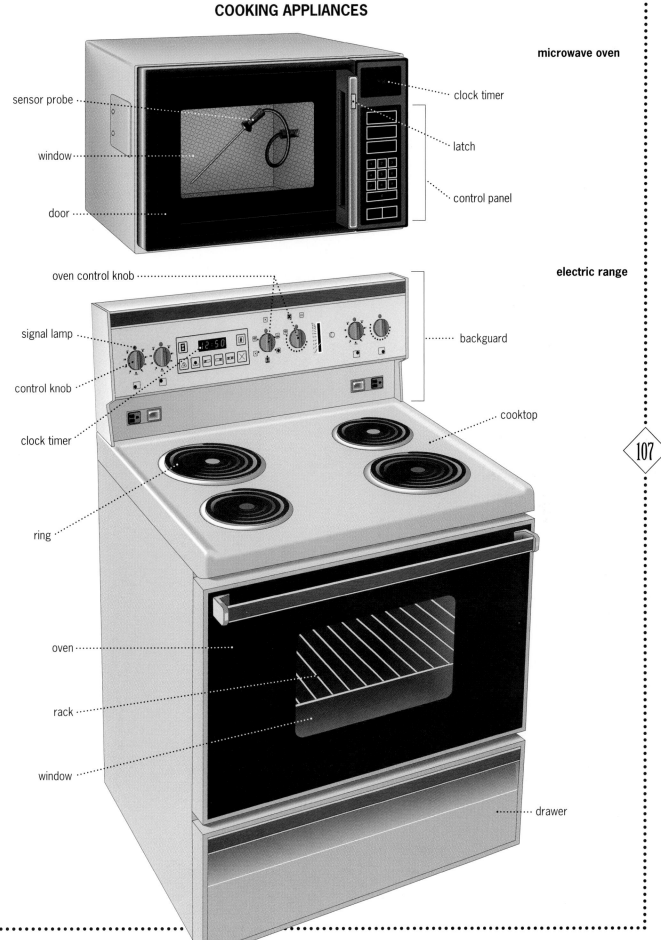

microwave oven

sensor probe

window

door

clock timer

latch

control panel

electric range

oven control knob

signal lamp

control knob

clock timer

backguard

cooktop

ring

oven

rack

window

drawer

107

CARPENTRY TOOLS

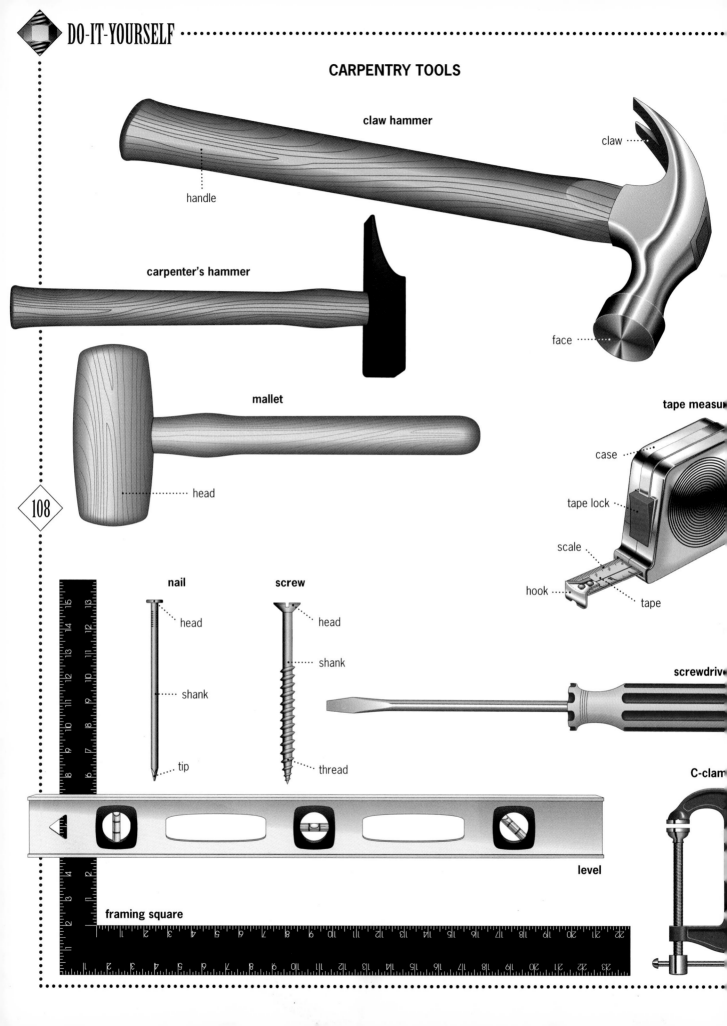

claw hammer

claw

handle

carpenter's hammer

face

mallet

tape measure

case

tape lock

scale

head

hook

tape

nail

screw

head

head

shank

shank

screwdriver

shank

tip

thread

C-clamp

level

framing square

handsaw

blade

tooth

handle

adjustable wrench

fixed jaw

thumbscrew

handle

movable jaw

handle

locking pliers

lever

spring

adjusting screw

release lever

jaw

rib joint pliers

adjustable channel

bolt

nut

head

threaded rod

long-nose pliers

slip joint pliers

handle

slip joint

ELECTRIC TOOLS

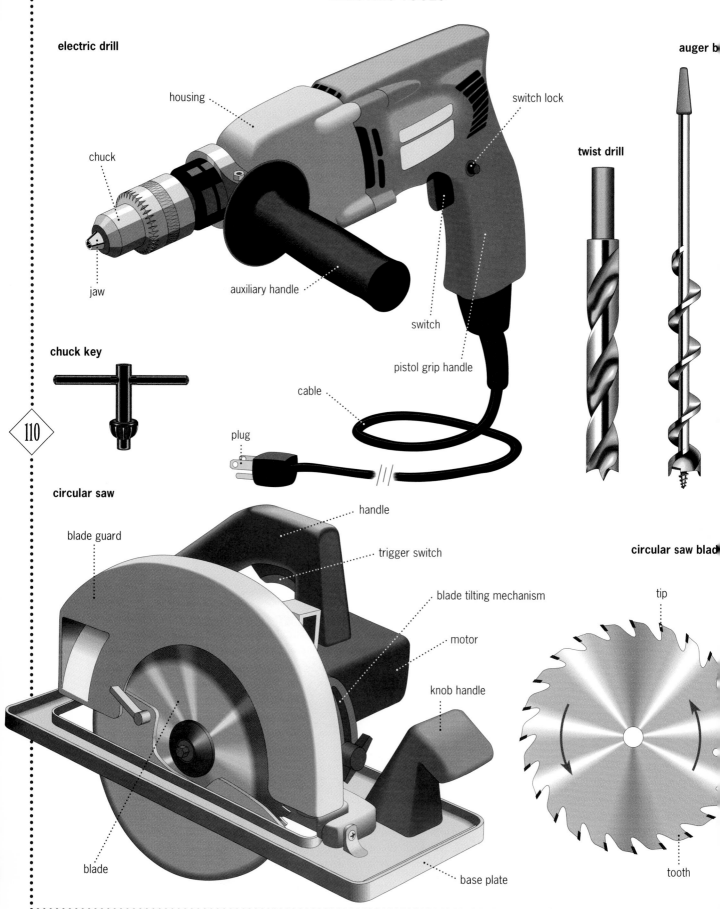

electric drill

housing

chuck

jaw

auxiliary handle

switch

pistol grip handle

switch lock

auger b

twist drill

chuck key

cable

plug

circular saw

handle

blade guard

trigger switch

blade tilting mechanism

motor

knob handle

circular saw blad

tip

blade

base plate

tooth

110

PAINTING UPKEEP

aint roller

tray

scraper

blade

roller frame

roller cover

extension ladder

brush

handle

bristles

side rail

pulley

locking device

tepladder

rung

platform ladder

hoisting rope

anti-slip shoe

111

MEN'S CLOTHING

shirt

collar point

collar

placket

breast pocket

front

cuff

button

shirttail

suspenders

adjustment slide

button loop

suspender clip

leather end

112

tie

rear apron

neck end

loop

front apron

belt

frame

punch hole

belt carrier

tongue

pants

waistband

pocket

fly

crease

cuff

vest

boxer shorts

briefs

fly

crotch

waistband

double-breasted jacket

collar

lining

breast welt pocket

sleeve

concealed pocket

flap

patch pocket

duffle coat

hood

frog

toggle fastening

cap

crown

peak

stocking cap

hunting cap

ear flap

jacket

snap fastener

elastic waistband

windbreacker

waistband

drawstring

WOMEN'S CLOTHING

toque

knitted hat

balaclava

peak

beret

suit

jacket

blouse

double-breasted jacket

114

skirt

overcoat

poncho

dress

jeans

ski pants

shorts

Bermuda shorts

footstrap

115

straight skirt

culottes

pleated skirt

WOMEN'S CLOTHING

pajamas

bra

shoulder strap ·········

cup ·········

pants

half-slip

bathrobe

SWEATERS

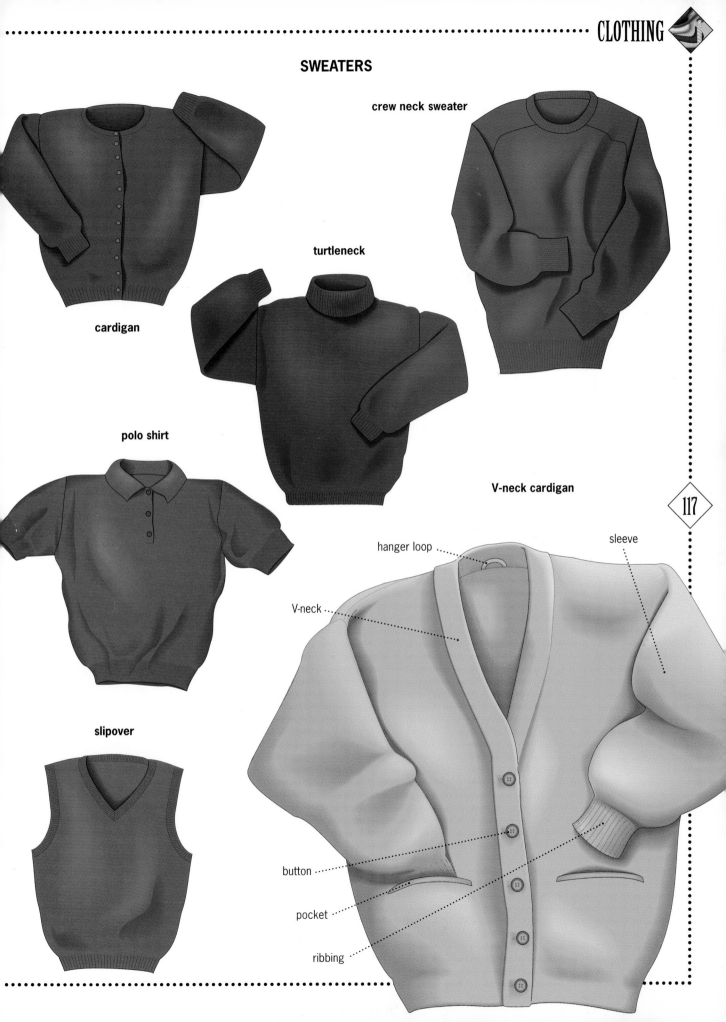

crew neck sweater

turtleneck

cardigan

polo shirt

V-neck cardigan

slipover

hanger loop

V-neck

sleeve

button

pocket

ribbing

GLOVES AND STOCKINGS

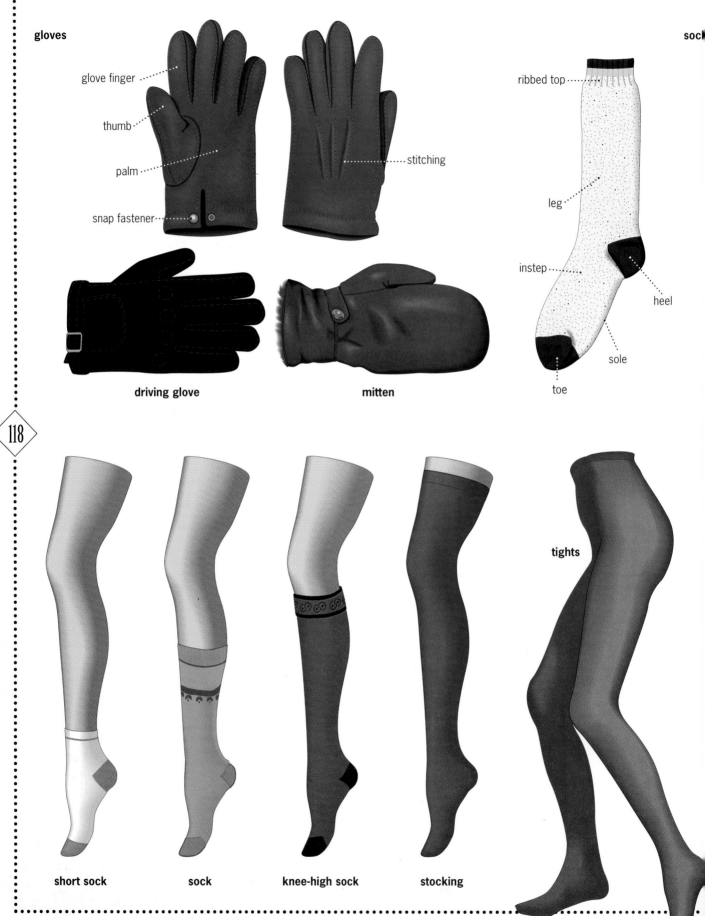

gloves

soc

glove finger

thumb

palm

snap fastener

stitching

driving glove

mitten

ribbed top

leg

instep

heel

sole

toe

118

short sock

sock

knee-high sock

stocking

tights

SHOES

heavy duty boot

slingback

ballerina

tennis shoe

pump

thigh-boot

espadrille

loafer

moccasin

clog

boot

ankle boot

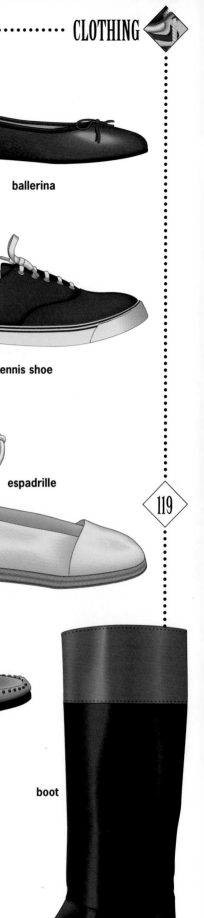

SPORTSWEAR

EXERCISE WEAR

tank top

swimsuit

leotard

TRACK SUIT

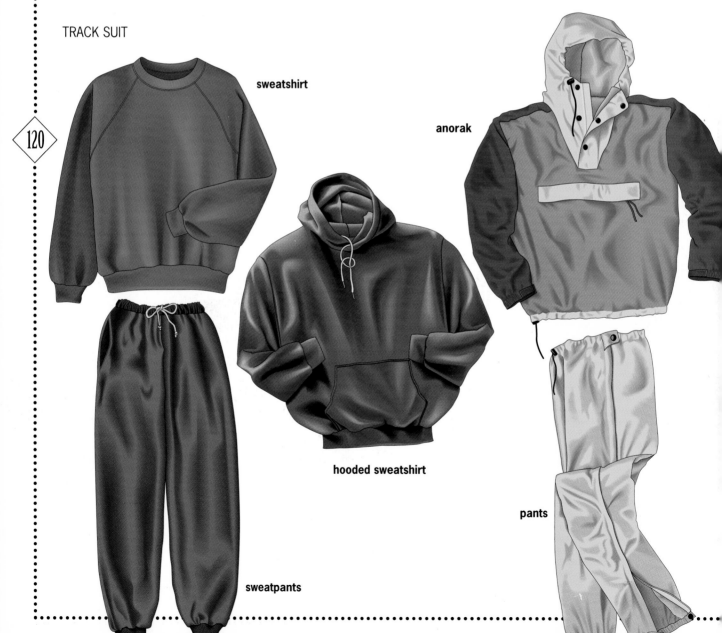

sweatshirt

anorak

hooded sweatshirt

pants

sweatpants

EXERCISE WEAR

footless tights

leg-warmer

swimming trunks

boxer shorts

running shoe

121

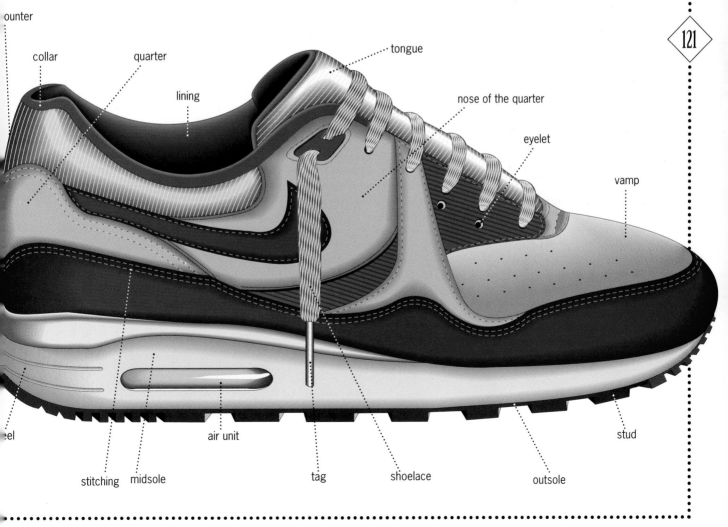

ounter

collar

quarter

lining

tongue

nose of the quarter

eyelet

vamp

el

air unit

stud

stitching   midsole

tag

shoelace

outsole

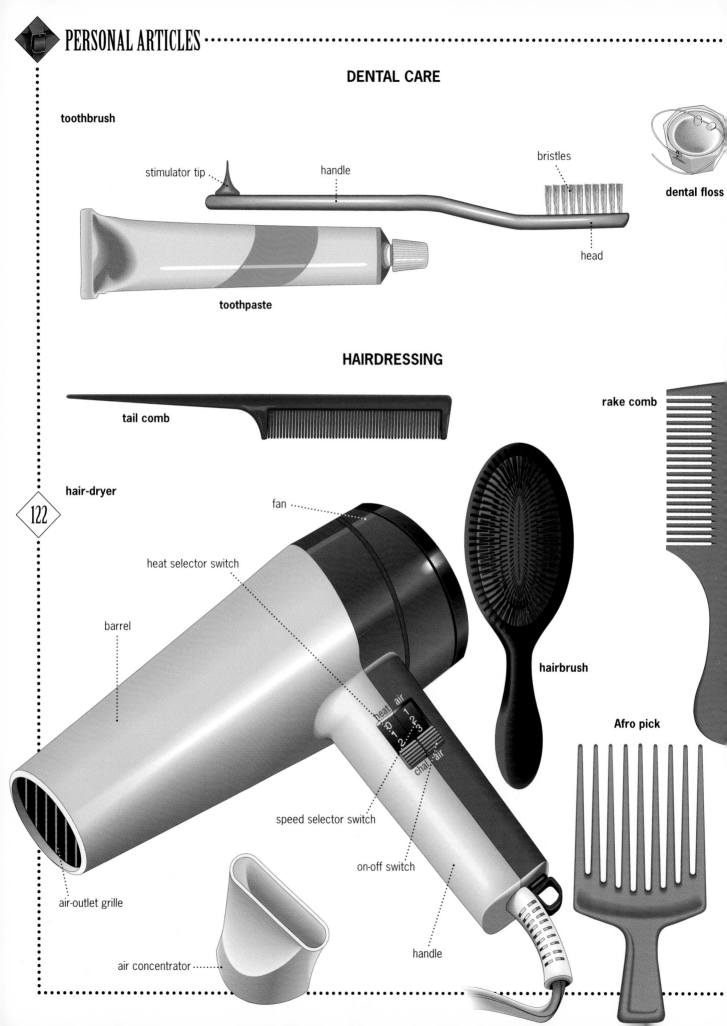

PERSONAL ARTICLES

DENTAL CARE

toothbrush

stimulator tip

handle

bristles

dental floss

head

toothpaste

HAIRDRESSING

tail comb

rake comb

hair-dryer

fan

heat selector switch

hairbrush

barrel

Afro pick

speed selector switch

on-off switch

air-outlet grille

handle

air concentrator

122

LEATHER GOODS

knapsack

drawstring bag

drawstring

key case

wallet

shoulder strap

front pocket

purse

GLASSES

glass lens   bridge   bar

rim   nose pad   temple

UMBRELLA

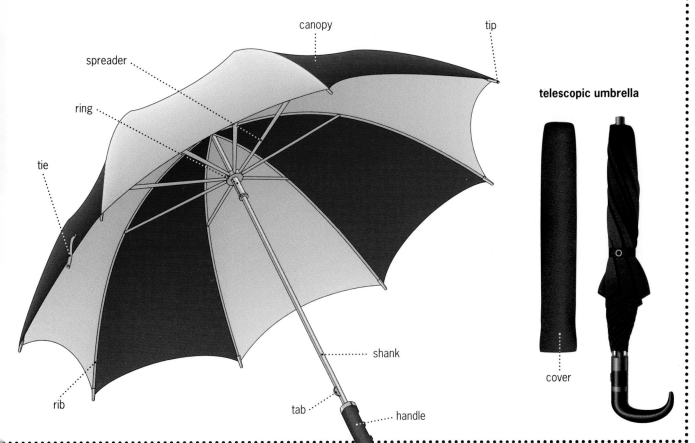

canopy   tip

spreader

ring

tie

rib

tab

handle

shank

telescopic umbrella

cover

COMMUNICATION BY TELEPHONE

telephone set

telephone answering machine

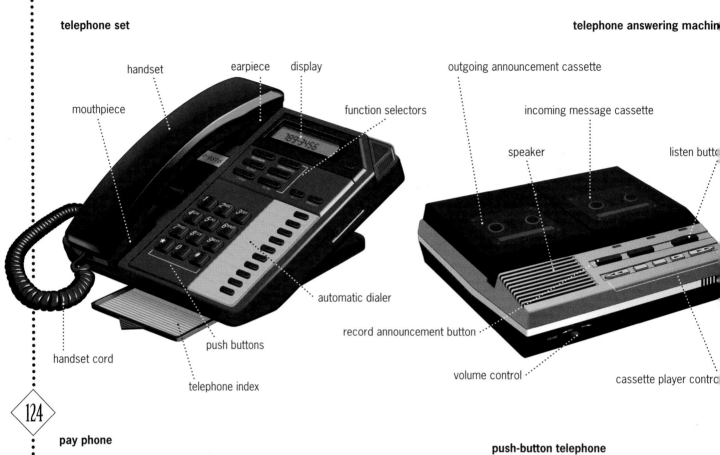

handset   earpiece   display

mouthpiece   function selectors

outgoing announcement cassette

incoming message cassette

speaker   listen button

automatic dialer

record announcement button

push buttons

handset cord

telephone index

volume control   cassette player control

124

pay phone

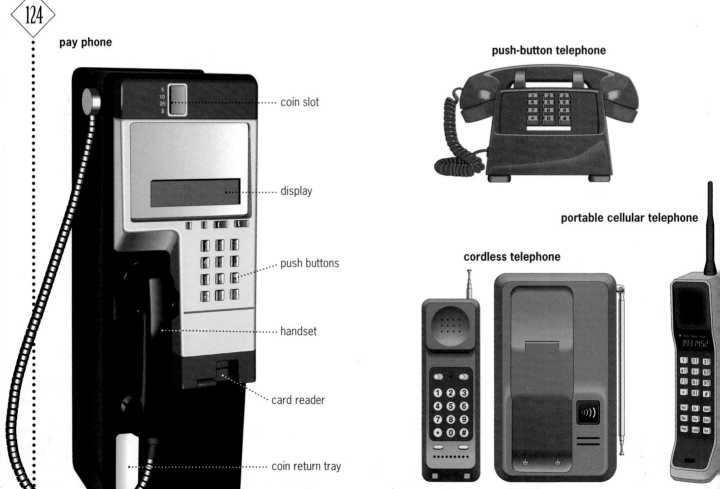

push-button telephone

portable cellular telephone

cordless telephone

coin slot

display

push buttons

handset

card reader

coin return tray

PHOTOGRAPHY

single lens reflex (slr) camera

accessory shoe

film rewind button

hot-shoe contact

film advance button

control dial

control panel

exposure button

film speed

remote control terminal

camera body

focus setting ring

shutter release button

objective lens

electronic flash

flashtube

photoelectric cell

mounting foot

rangefinder; compact camera

perforation

cassette film

film leader

Polaroid® Land camera

ocket camera

cartridge film

film pack

125

TELEVISION

television set

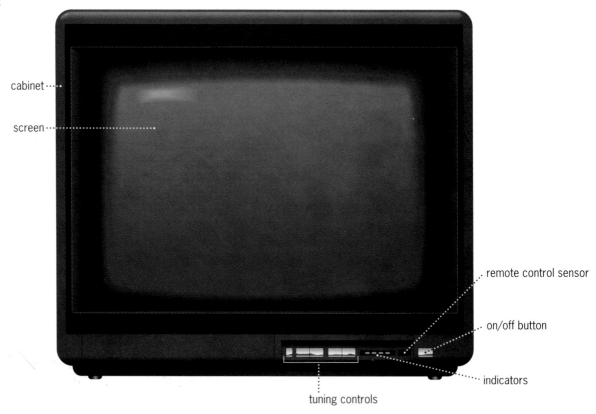

cabinet

screen

remote control sensor

on/off button

indicators

tuning controls

remote control

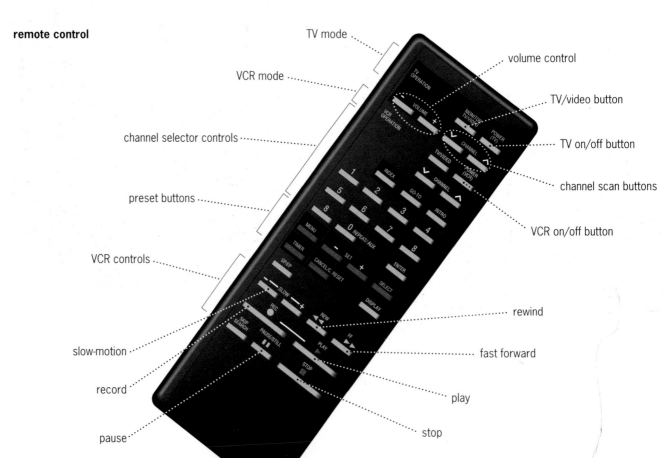

TV mode

VCR mode

channel selector controls

preset buttons

VCR controls

slow-motion

record

pause

volume control

TV/video button

TV on/off button

channel scan buttons

VCR on/off button

rewind

fast forward

play

stop

VIDEO

videocassette recorder

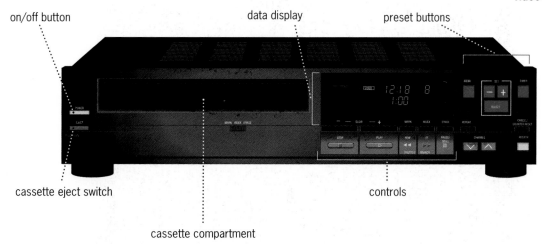

on/off button

data display

preset buttons

cassette eject switch

controls

cassette compartment

video camera

accessory shoe

eyepiece

power zoom button

electronic viewfinder

cassette eject switch

videotape operation controls

viewfinder adjustment keys

built-in microphone

battery

zoom lens

data display

shooting adjustment keys

edit/search buttons

cassette compartment

battery eject switch

STEREO SYSTEM

SYSTEM COMPONENTS

tuner

FM antenna

AM antenna

turntable

compact disc player

cassette tape deck

amplifier

128

graphic equalizer

loudspeakers

left channel

right channel

headphone

tweeter

midrange

headband

ear cushion

woofer

adjusting band

diaphragm; cone

speaker cover

earphone

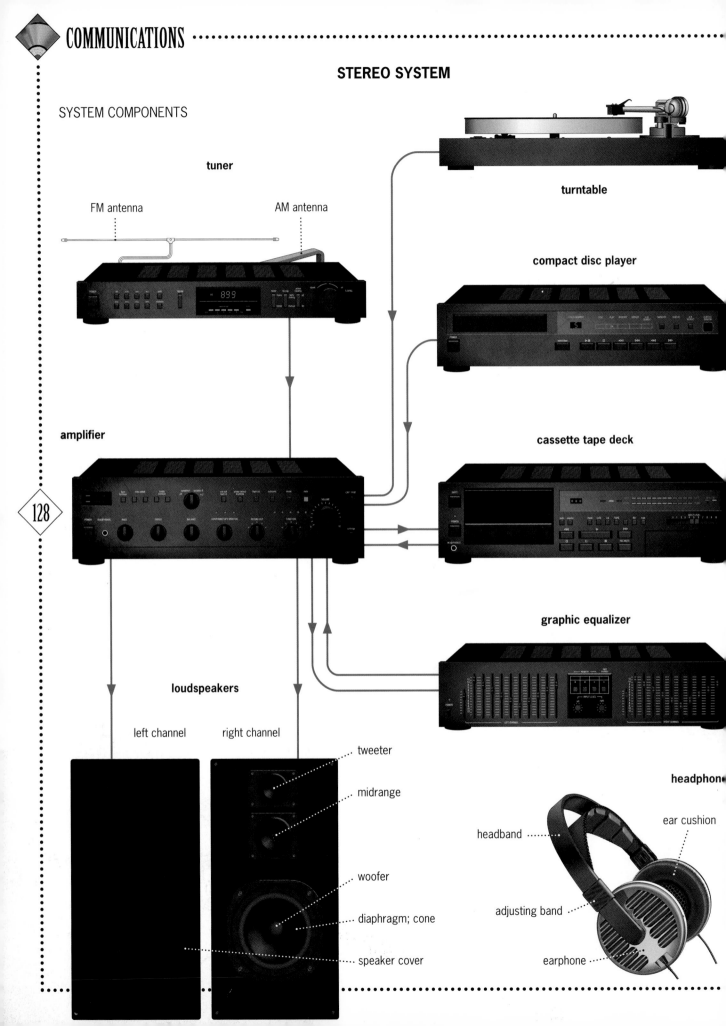

PORTABLE SOUND SYSTEMS

portable CD AM/FM cassette recorder

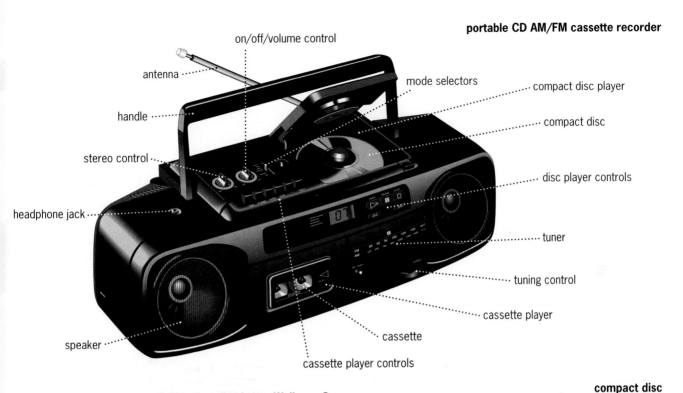

on/off/volume control

antenna

mode selectors

compact disc player

handle

compact disc

stereo control

disc player controls

headphone jack

tuner

tuning control

cassette player

cassette

speaker

cassette player controls

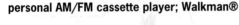

personal AM/FM cassette player; Walkman®

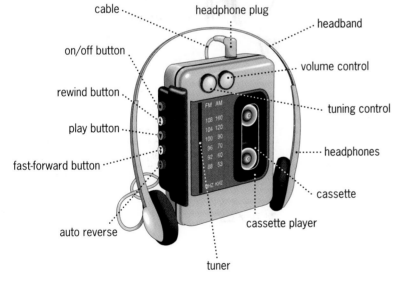

cable

headphone plug

headband

on/off button

volume control

rewind button

tuning control

play button

headphones

fast-forward button

cassette

auto reverse

cassette player

tuner

compact disc

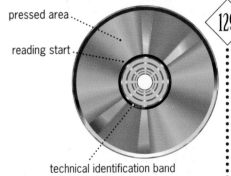

pressed area

reading start

technical identification band

129

record

spiral-in groove

spiral

band

tail-out groove

label

centre hole

cassette

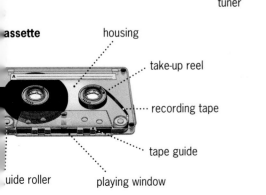

housing

take-up reel

recording tape

tape guide

guide roller

playing window

CAR

body

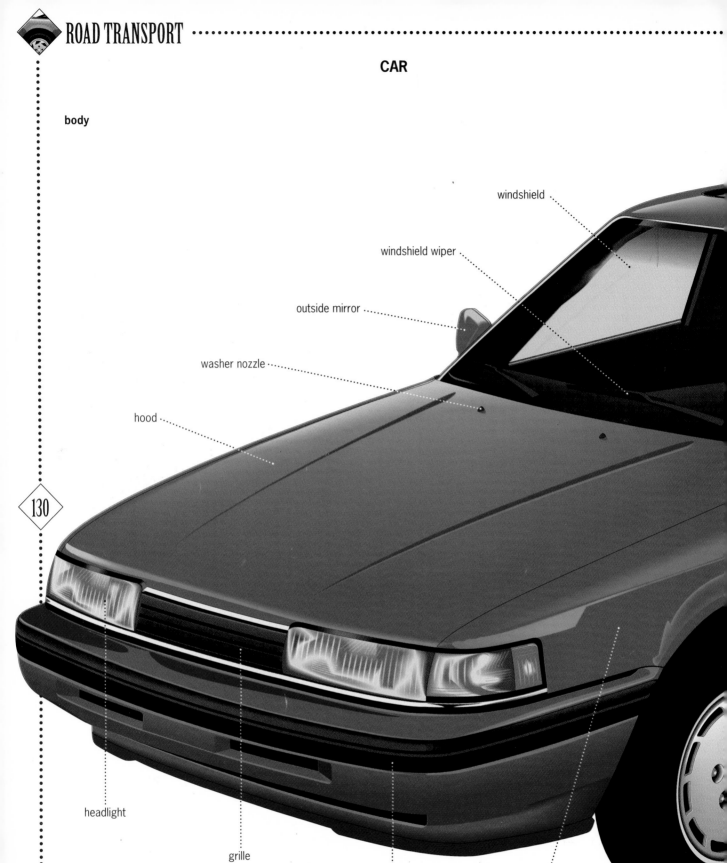

windshield

windshield wiper

outside mirror

washer nozzle

hood

headlight

grille

bumper

fender

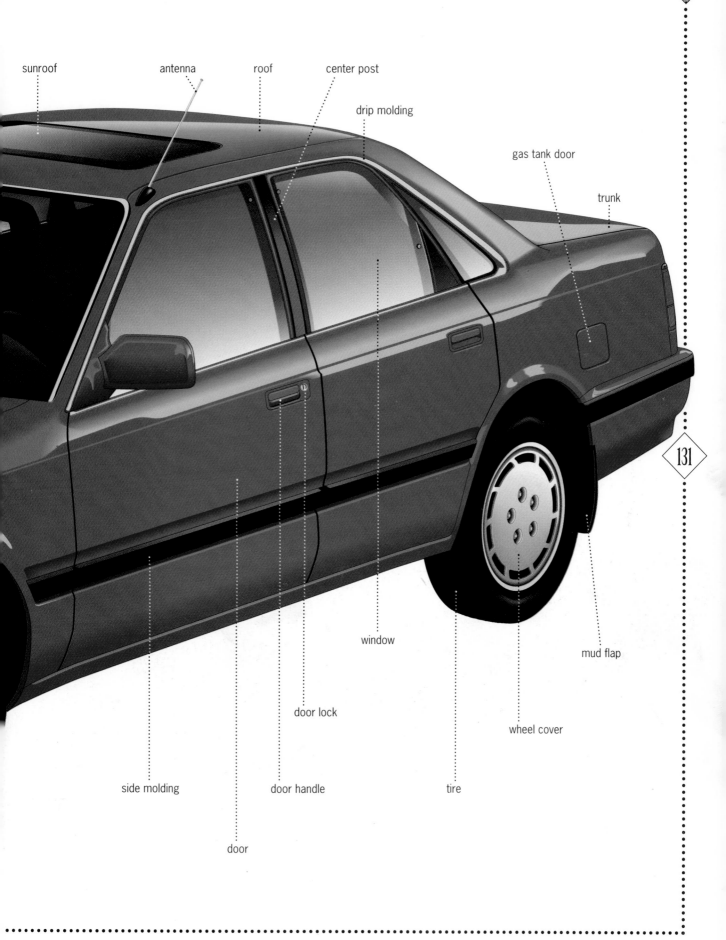

sunroof

antenna

roof

center post

drip molding

gas tank door

trunk

side molding

door

door handle

door lock

window

tire

wheel cover

mud flap

CAR

dashboard

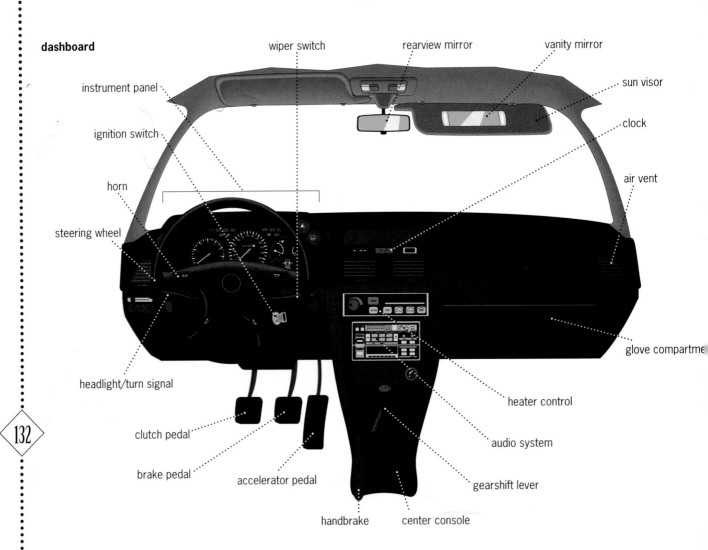

wiper switch

rearview mirror

vanity mirror

instrument panel

sun visor

ignition switch

clock

air vent

horn

steering wheel

headlight/turn signal

glove compartment

clutch pedal

heater control

brake pedal

audio system

accelerator pedal

gearshift lever

handbrake

center console

instrument panel

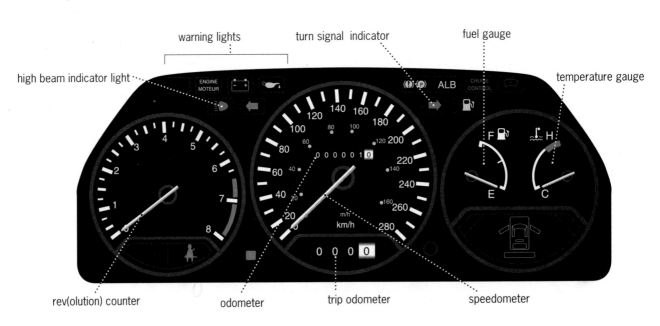

warning lights

turn signal indicator

fuel gauge

high beam indicator light

temperature gauge

rev(olution) counter

odometer

trip odometer

speedometer

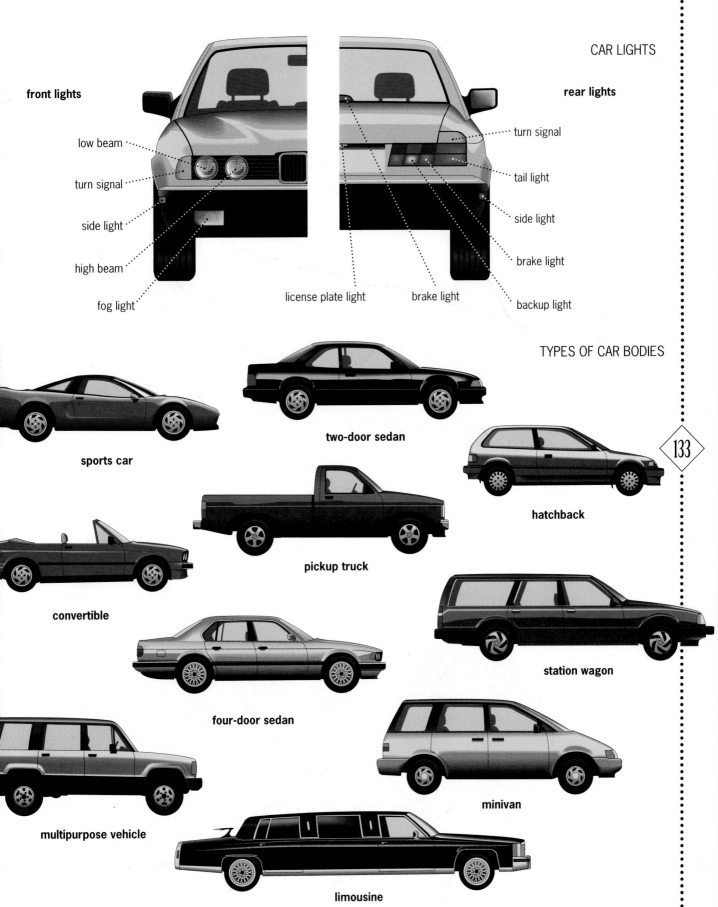

CAR LIGHTS

front lights

- low beam
- turn signal
- side light
- high beam
- fog light

rear lights

- turn signal
- tail light
- side light
- brake light
- backup light

license plate light

brake light

TYPES OF CAR BODIES

133

sports car

two-door sedan

hatchback

convertible

pickup truck

station wagon

four-door sedan

minivan

multipurpose vehicle

limousine

TRUCKING

tractor unit

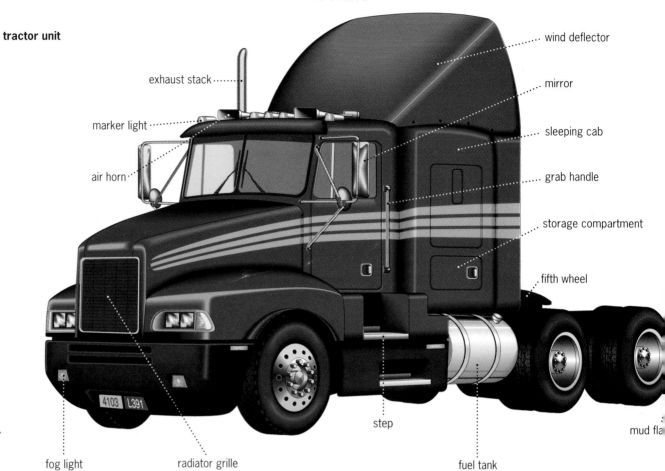

exhaust stack

marker light

air horn

wind deflector

mirror

sleeping cab

grab handle

storage compartment

fifth wheel

step

mud fla

fog light

radiator grille

fuel tank

4103 L391

service station

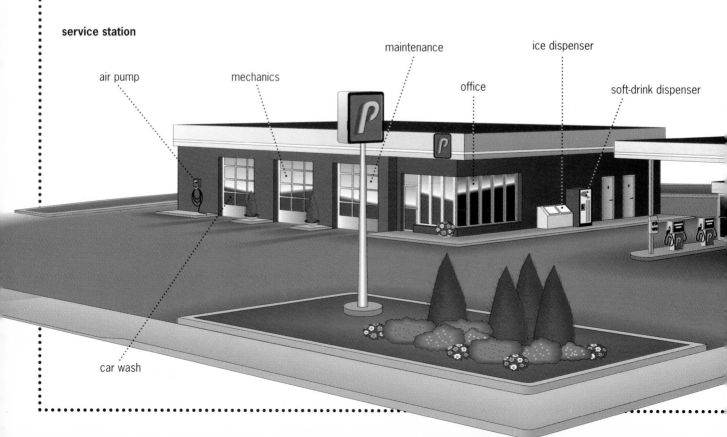

air pump

mechanics

maintenance

office

ice dispenser

soft-drink dispenser

car wash

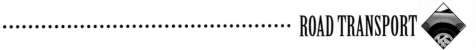

MOTORCYCLE

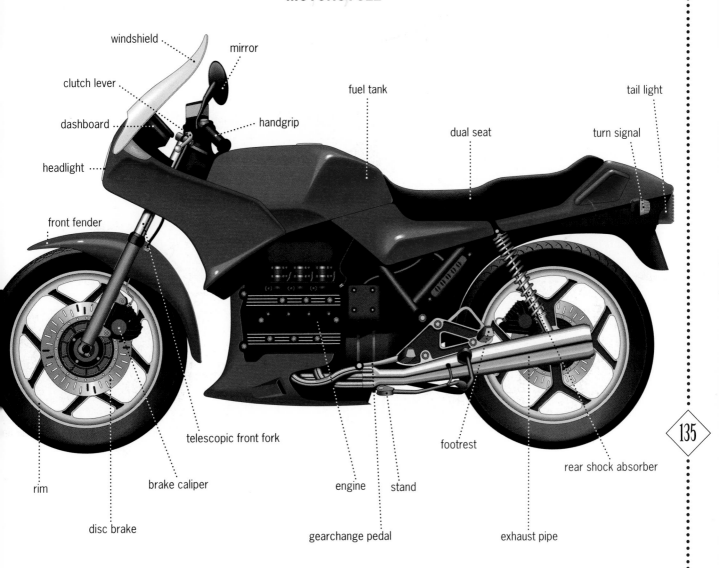

windshield

mirror

clutch lever

fuel tank

tail light

dashboard

handgrip

dual seat

turn signal

headlight

front fender

telescopic front fork

rim

brake caliper

disc brake

engine

stand

footrest

rear shock absorber

gearchange pedal

exhaust pipe

135

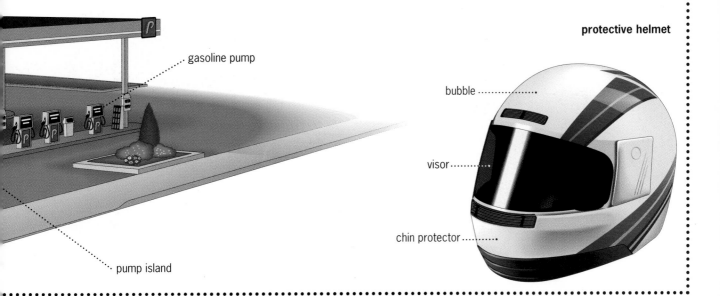

osk

gasoline pump

pump island

protective helmet

bubble

visor

chin protector

BICYCLE

saddle

seat post

tire pump

crossbar

carrier

rear brake

generator

water bottle clip

reflector

front derailleur

rear light

water bottle

chain wheel

crank

mudguard

chain guide

toe clip

rear derailleur

pedal

drive chain

bicycle bag

lock

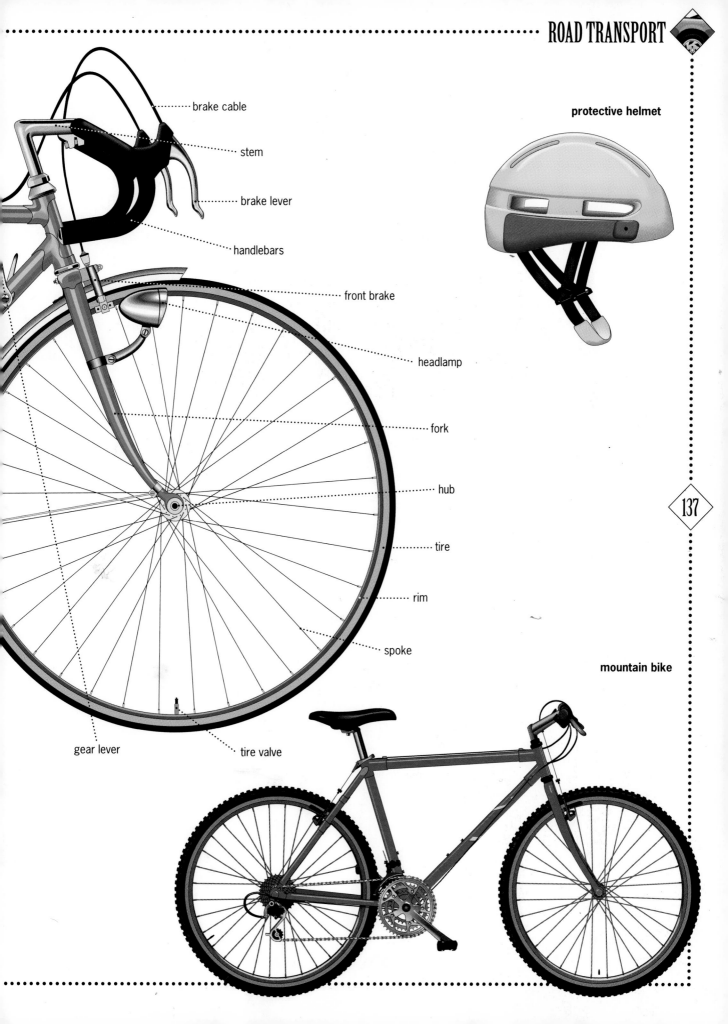

brake cable

stem

brake lever

handlebars

front brake

headlamp

fork

hub

tire

rim

spoke

gear lever

tire valve

protective helmet

mountain bike

137

DIESEL-ELECTRIC LOCOMOTIVE

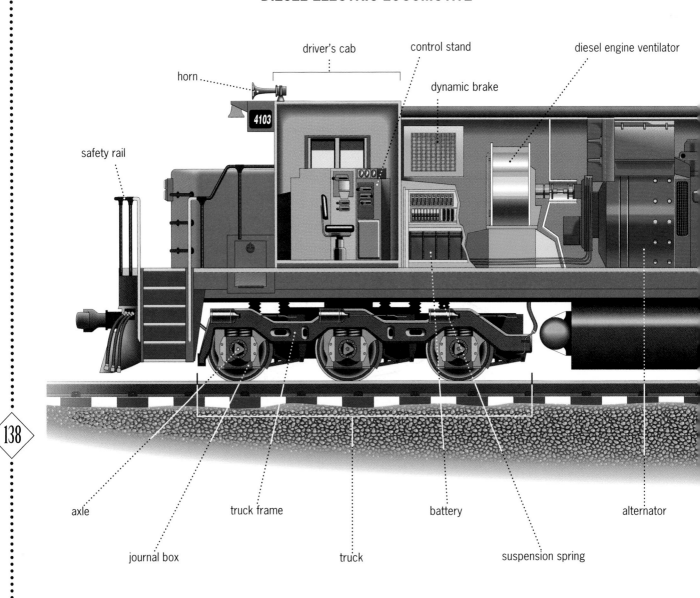

driver's cab

control stand

diesel engine ventilator

horn

dynamic brake

4103

safety rail

axle

truck frame

battery

alternator

journal box

truck

suspension spring

TYPES OF FREIGHT CARS

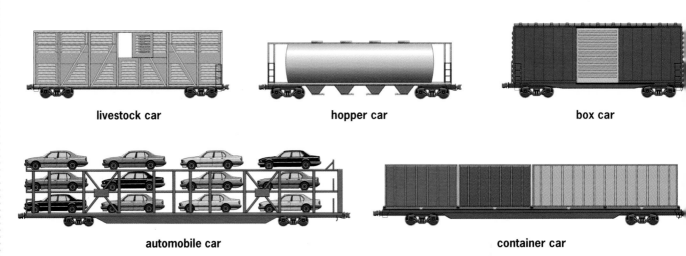

livestock car

hopper car

box car

automobile car

container car

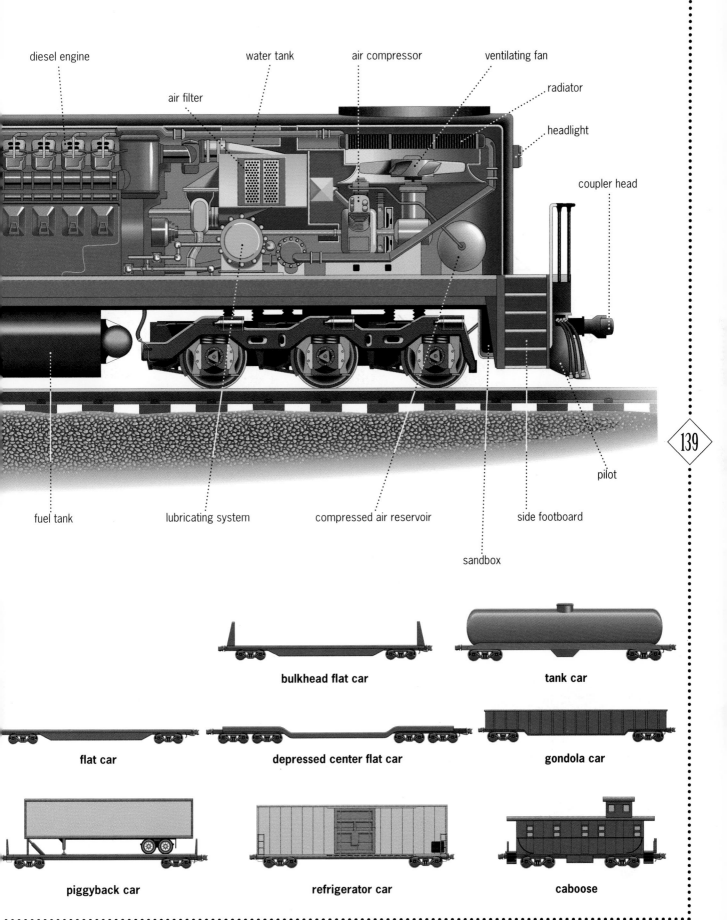

diesel engine

air filter

water tank

air compressor

ventilating fan

radiator

headlight

coupler head

fuel tank

lubricating system

compressed air reservoir

side footboard

pilot

sandbox

bulkhead flat car

tank car

flat car

depressed center flat car

gondola car

piggyback car

refrigerator car

caboose

HIGHWAY CROSSING

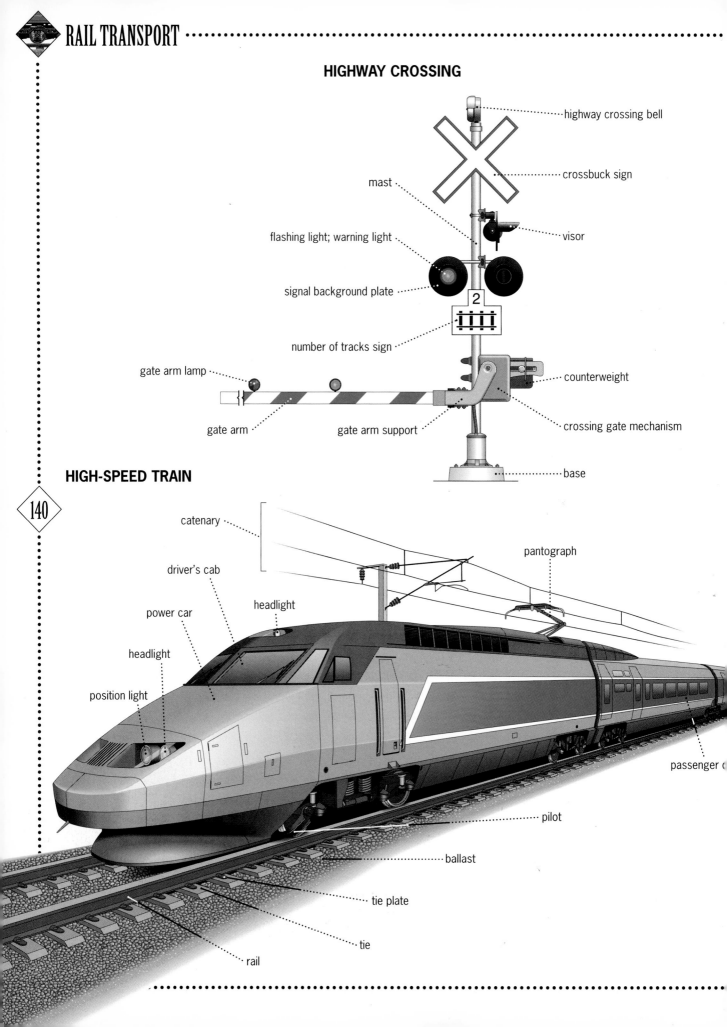

highway crossing bell

crossbuck sign

mast

flashing light; warning light

visor

signal background plate

2

number of tracks sign

gate arm lamp

counterweight

crossing gate mechanism

gate arm

gate arm support

base

HIGH-SPEED TRAIN

catenary

pantograph

driver's cab

power car

headlight

headlight

position light

passenger c

pilot

ballast

tie plate

tie

rail

FOUR-MASTED BARK

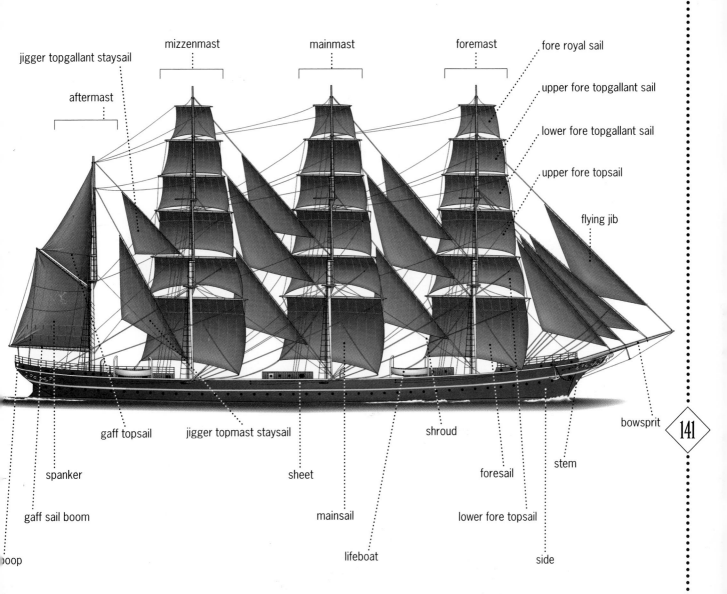

jigger topgallant staysail

aftermast

mizzenmast

mainmast

foremast

fore royal sail

upper fore topgallant sail

lower fore topgallant sail

upper fore topsail

flying jib

gaff topsail

jigger topmast staysail

shroud

bowsprit

141

spanker

sheet

foresail

stem

gaff sail boom

mainsail

lower fore topsail

side

poop

lifeboat

HOVERCRAFT

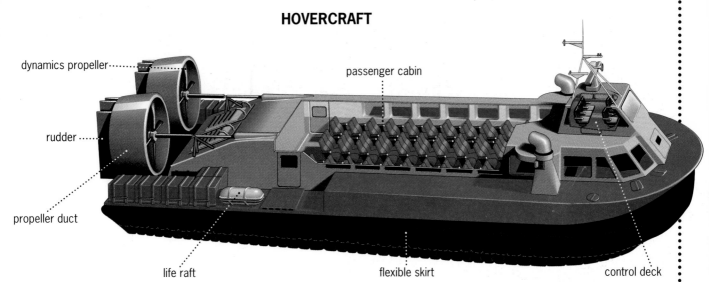

dynamics propeller

passenger cabin

rudder

propeller duct

life raft

flexible skirt

control deck

CRUISE LINER

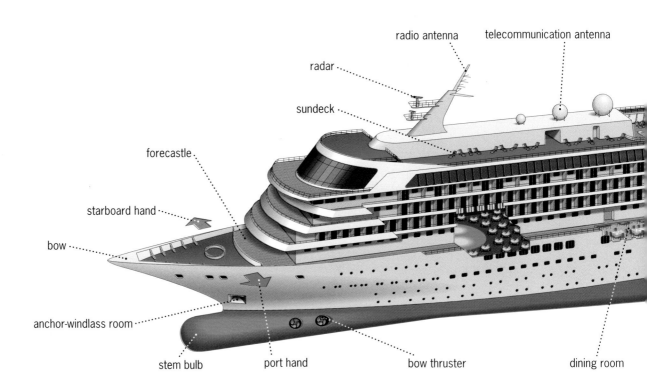

radio antenna

telecommunication antenna

radar

sundeck

forecastle

starboard hand

bow

anchor-windlass room

stem bulb

port hand

bow thruster

dining room

HARBOR

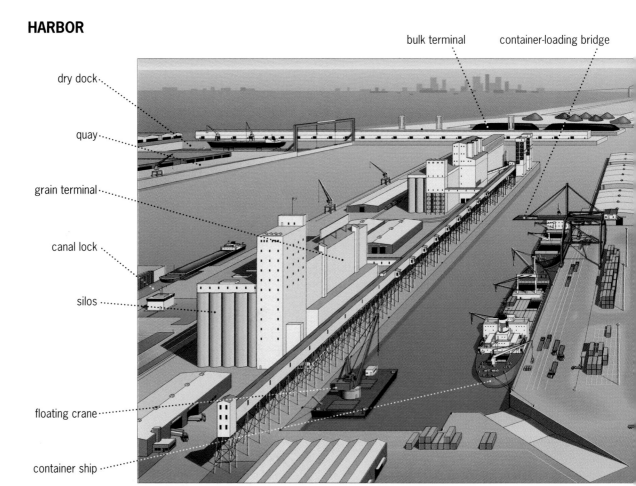

bulk terminal

container-loading bridge

dry dock

quay

grain terminal

canal lock

silos

floating crane

container ship

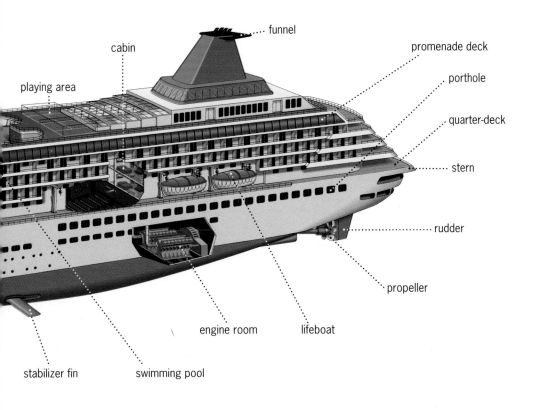

funnel

cabin

playing area

promenade deck

porthole

quarter-deck

stern

rudder

propeller

engine room

lifeboat

stabilizer fin

swimming pool

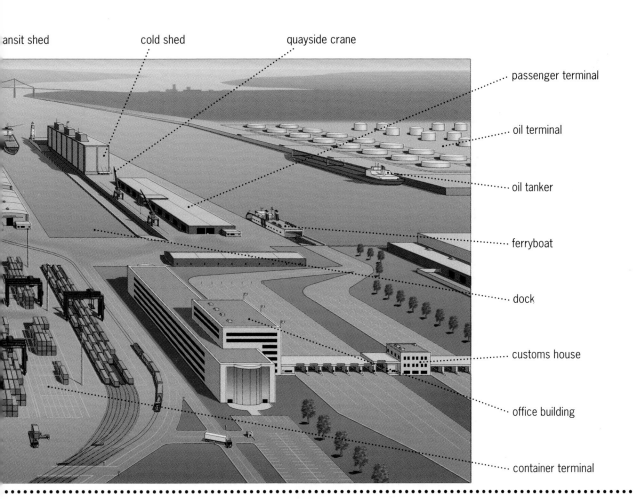

ansit shed

cold shed

quayside crane

passenger terminal

oil terminal

oil tanker

ferryboat

dock

customs house

office building

container terminal

PLANE

TYPES OF WING SHAPES

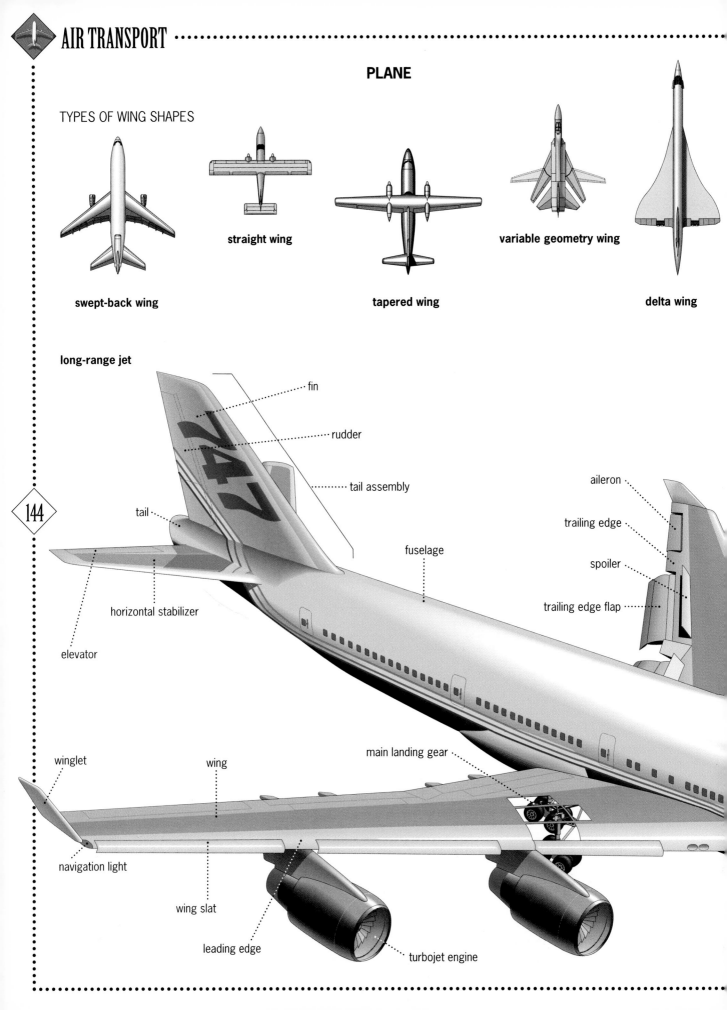

straight wing

variable geometry wing

swept-back wing

tapered wing

delta wing

long-range jet

fin

rudder

tail assembly

aileron

trailing edge

spoiler

trailing edge flap

fuselage

tail

horizontal stabilizer

elevator

winglet

wing

main landing gear

navigation light

wing slat

leading edge

turbojet engine

HELICOPTER

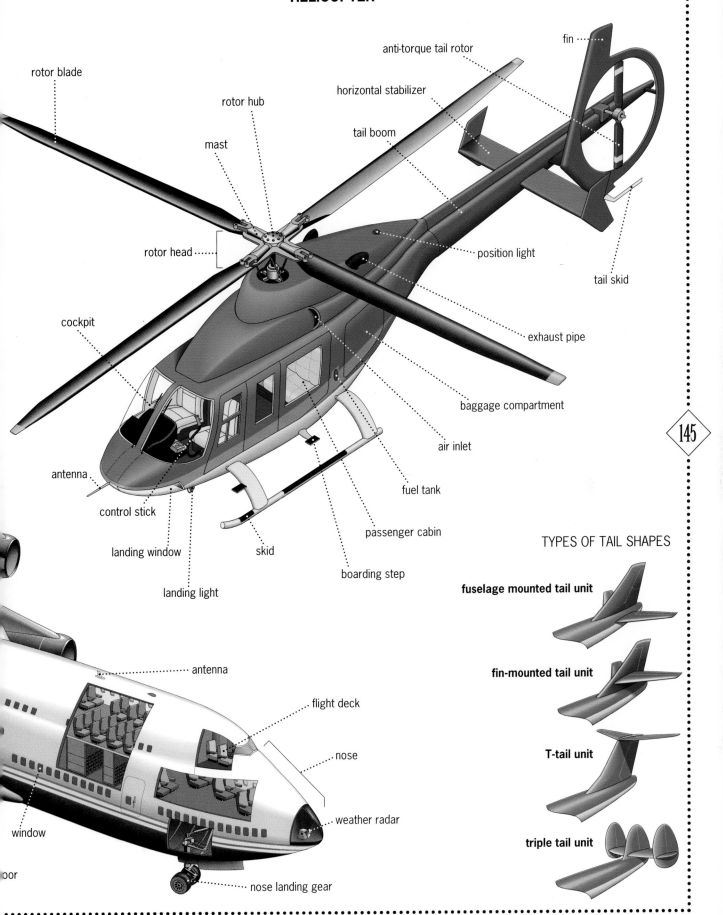

rotor blade

anti-torque tail rotor

fin

rotor hub

horizontal stabilizer

mast

tail boom

rotor head

position light

tail skid

cockpit

exhaust pipe

baggage compartment

air inlet

antenna

fuel tank

control stick

passenger cabin

landing window

skid

landing light

boarding step

145

TYPES OF TAIL SHAPES

fuselage mounted tail unit

fin-mounted tail unit

T-tail unit

triple tail unit

antenna

flight deck

nose

weather radar

window

door

nose landing gear

AIRPORT

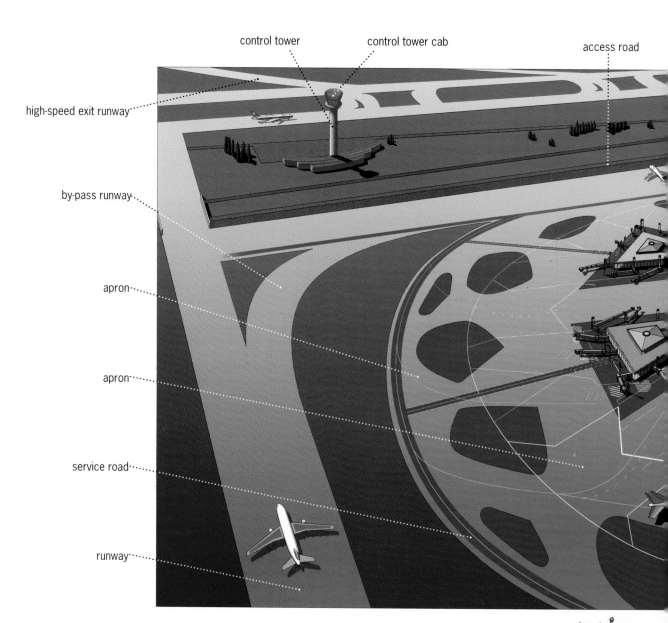

control tower

control tower cab

access road

high-speed exit runway

by-pass runway

apron

apron

service road

runway

AIRPORT GROUND EQUIPMENT

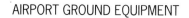

tow bar

tow tractor

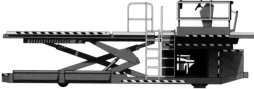

container/pallet loader

universal step

baggage conveyor

wheel chock

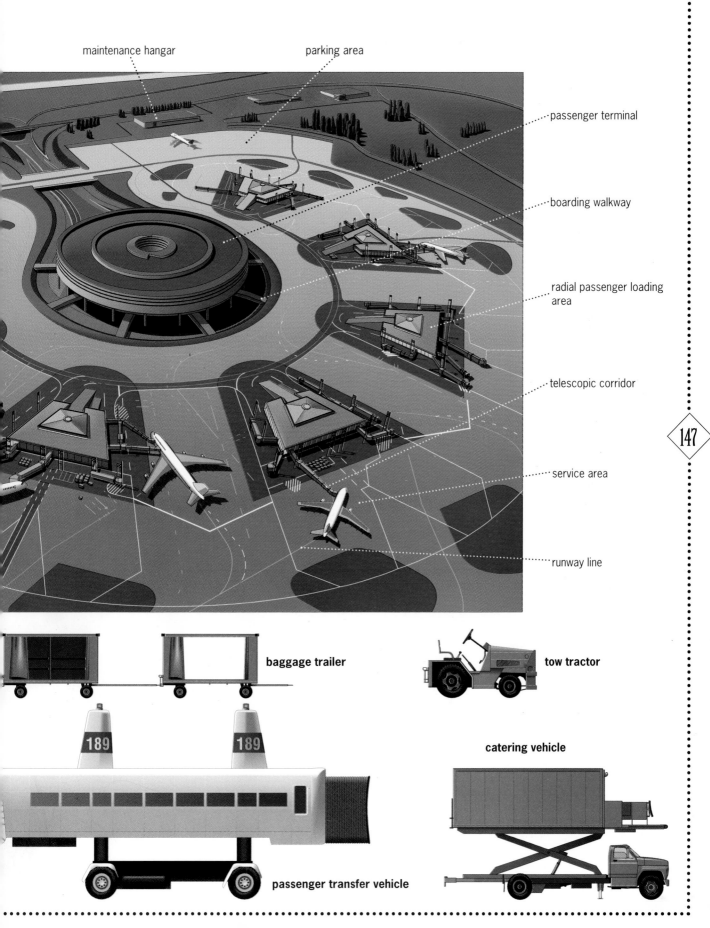

maintenance hangar

parking area

passenger terminal

boarding walkway

radial passenger loading area

telescopic corridor

service area

runway line

147

baggage trailer

tow tractor

189   189

catering vehicle

passenger transfer vehicle

SPACE SHUTTLE

space shuttle at takeoff

external tank

booster parachute

solid rocket booster

shuttle

nozzle

space shuttle in orbit

rudder

scientific instruments

hatch

observation window

maneuvering engine

main engines

fuel tanks

body flap

elevon

spacelab

insulation tiles

wing

radiator panel

cargo bay door

148

SPACESUIT

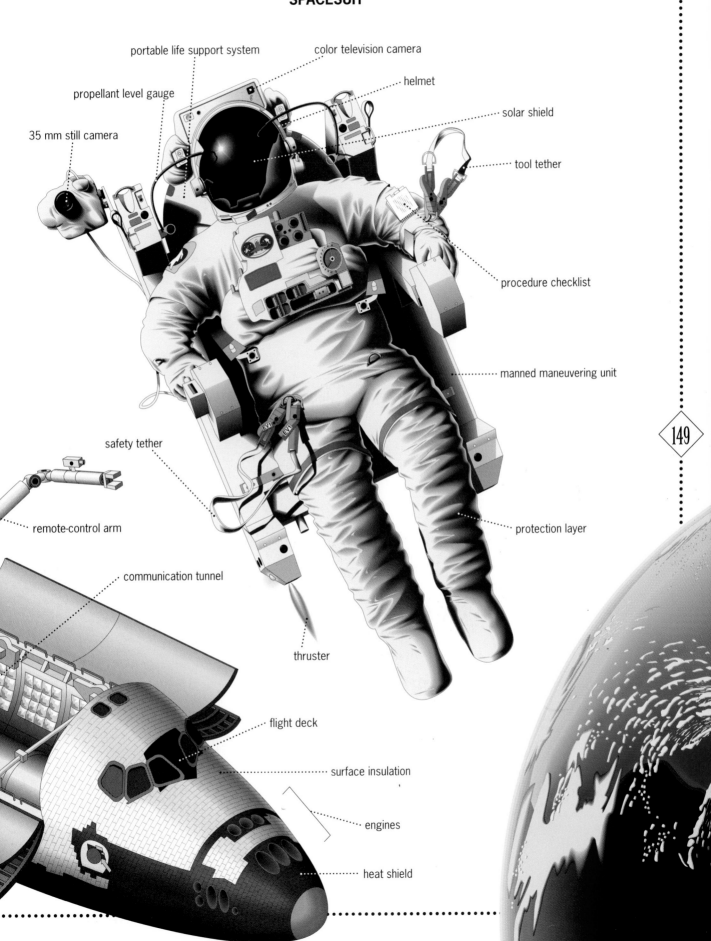

portable life support system

color television camera

helmet

propellant level gauge

solar shield

35 mm still camera

tool tether

procedure checklist

manned maneuvering unit

safety tether

remote-control arm

protection layer

communication tunnel

thruster

flight deck

surface insulation

engines

heat shield

SCHOOL SUPPLIES

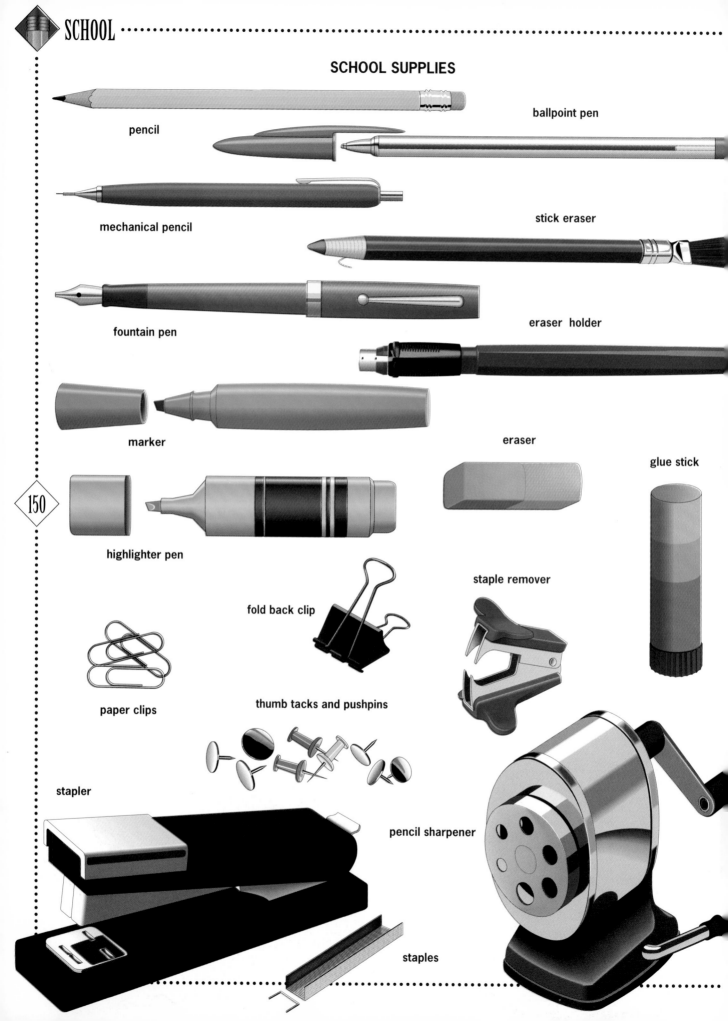

pencil

ballpoint pen

mechanical pencil

stick eraser

fountain pen

eraser holder

marker

eraser

glue stick

highlighter pen

staple remover

fold back clip

paper clips

thumb tacks and pushpins

stapler

pencil sharpener

staples

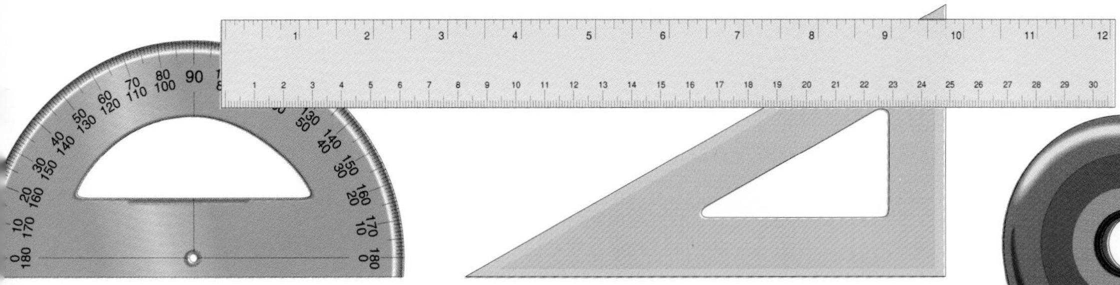

ruler

protractor

set square

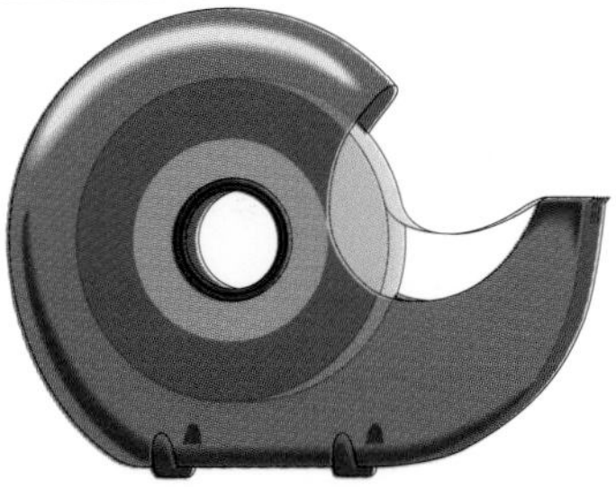

tape dispenser

ring binder

spiral bound notebook

loose-leaf paper

notebook

notepad

briefcase

satchel

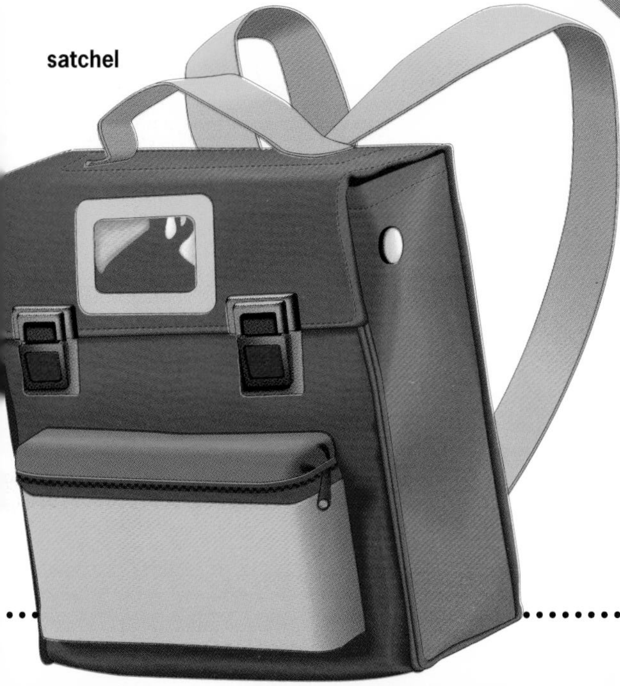

SCHOOL EQUIPMENT

blackboard

a b c

1 2 3

152

overhead projector

mirror

projection head

optical lens

optical stage

globe of Earth

meridian band

globe

base

axis of rotation

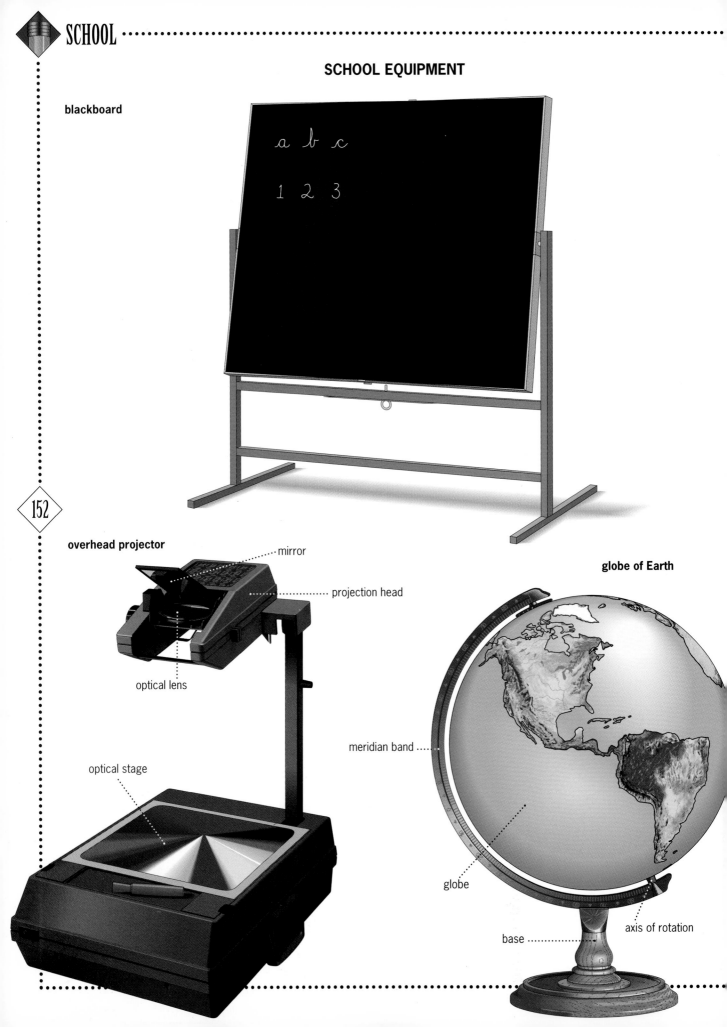

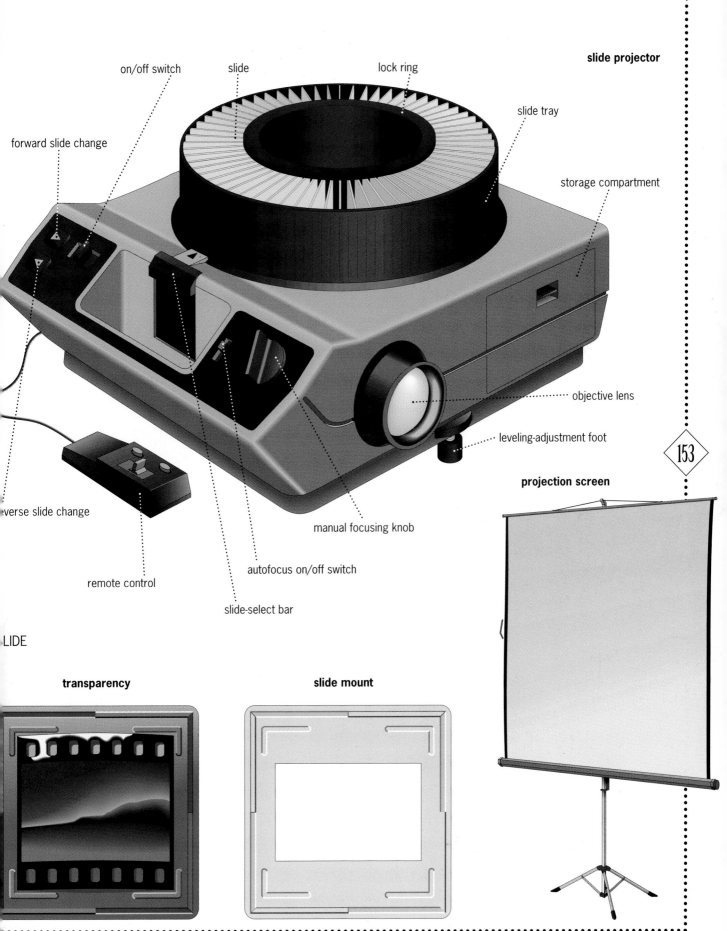

slide projector

on/off switch

slide

lock ring

slide tray

forward slide change

storage compartment

objective lens

leveling-adjustment foot

153

projection screen

reverse slide change

manual focusing knob

remote control

autofocus on/off switch

slide-select bar

SLIDE

transparency

slide mount

SCHOOL EQUIPMENT

pocket calculator

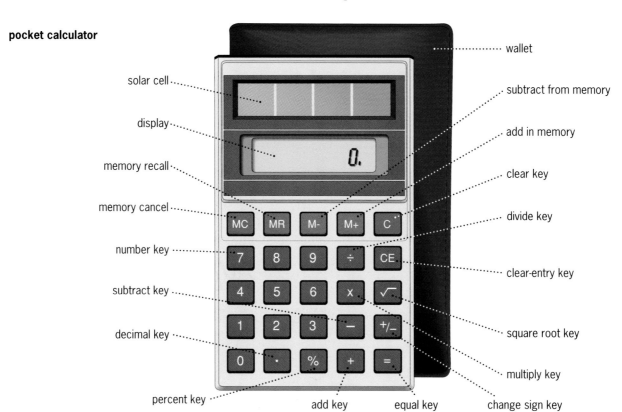

solar cell
display
memory recall
memory cancel
number key
subtract key
decimal key
percent key
add key
equal key

wallet
subtract from memory
add in memory
clear key
divide key
clear-entry key
square root key
multiply key
change sign key

personal computer

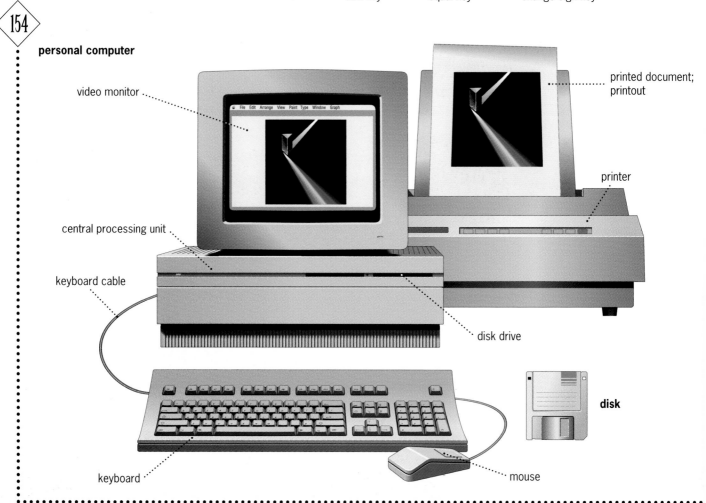

video monitor
central processing unit
keyboard cable
keyboard

printed document; printout
printer
disk drive
disk
mouse

File Edit Arrange View Paint Type Window Graph

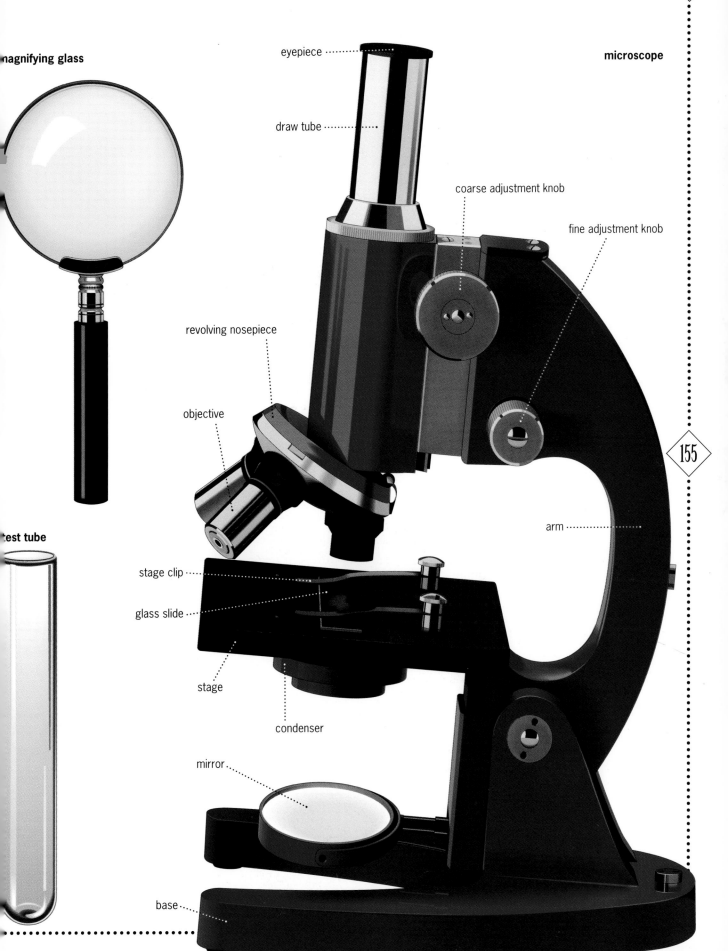

magnifying glass

microscope

eyepiece

draw tube

coarse adjustment knob

fine adjustment knob

revolving nosepiece

objective

test tube

arm

stage clip

glass slide

stage

condenser

mirror

base

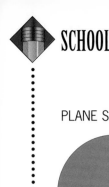

GEOMETRY

PLANE SURFACES

circle

square

triangle

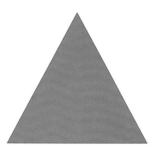

rhombus

rectangle   trapezoid   parallelogram

 156

SOLIDS

sphere

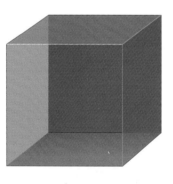

cube

cone

pyramid

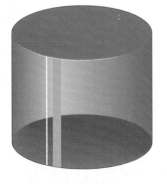

cylinder

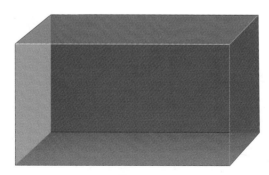

parallelepiped

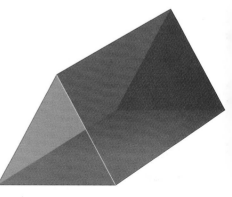

prism

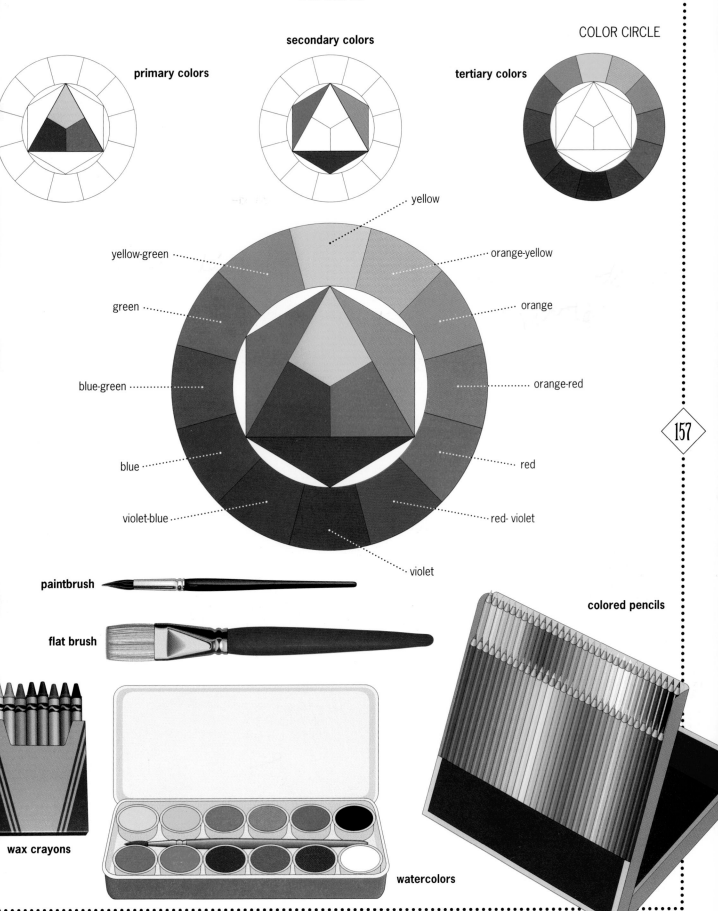

DRAWING

COLOR CIRCLE

primary colors

secondary colors

tertiary colors

yellow

yellow-green

orange-yellow

green

orange

blue-green

orange-red

blue

red

violet-blue

red- violet

violet

paintbrush

flat brush

colored pencils

wax crayons

watercolors

TRADITIONAL MUSICAL INSTRUMENTS

balalaika

mandolin

zither

lyre

soundboard

triangular body

open strings

melody strings

pear-shaped body

panpipes

bagpipe

158

banjo

blowpipe; mouthpipe

drone pipe

circular body

harmonica

bellows

accordion

bass keyboard

treble keyboard

windbag

treble register

bass register

chanter

KEYBOARD INSTRUMENTS

upright piano

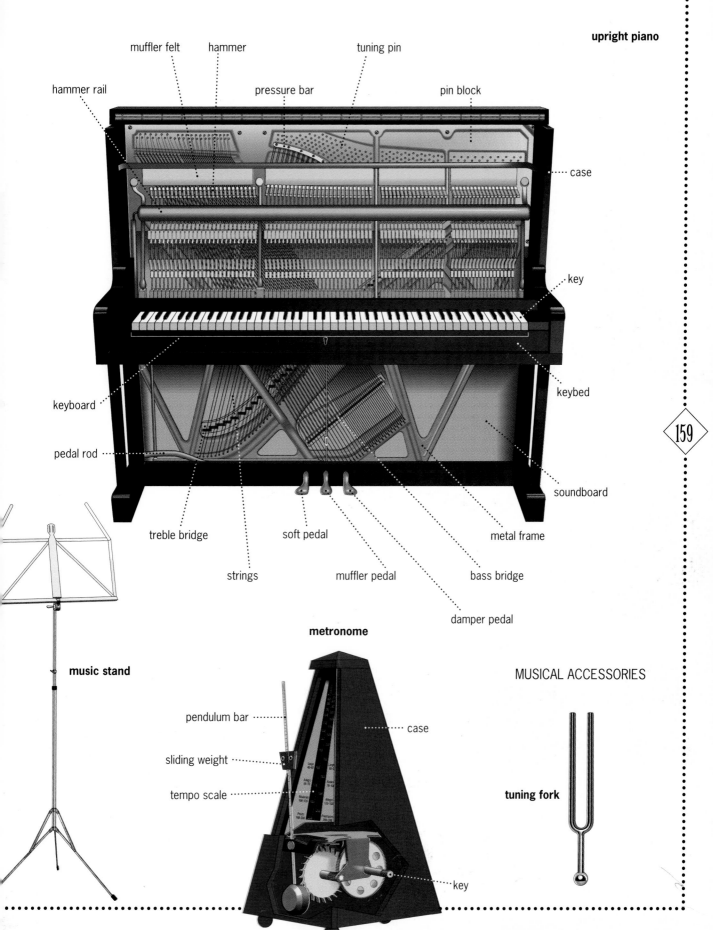

muffler felt

hammer

tuning pin

hammer rail

pressure bar

pin block

case

key

keyboard

keybed

pedal rod

soundboard

treble bridge

soft pedal

metal frame

strings

muffler pedal

bass bridge

damper pedal

159

music stand

metronome

MUSICAL ACCESSORIES

pendulum bar

case

sliding weight

tempo scale

tuning fork

key

MUSICAL NOTATION

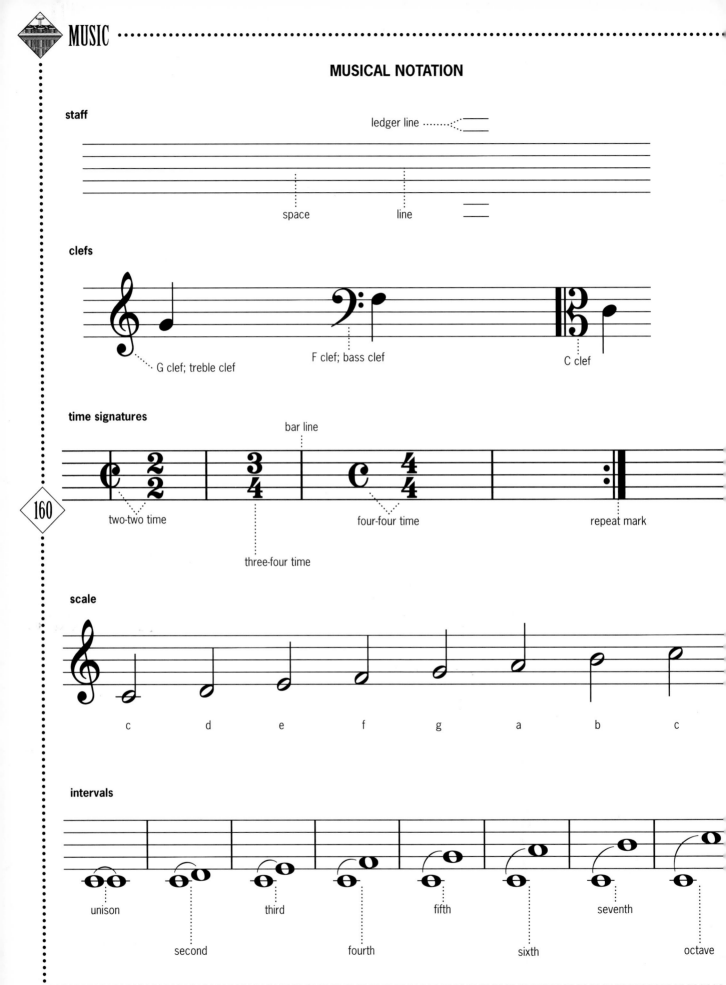

staff

ledger line

space line

clefs

G clef; treble clef

F clef; bass clef

C clef

time signatures

bar line

two-two time

three-four time

four-four time

repeat mark

scale

c d e f g a b c

intervals

unison

second

third

fourth

fifth

sixth

seventh

octave

note symbols

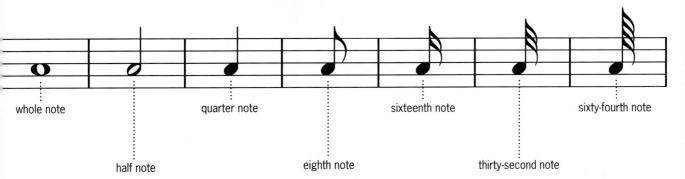

whole note | quarter note | sixteenth note | sixty-fourth note

half note | eighth note | thirty-second note

rest symbols

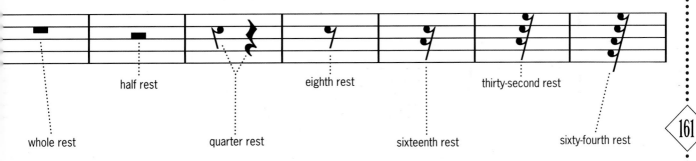

half rest | eighth rest | thirty-second rest

whole rest | quarter rest | sixteenth rest | sixty-fourth rest

accidentals

natural

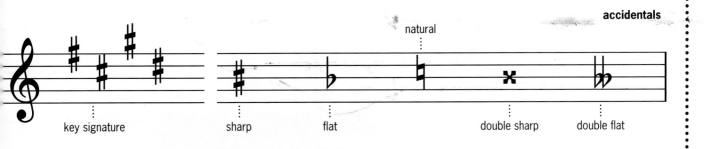

key signature | sharp | flat | double sharp | double flat

ornaments

appoggiatura | trill | turn | mordent

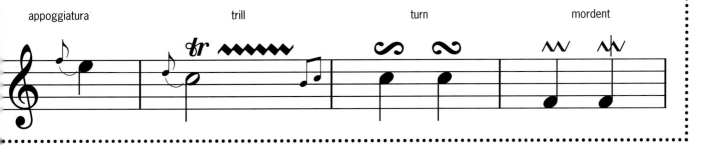

STRINGED INSTRUMENTS

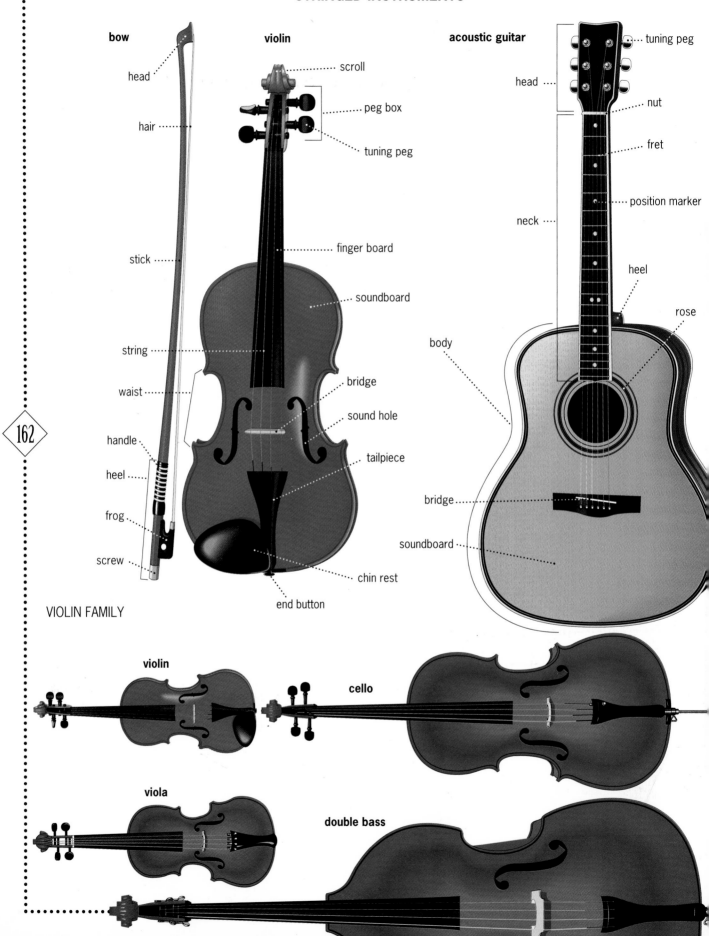

bow

head

hair

stick

string

waist

handle

heel

frog

screw

violin

scroll

peg box

tuning peg

finger board

soundboard

bridge

sound hole

tailpiece

chin rest

end button

acoustic guitar

tuning peg

head

nut

fret

position marker

neck

heel

rose

body

bridge

soundboard

VIOLIN FAMILY

violin

cello

viola

double bass

electric guitar

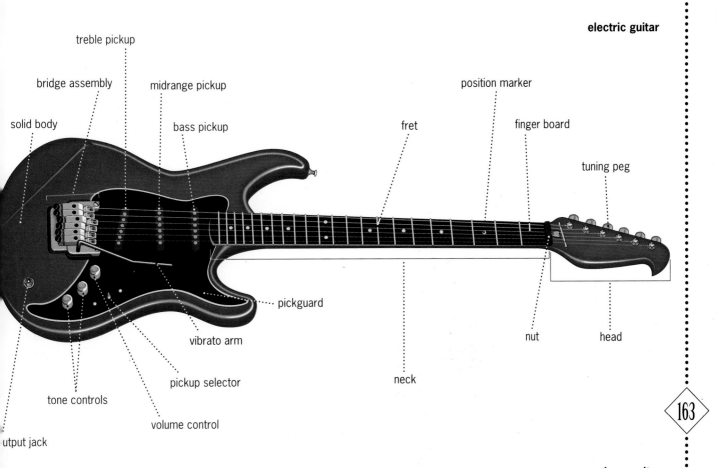

treble pickup

bridge assembly

midrange pickup

solid body

bass pickup

position marker

fret

finger board

tuning peg

pickguard

vibrato arm

nut

head

pickup selector

neck

tone controls

output jack

volume control

bass guitar

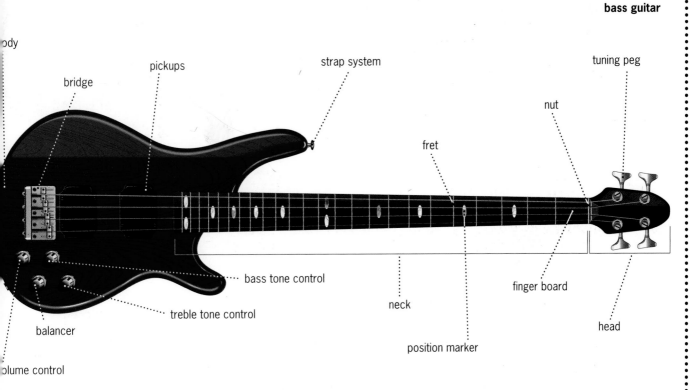

body

pickups

bridge

strap system

tuning peg

nut

fret

bass tone control

finger board

treble tone control

neck

balancer

head

volume control

position marker

WIND INSTRUMENTS

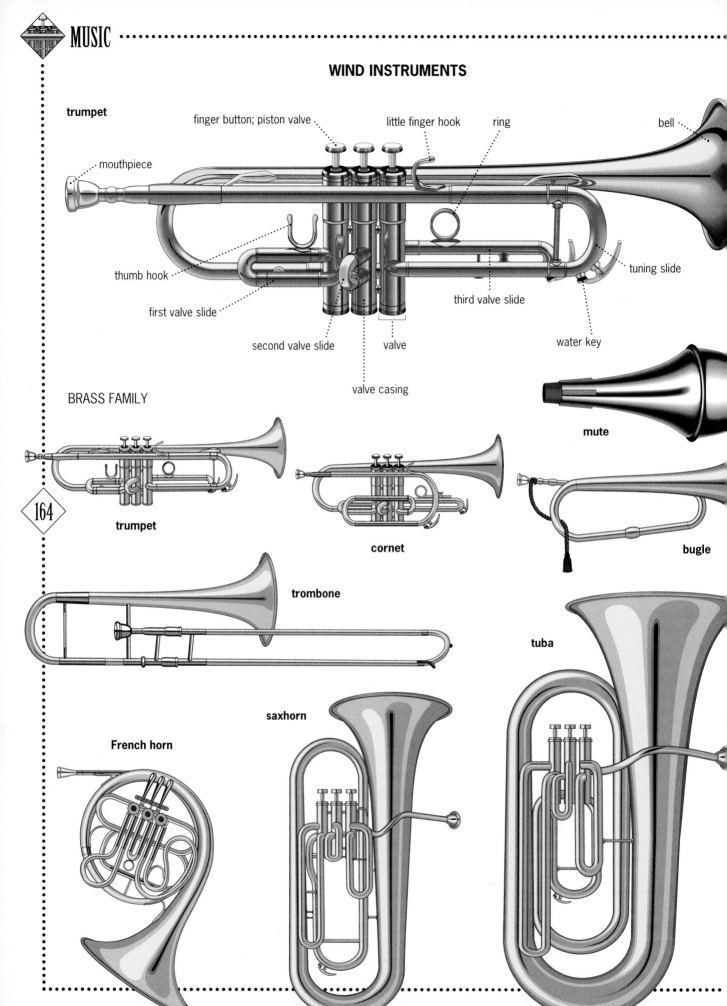

trumpet

finger button; piston valve

little finger hook

ring

bell

mouthpiece

thumb hook

first valve slide

second valve slide

valve

valve casing

third valve slide

tuning slide

water key

mute

BRASS FAMILY

trumpet

cornet

bugle

164

trombone

tuba

saxhorn

French horn

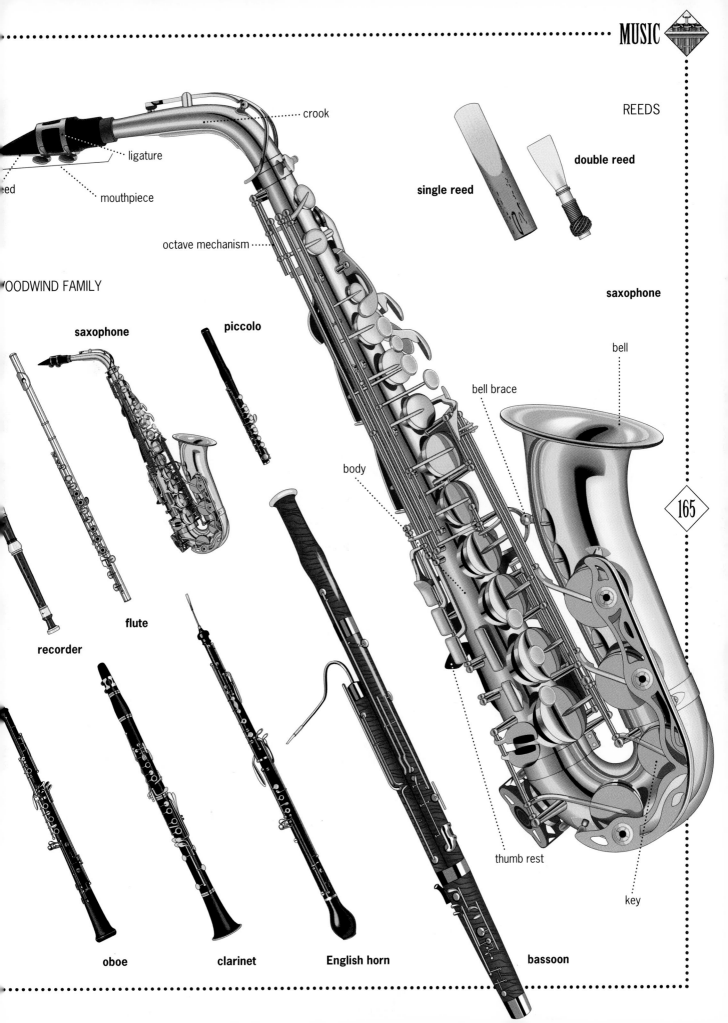

crook

ligature

ed

mouthpiece

octave mechanism

REEDS

double reed

single reed

saxophone

WOODWIND FAMILY

bell

saxophone

piccolo

bell brace

body

165

flute

recorder

thumb rest

key

oboe

clarinet

English horn

bassoon

PERCUSSION INSTRUMENTS

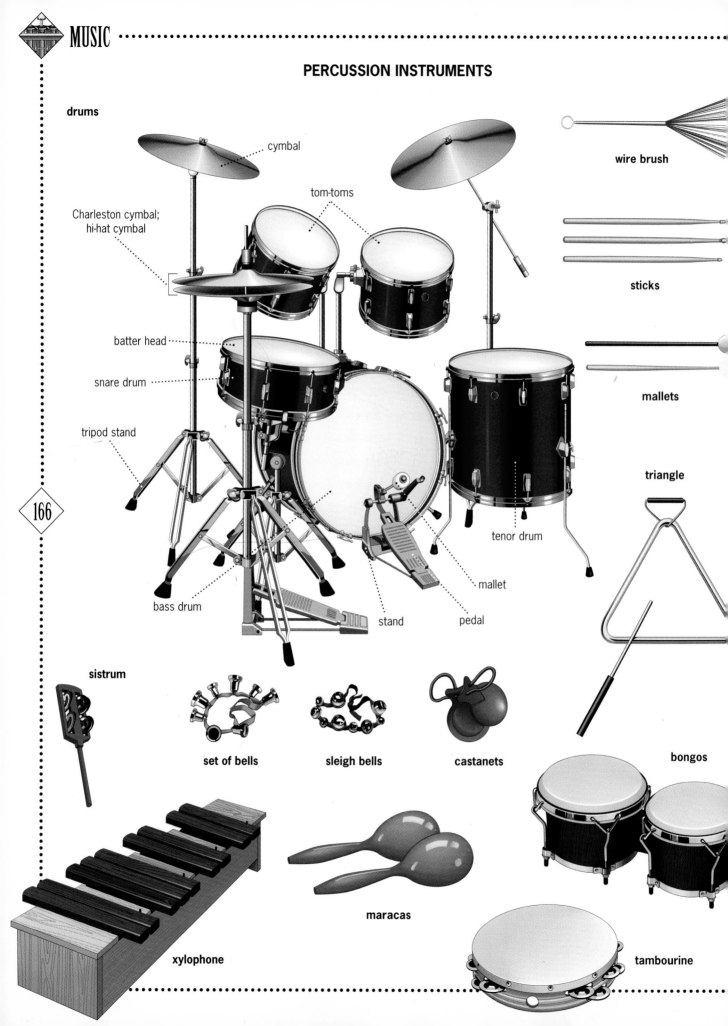

drums

cymbal

tom-toms

Charleston cymbal;
hi-hat cymbal

batter head

snare drum

tripod stand

166

bass drum

stand

pedal

mallet

tenor drum

wire brush

sticks

mallets

triangle

sistrum

set of bells

sleigh bells

castanets

bongos

maracas

xylophone

tambourine

SYMPHONY ORCHESTRA

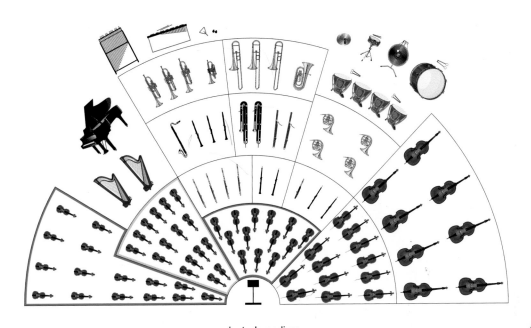

conductor's podium

tubular bells

xylophone

bass drum

harp

piano

flute

oboe

piccolo

English horn

first violin

second violin

viola

cello

double bass

bass clarinet

clarinet

contrabassoon

bassoon

French horn

cornet

trumpet

trombone

tuba

triangle

snare drum

cymbals

castanets

kettledrum

gong

167

BASEBALL

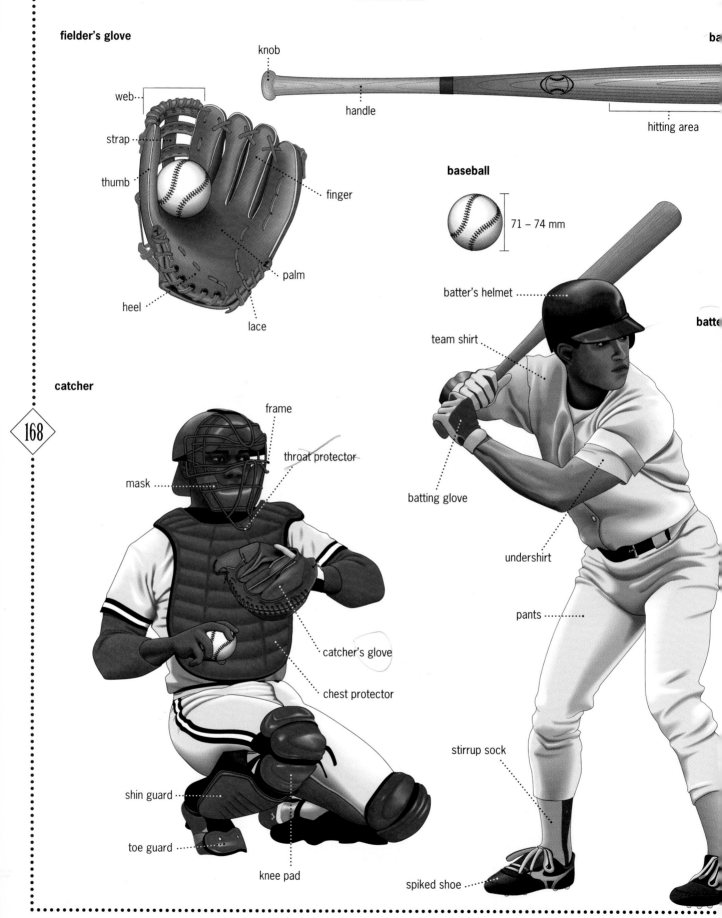

fielder's glove

web

strap

thumb

heel

knob

handle

finger

palm

lace

baseball

71 – 74 mm

ba

hitting area

catcher

frame

throat protector

mask

batter's helmet

team shirt

batting glove

undershirt

pants

batt

catcher's glove

chest protector

shin guard

toe guard

knee pad

stirrup sock

spiked shoe

eld

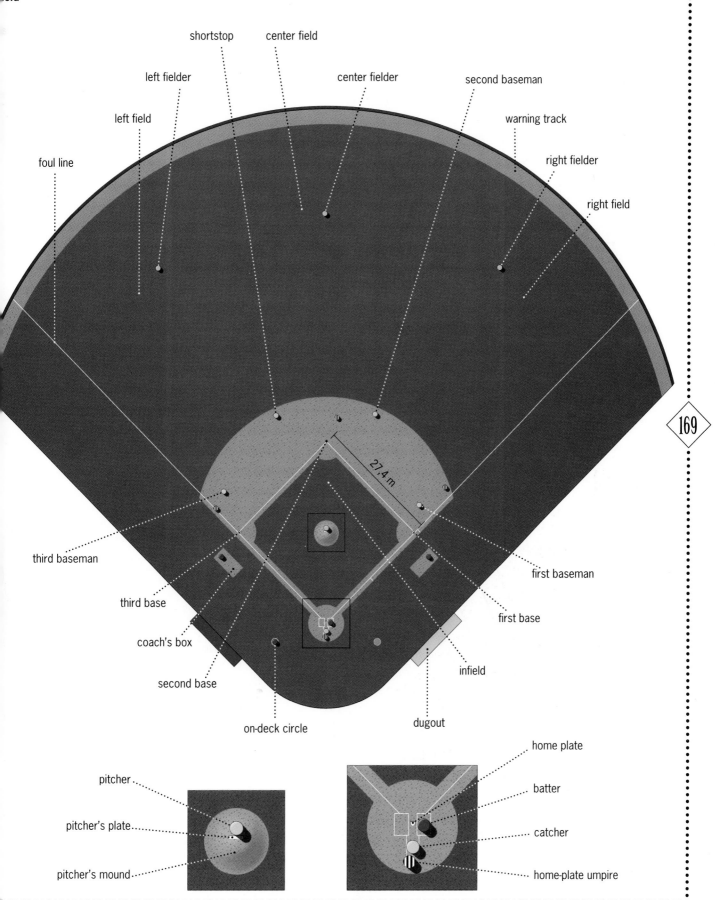

shortstop

center field

left fielder

center fielder

second baseman

left field

warning track

foul line

right fielder

right field

27,4 m

third baseman

first baseman

third base

first base

coach's box

second base

on-deck circle

dugout

infield

home plate

pitcher

batter

pitcher's plate

catcher

pitcher's mound

home-plate umpire

AMERICAN FOOTBALL

American football player

helmet

chin strap

player's number

team shirt

wristband

pants

sock

cleated shoe

footba

279 – 286 mm

protective equipme

helmet

face mask

shoulder pad

chest protector

arm guard

rib pad

elbow pad

hip pad

lumbar pad

protective cup

thigh pad

knee pad

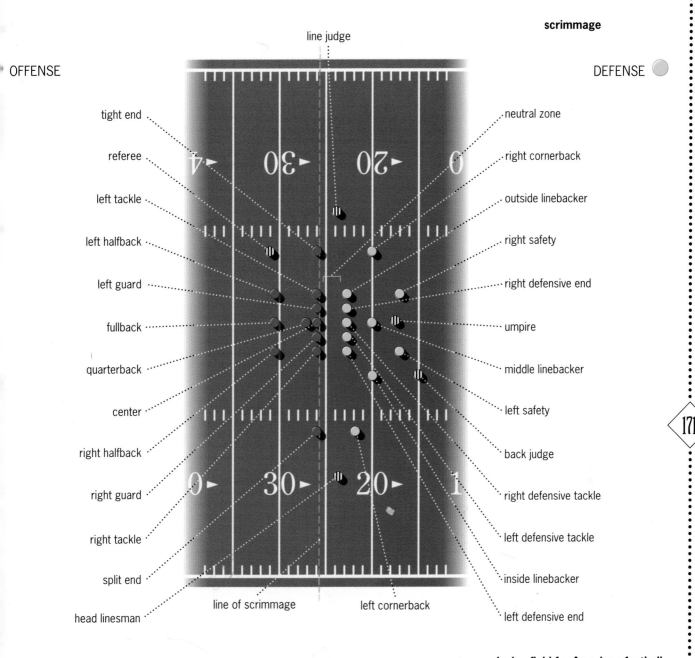

scrimmage

OFFENSE

DEFENSE

line judge

tight end

referee

left tackle

left halfback

left guard

fullback

quarterback

center

right halfback

right guard

right tackle

split end

head linesman

line of scrimmage

left cornerback

neutral zone

right cornerback

outside linebacker

right safety

right defensive end

umpire

middle linebacker

left safety

back judge

right defensive tackle

left defensive tackle

inside linebacker

left defensive end

171

playing field for American football

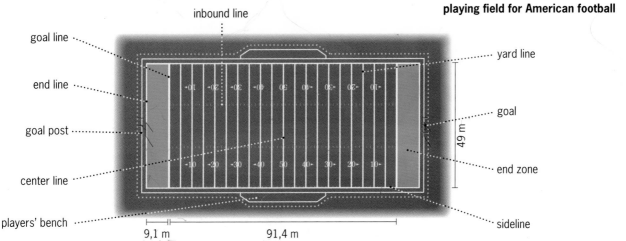

inbound line

goal line

end line

goal post

center line

players' bench

yard line

goal

end zone

sideline

49 m

9,1 m

91,4 m

SOCCER

soccer player

soccer ball

team shirt

218 mm

shorts

shin guard

soccer shoe

interchangeable studs

172

playing field

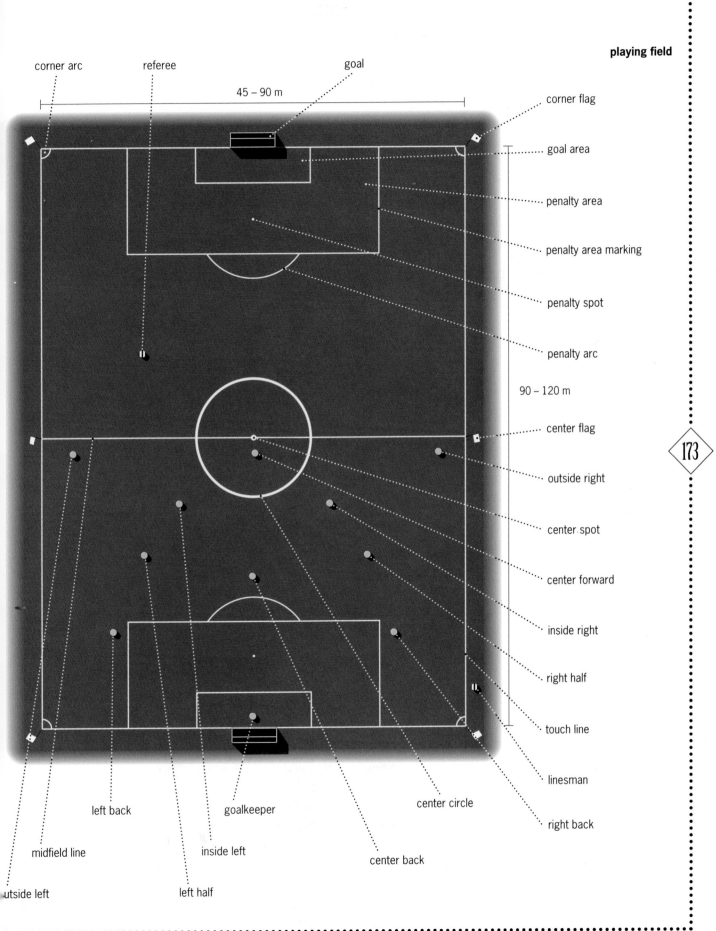

corner arc

referee

goal

45 – 90 m

corner flag

goal area

penalty area

penalty area marking

penalty spot

penalty arc

90 – 120 m

center flag

outside right

center spot

center forward

inside right

right half

touch line

linesman

right back

center circle

goalkeeper

left back

midfield line

inside left

outside left

left half

center back

CRICKET

cricket player

bat

glove

wicket-keeper

batsman

fielders

pitch

field

umpire

bowler

umpire

batsman

wicket

bail

stump

pad

cricket shoe

studs

cricket ball

70 – 73 mm

bat

handle

willow

groove

174

FIELD HOCKEY

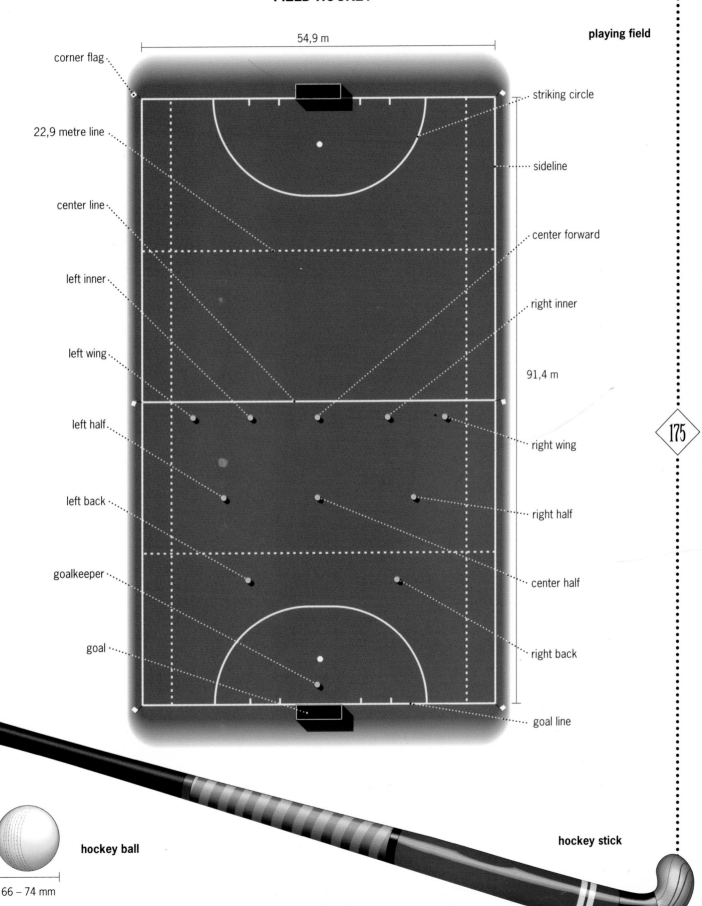

54,9 m

corner flag

striking circle

22,9 metre line

sideline

center line

center forward

left inner

right inner

left wing

91,4 m

left half

right wing

left back

right half

goalkeeper

center half

goal

right back

goal line

175

hockey ball

hockey stick

66 – 74 mm

ICE HOCKEY

rink

26 – 30 m

puck

25 mm

76 mm

goal line

goal crease

goal

face-off circle

face-off spot

attacking zone

blue line

referee

neutral zone

center line

61 m

penalty bench

officials' bench

players' bench

left wing

right wing

center

linesman

left defense

center face-off circle

defending zone

right defense

boards

goalkeeper

goal judge

rink corner

ICE HOCKEY

player's stick

butt end

shoulder pad

protective girdle

protective cup

shin pad

shaft

blade

eel

helmet

elbow pad

cuff

glove

knee pad

skate

goalkeeper

face mask

throat protector

arm pad

body pad

back pad

pants

catch glove

goalkeeper's pad

skate

goalkeeper's stick

blade

BASKETBALL

court

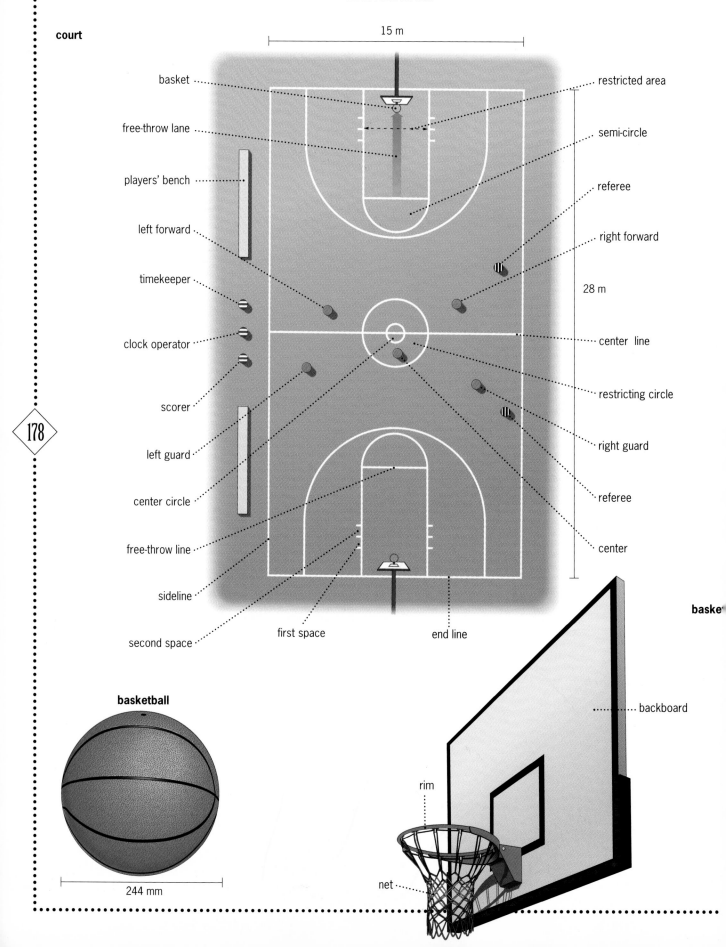

15 m

basket

restricted area

free-throw lane

semi-circle

players' bench

referee

left forward

right forward

timekeeper

28 m

clock operator

center line

scorer

restricting circle

left guard

right guard

center circle

referee

free-throw line

center

sideline

first space

end line

second space

basketball

244 mm

baske

backboard

rim

net

VOLLEYBALL

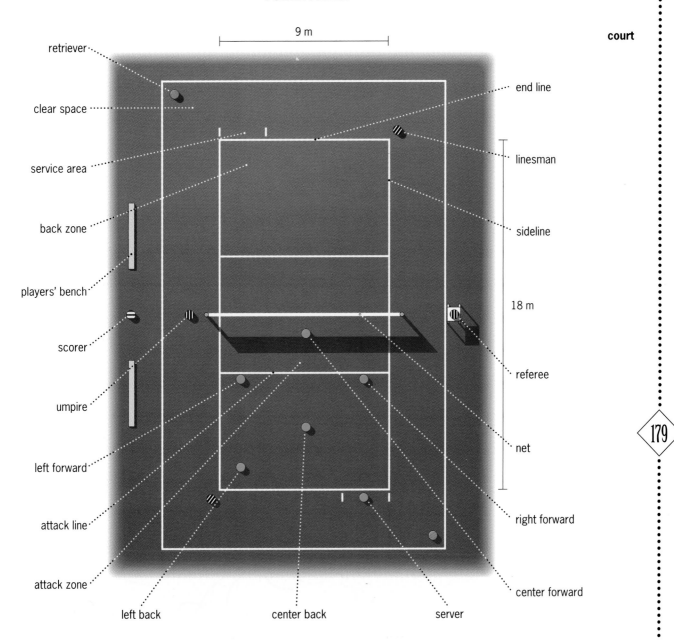

9 m

retriever

clear space

service area

back zone

players' bench

scorer

umpire

left forward

attack line

attack zone

end line

linesman

sideline

18 m

referee

net

right forward

center forward

left back

center back

server

179

volleyball

206 – 213 mm

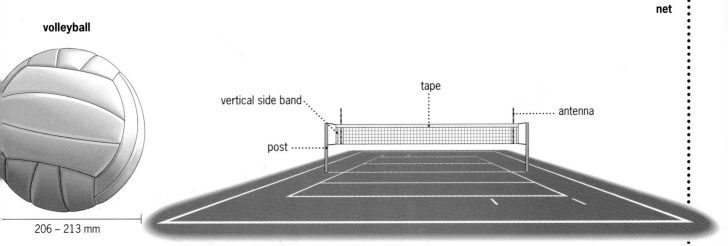

tape

vertical side band

antenna

post

VOLLEYBALL

TENNIS

court

8,23 m

linesman

center mark

receiver

baseline

backcourt

service line

forecourt

service judge

singles sideline

center service line

23,8 m

umpire

net judge

left service court

net

alley

right service court

server

foot fault judge

ball boy

doubles sideline

11 m

net

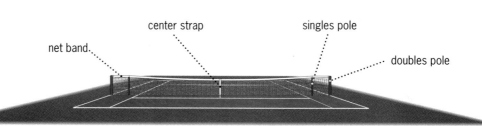

net band

center strap

singles pole

doubles pole

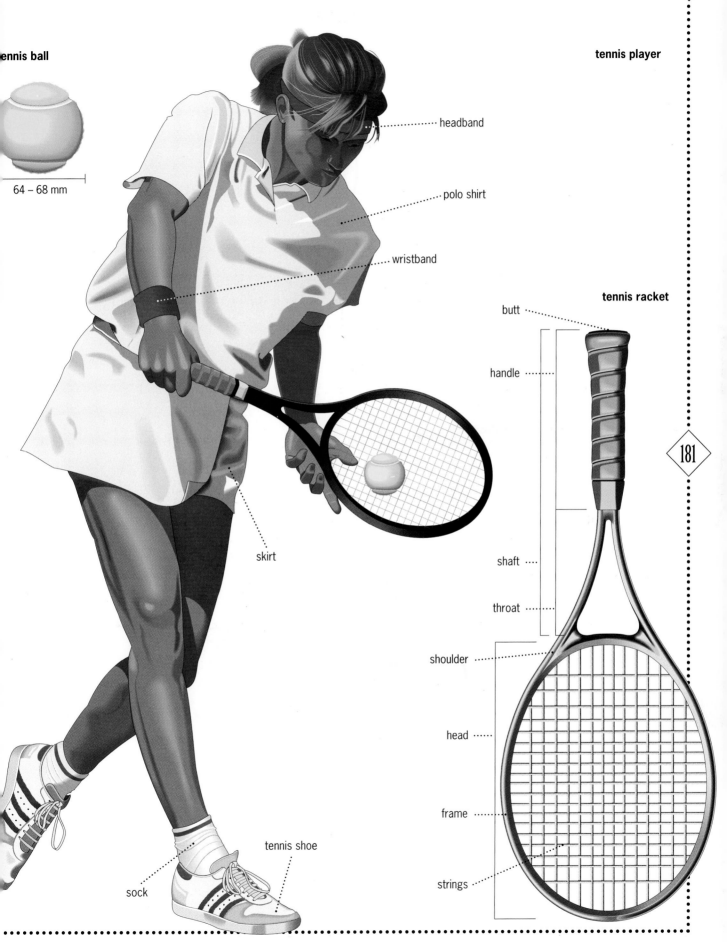

tennis ball

64 – 68 mm

tennis player

headband

polo shirt

wristband

tennis racket

butt

handle

skirt

shaft

throat

shoulder

head

frame

tennis shoe

strings

sock

SWIMMING

competitive course

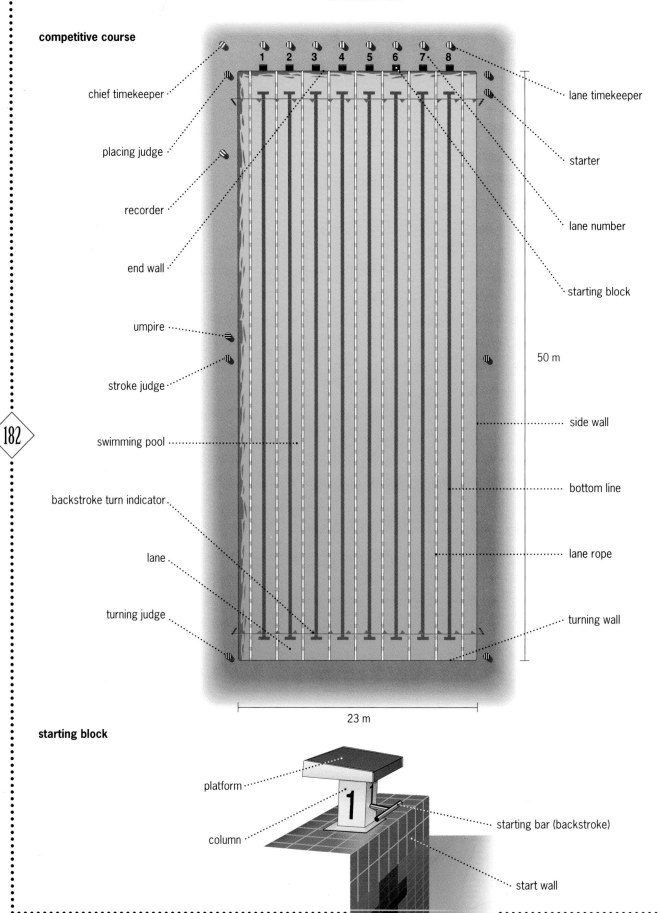

chief timekeeper

placing judge

recorder

end wall

umpire

stroke judge

swimming pool

backstroke turn indicator

lane

turning judge

lane timekeeper

starter

lane number

starting block

side wall

bottom line

lane rope

turning wall

50 m

23 m

starting block

platform

column

starting bar (backstroke)

start wall

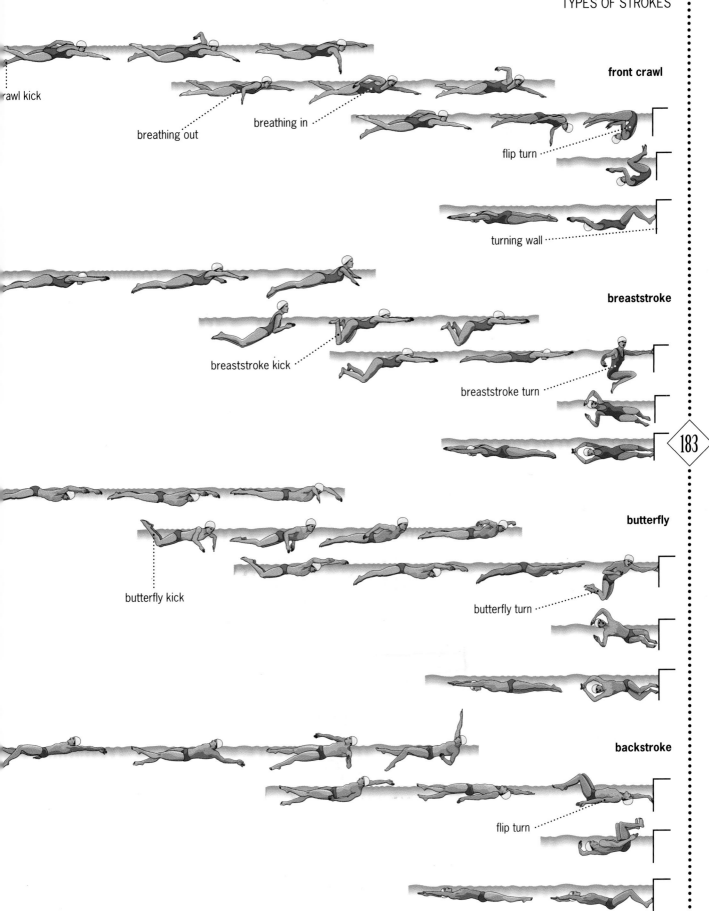

...awl kick

breathing out

breathing in

front crawl

flip turn

turning wall

breaststroke

breaststroke kick

breaststroke turn

butterfly

butterfly kick

butterfly turn

backstroke

flip turn

SAILBOARD

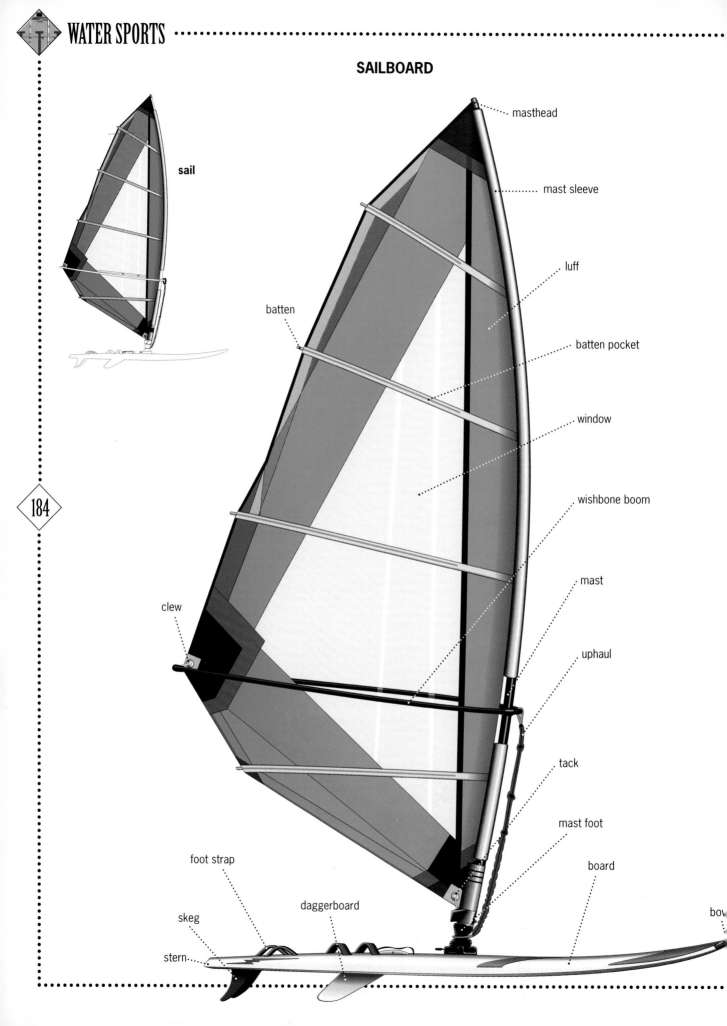

sail

masthead

mast sleeve

luff

batten

batten pocket

window

wishbone boom

mast

uphaul

clew

tack

mast foot

foot strap

board

daggerboard

skeg

bow

stern

SKATING

roller-skate

inner boot

upper shell

adjusting buckle

boot

axle

wheel

truck

heel stop

figure skate

hook

backstay

eyelet

boot

stanchion

edge

blade

tongue

lace

sole

toe pick

speed skate

hockey skate

tendon guard

boot

toe box

point

blade

skate guard

SKIING

alpine skier

ski boot

ski hat

ski goggles

ski suit

ski glove

tongue

upper strap

buckle

adjusting catch

lower shell

upper shell   hinge

wrist strap

ski pole

basket

handle

186

edge

tip

shovel

bottom

ski stop

groove

toe piece

ski boot   ski

heel piece

cross-country ski

heelplate   toe binding

tail   toeplate   clamp   shov

safety binding

anti-friction pad

brake pedal

manual release

ski stop

heel-piece

toe-piece

cross-country skier

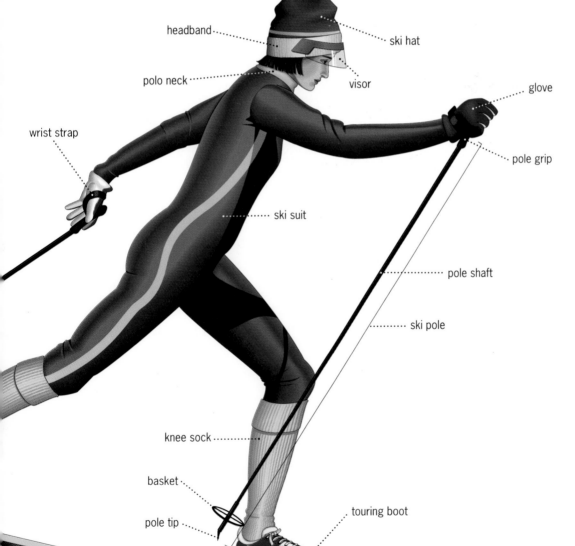

headband

ski hat

polo neck

visor

wrist strap

glove

pole grip

ski suit

pole shaft

ski pole

knee sock

basket

touring boot

pole tip

cross-country ski

187

GYMNASTICS

pommel horse

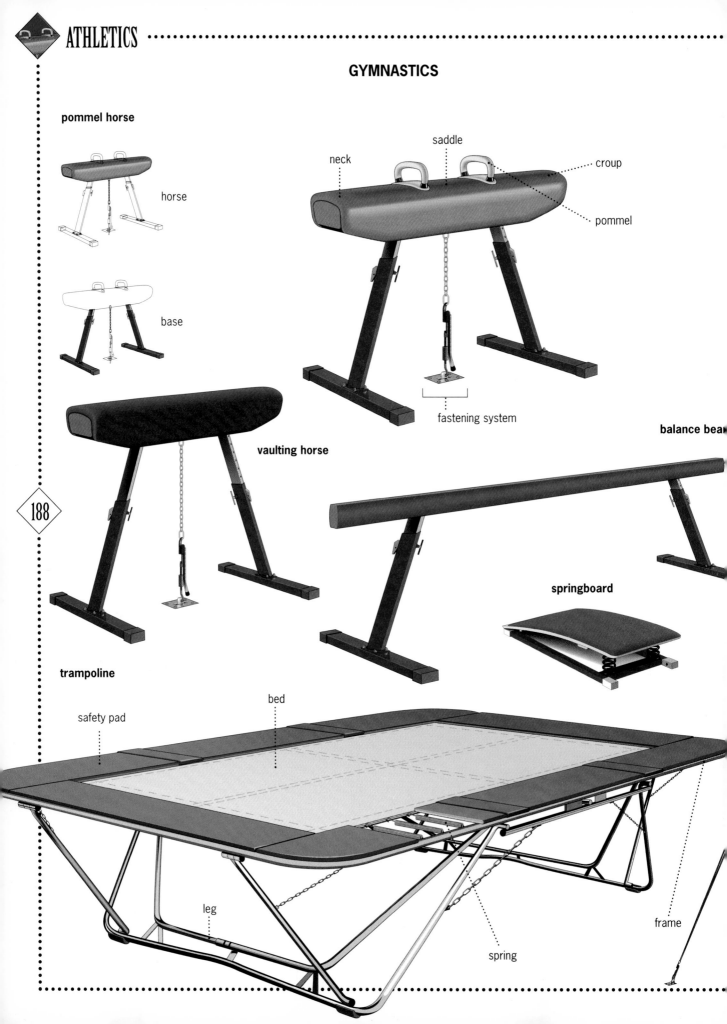

horse

base

neck

saddle

croup

pommel

fastening system

vaulting horse

balance bea

springboard

188

trampoline

safety pad

bed

leg

frame

spring

symmetrical bars

horizontal bar; high bar

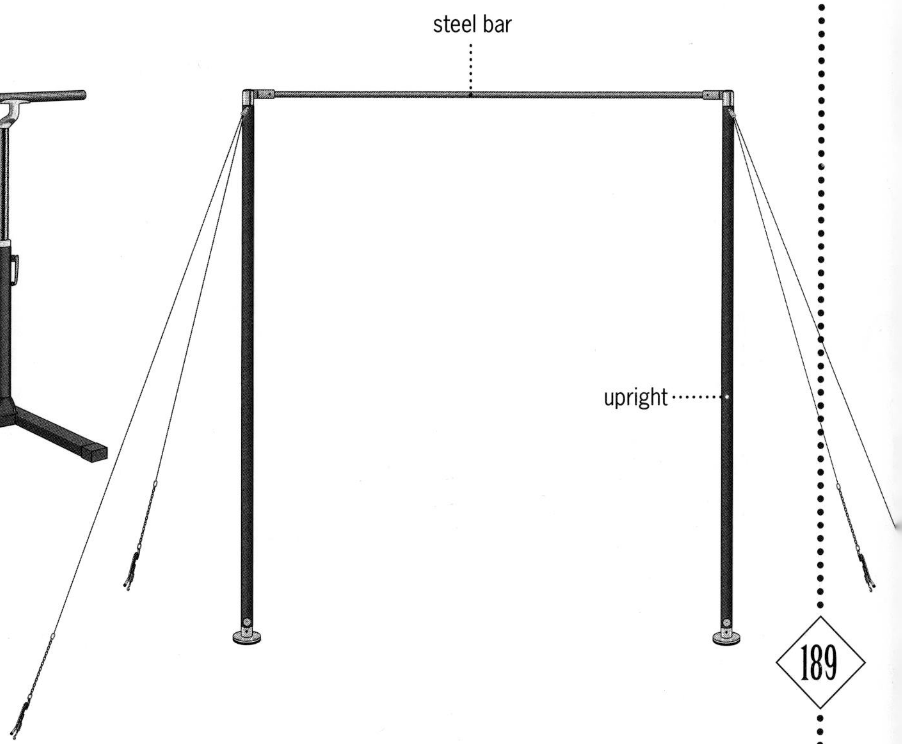

steel bar

upright

ngs

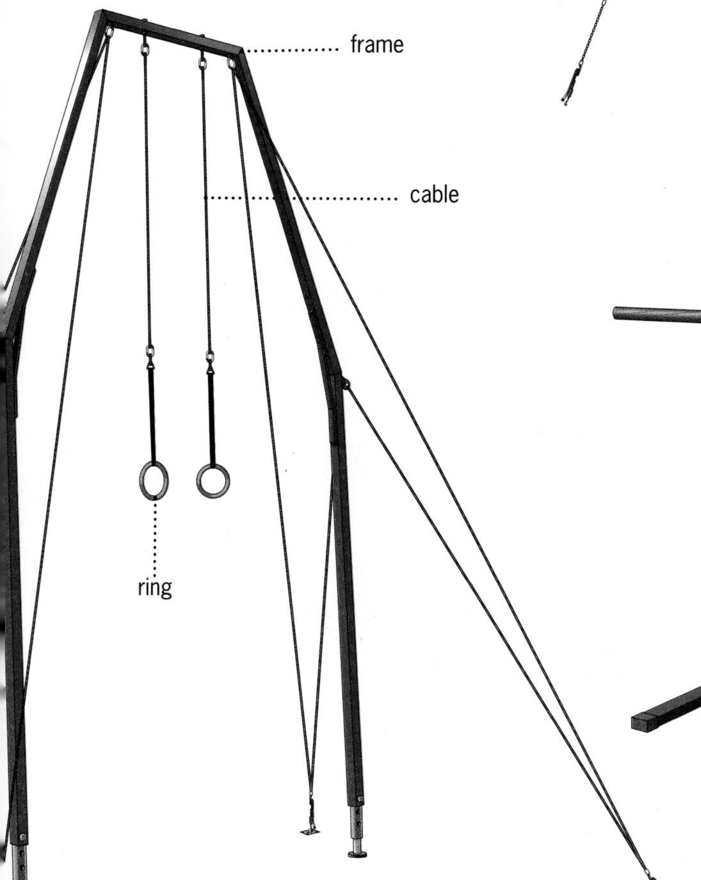

frame

cable

parallel bars

ring

TENTS

two-person tent

rainfly

door

awning

guy line

strainer

zipper

inner tent

stake

MAJOR TYPES OF TENTS

wagon tent

wall tent

pup tent

dome tent

pop-up tent

family tent

one-person tent

SLEEPING EQUIPMENT

foam pad

self-inflating mattress

BEDS AND MATTRESSES

inflator

inflator-deflator

folding cot

SLEEPING BAGS

rectangular

semi-mummy

air mattress

mummy

CAMPING EQUIPMENT

Swiss army knife

scissors

ruler

fish scaler

magnifier

file

small blade

cross-tip screwdriver

bottle opener

screwdriver

screwdriver

nail nick

large blade

awl

can opener

corkscrew

leather sheath

knife

flashlight

hatchet

sheath

plate

COOKING SET

coffee pot

frying pan

cup

canteen

handle

saucepa

backpack

top flap

shoulder strap

side compression strap

internal frame

waist belt

tightening buckle

strap loop

front compression strap

first aid kit

magnetic compass

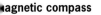

cover

sight

sighting mirror

sighting line

magnetic needle

pivot

scale

edge

compass card

graduated dial

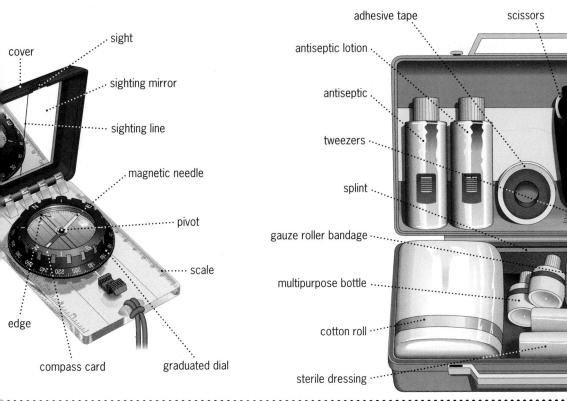

adhesive tape

antiseptic lotion

antiseptic

tweezers

splint

gauze roller bandage

multipurpose bottle

cotton roll

sterile dressing

scissors

small bandage

CARD GAMES

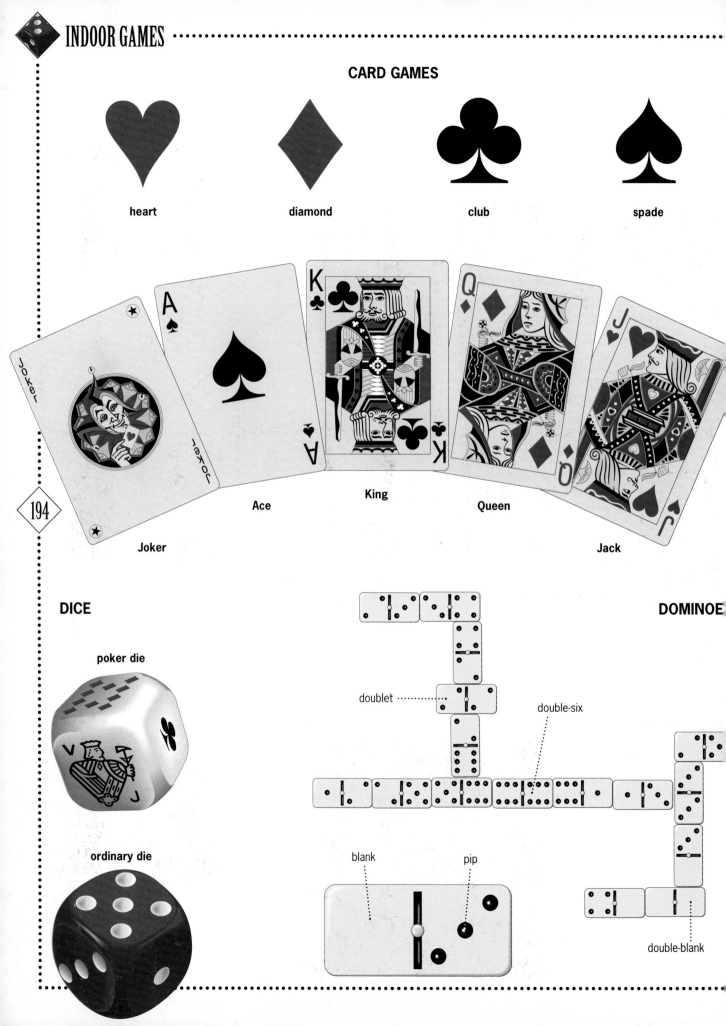

heart

diamond

club

spade

Joker

Ace

King

Queen

Jack

194

DICE

poker die

ordinary die

DOMINOE

doublet

double-six

blank

pip

double-blank

CHESS

chessboard

MEN

Queen's side   King's side

Black

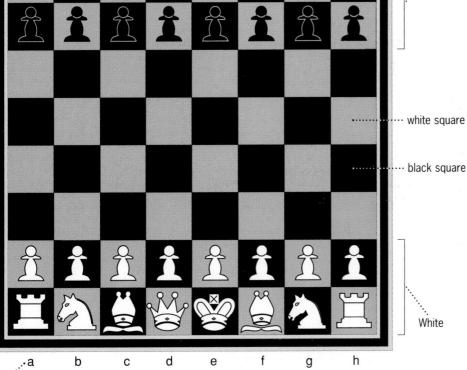

white square

black square

White

a b c d e f g h

chess notation

Pawn

Knight

Bishop

Rook

types of movements

vertical movement

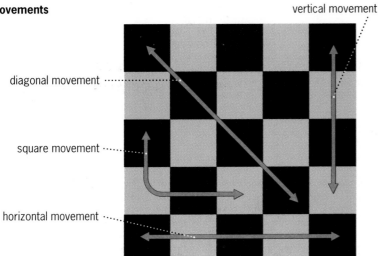

diagonal movement

square movement

horizontal movement

Queen

King

BACKGAMMON

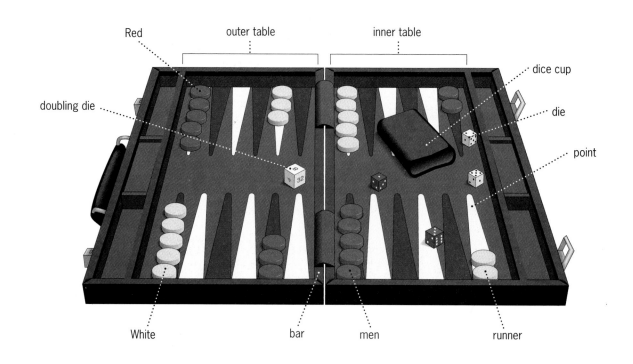

Red

outer table

inner table

dice cup

doubling die

die

point

White

bar

men

runner

CHECKERS

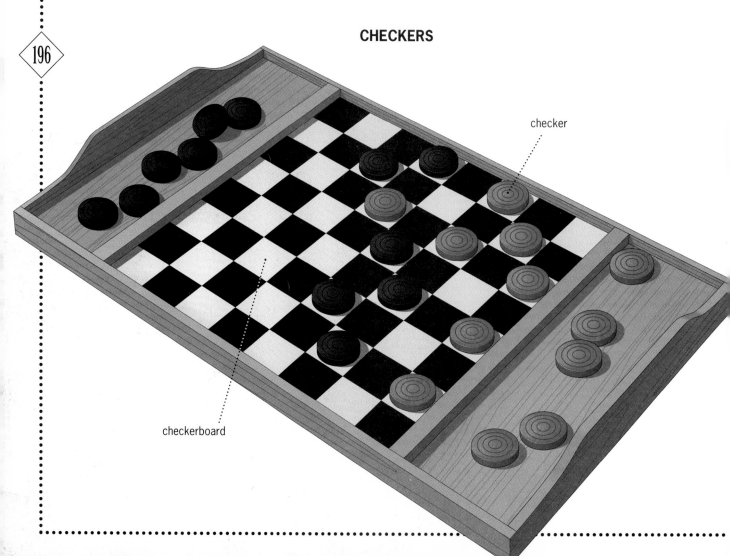

checker

checkerboard

VIDEO ENTERTAINMENT SYSTEM

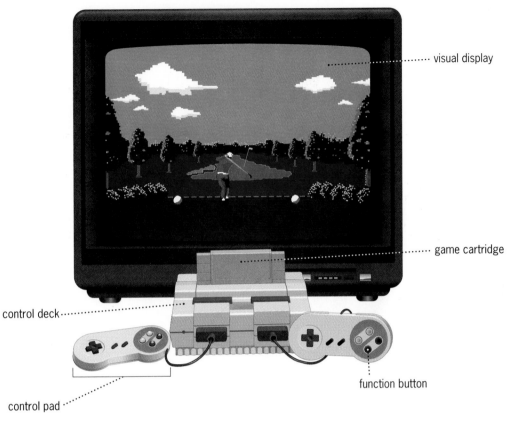

visual display

game cartridge

control deck

function button

control pad

GAME OF DARTS

dart

dartboard

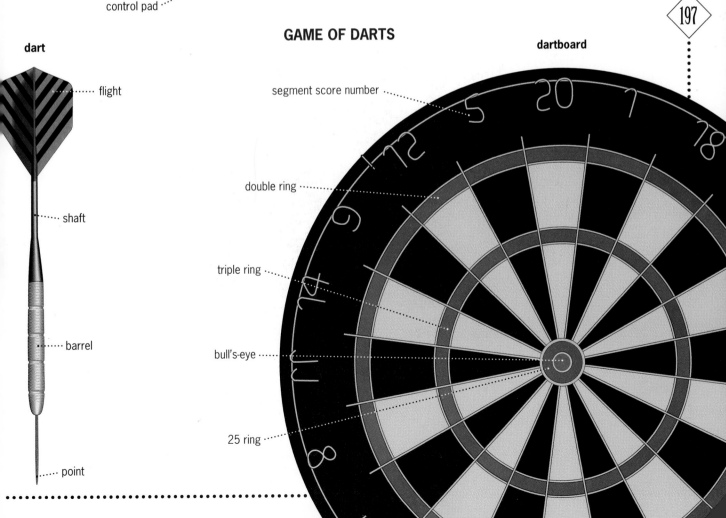

flight

segment score number

shaft

double ring

triple ring

barrel

bull's-eye

25 ring

point

MEASURE OF TIME

stopwatch

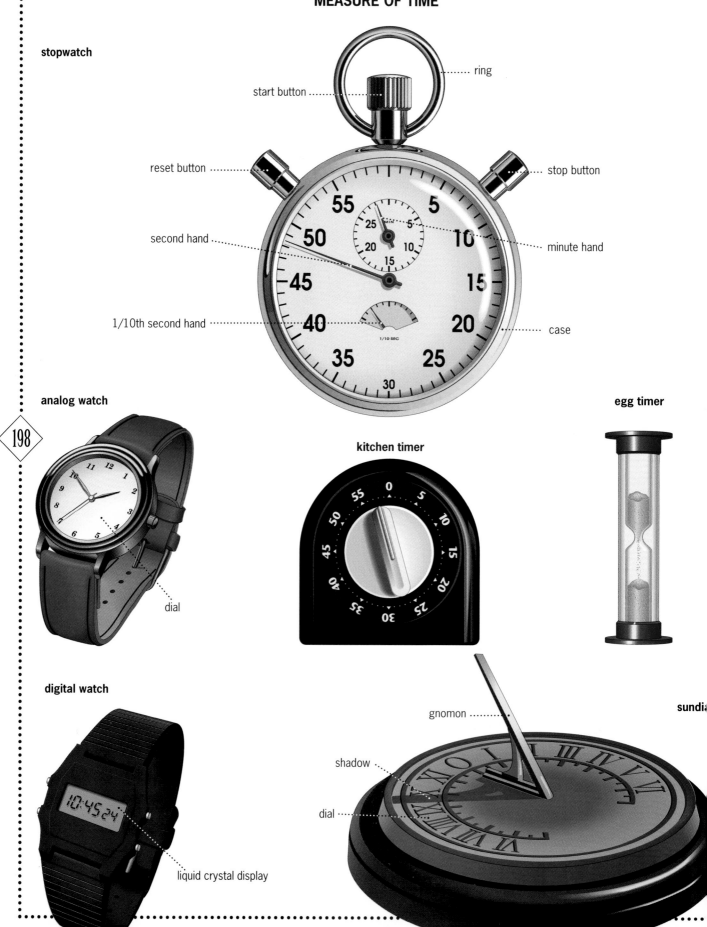

ring

start button

reset button

stop button

55

5

50

10

second hand

minute hand

25 MIN 5

20 10

15

45

15

1/10th second hand

40

20

1/10 SEC

case

35

25

30

analog watch

198

12
11 1
10 2
9 3
8 4
7 5
6

dial

kitchen timer

0
55 5
50 10
45 15
40 20
35 25
30

egg timer

digital watch

10:45 24

liquid crystal display

gnomon

sundial

shadow

dial

MEASURE OF TEMPERATURE

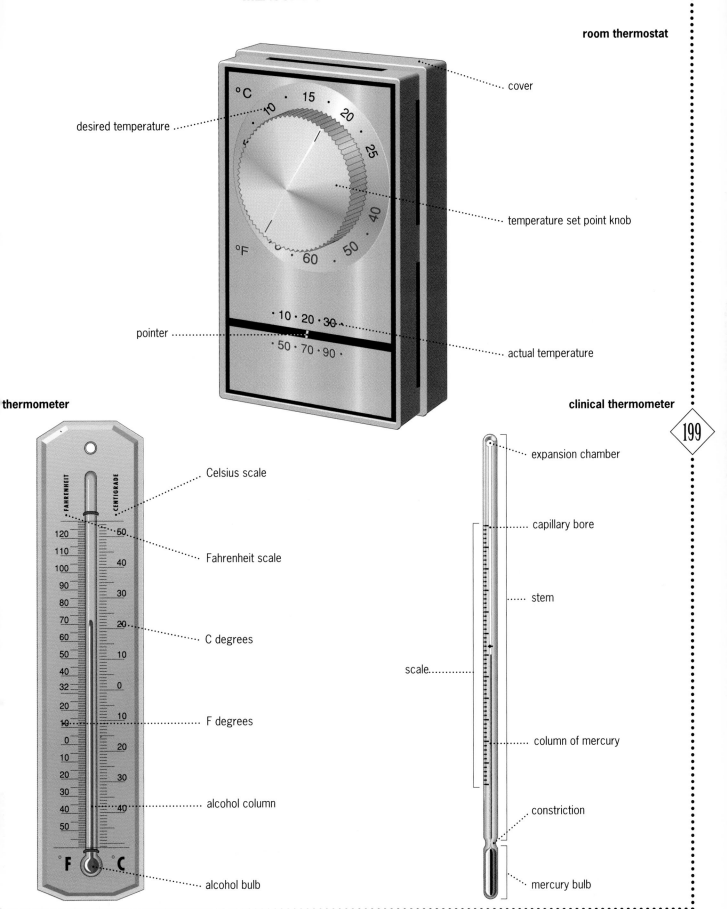

cover

desired temperature

°C

15

10

20

25

40

°F

60

50

temperature set point knob

pointer

• 10 • 20 • 30 •

• 50 • 70 • 90 •

actual temperature

thermometer

FAHRENHEIT   CENTIGRADE

Celsius scale

Fahrenheit scale

120   50
110   40
100
90   30
80
70   20
60
50   10
40
32   0
20
10   10
0
10   20
20
30   30
40
50   40

°F   °C

C degrees

F degrees

alcohol column

alcohol bulb

clinical thermometer

expansion chamber

capillary bore

stem

scale

column of mercury

constriction

mercury bulb

MEASURE OF WEIGHT

balance

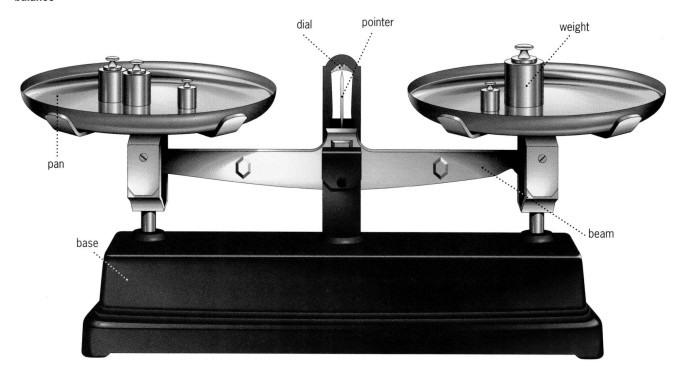

dial

pointer

weight

pan

base

beam

200

steelyard

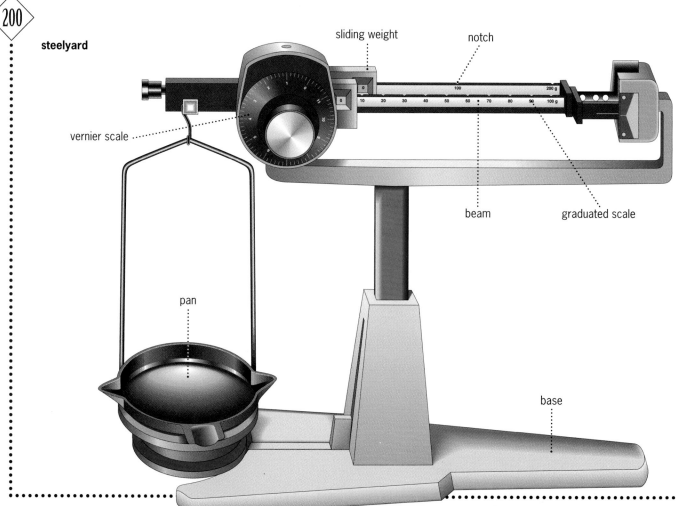

sliding weight

notch

vernier scale

100

200 g

10   20   30   40   50   60   70   80   90   100 g

pan

beam

graduated scale

base

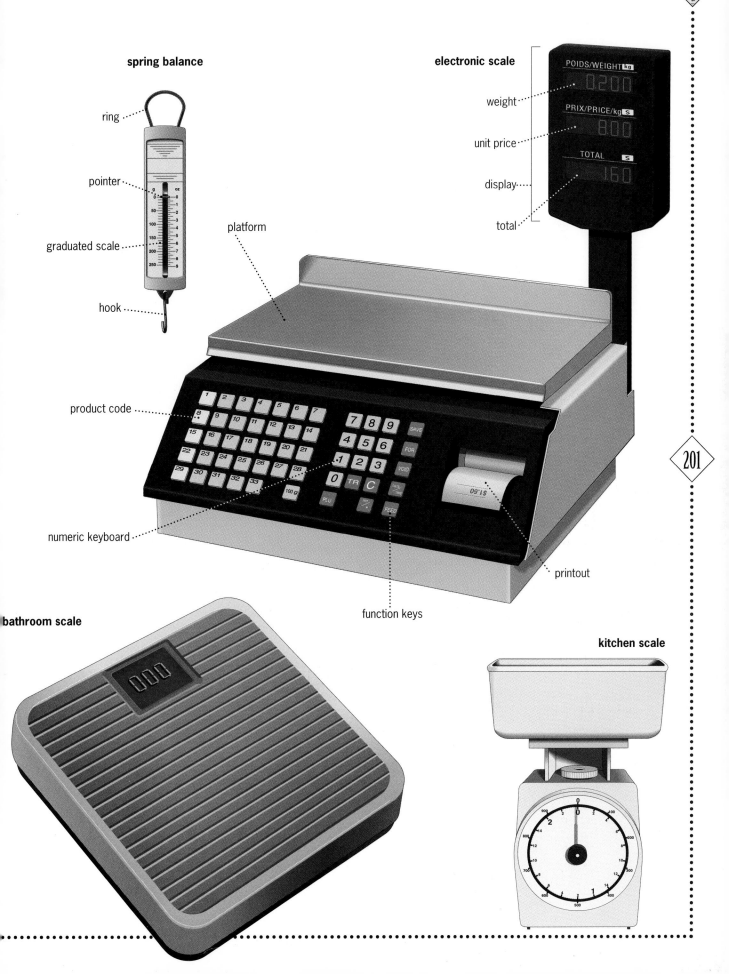

spring balance

ring

pointer

graduated scale

hook

platform

electronic scale

weight

unit price

display

total

POIDS/WEIGHT kg

0.200

PRIX/PRICE/kg S

8.00

TOTAL S

1.60

product code

numeric keyboard

SAVE

FOR

VOID

TR C

PLU

FEED

100 g

function keys

printout

$1.60

bathroom scale

kitchen scale

OIL

PROSPECTING

surface prospecting

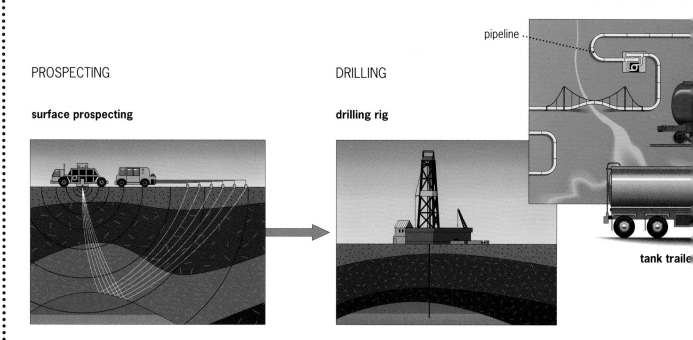

pipeline

DRILLING

drilling rig

tank traile

offshore prospecting

production platform

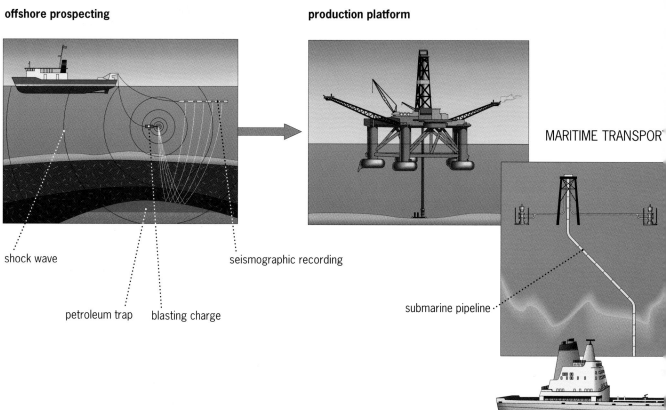

shock wave

seismographic recording

petroleum trap   blasting charge

MARITIME TRANSPOR

submarine pipeline

REFINERY PRODUCTS

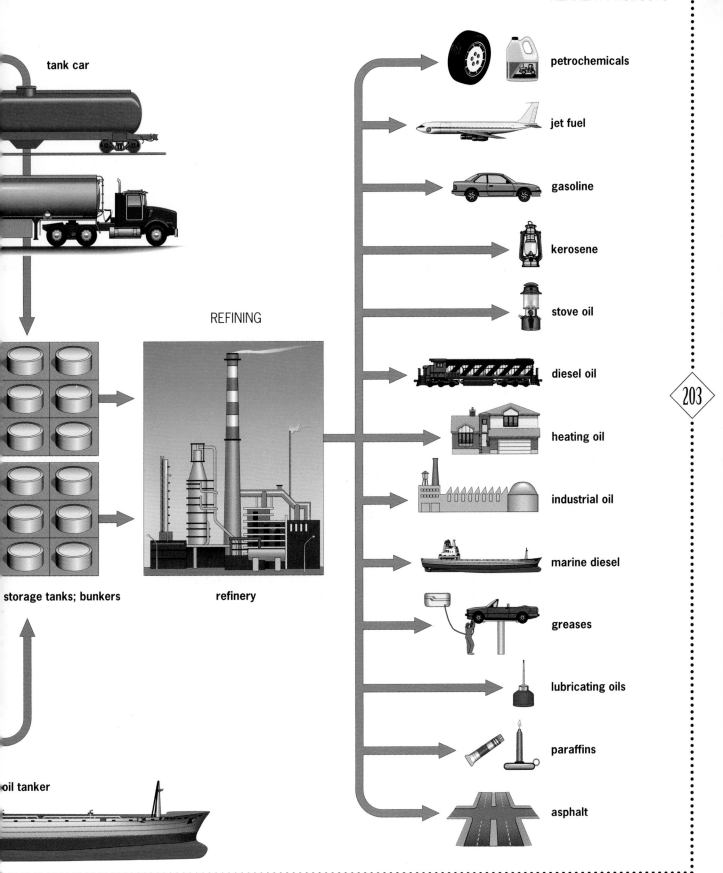

tank car

REFINING

storage tanks; bunkers

refinery

oil tanker

petrochemicals

jet fuel

gasoline

kerosene

stove oil

diesel oil

heating oil

industrial oil

marine diesel

greases

lubricating oils

paraffins

asphalt

HYDROELECTRIC ENERGY

hydroelectric complex

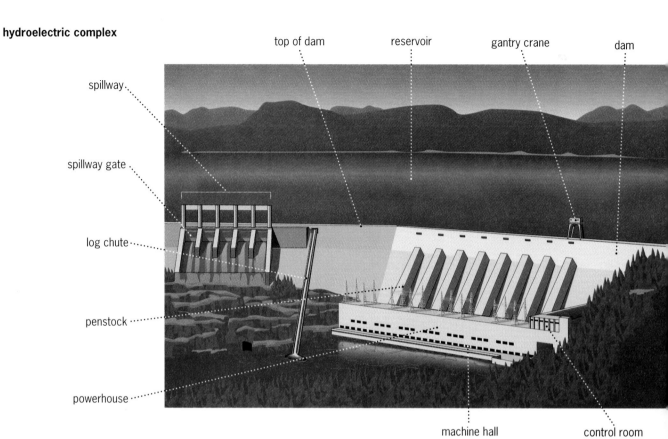

spillway

spillway gate

log chute

penstock

powerhouse

top of dam

reservoir

gantry crane

dam

machine hall

control room

cross section of hydroelectric power station

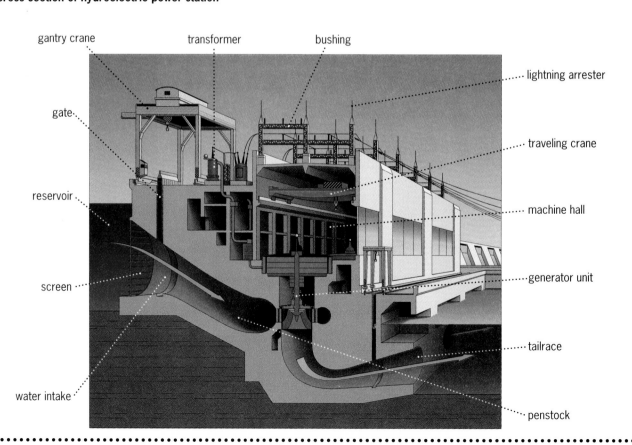

gantry crane

transformer

bushing

lightning arrester

gate

traveling crane

reservoir

machine hall

screen

generator unit

water intake

tailrace

penstock

electric circuit

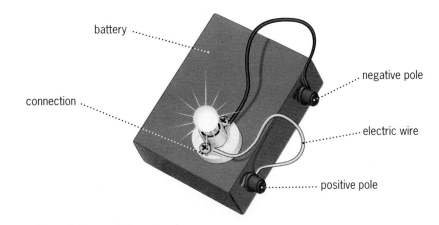

battery

connection

negative pole

electric wire

positive pole

steps in production of electricity

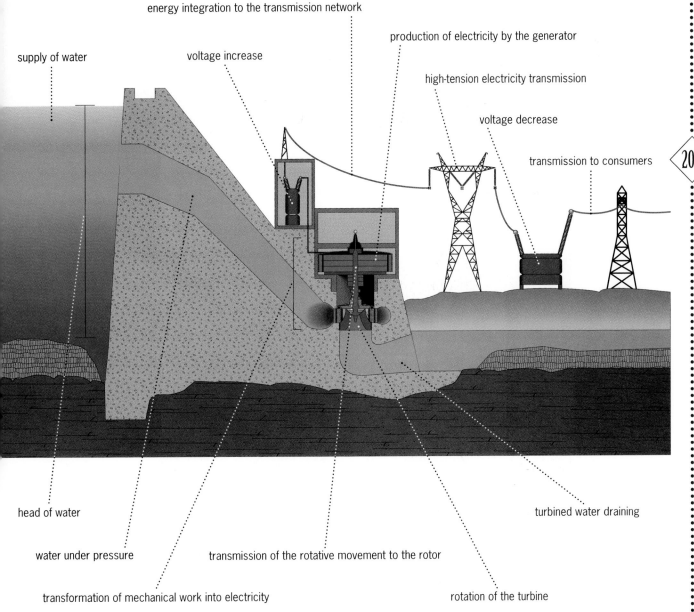

supply of water

energy integration to the transmission network

voltage increase

production of electricity by the generator

high-tension electricity transmission

voltage decrease

transmission to consumers

head of water

turbined water draining

water under pressure

transmission of the rotative movement to the rotor

transformation of mechanical work into electricity

rotation of the turbine

NUCLEAR ENERGY

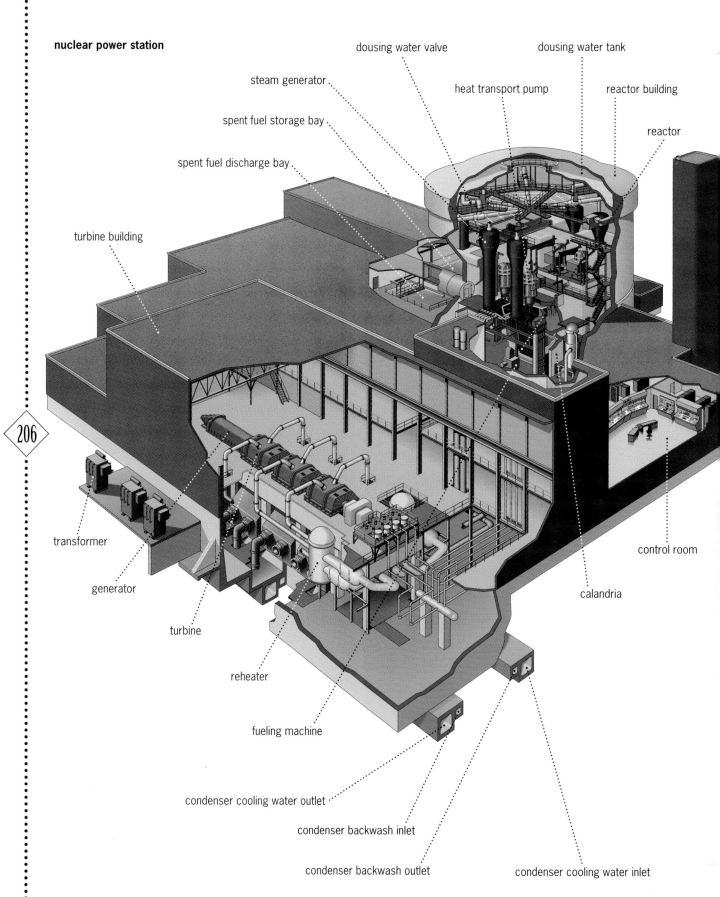

nuclear power station

dousing water valve

dousing water tank

steam generator

heat transport pump

reactor building

spent fuel storage bay

reactor

spent fuel discharge bay

turbine building

transformer

control room

generator

calandria

turbine

reheater

fueling machine

condenser cooling water outlet

condenser backwash inlet

condenser backwash outlet

condenser cooling water inlet

production of electricity from nuclear energy

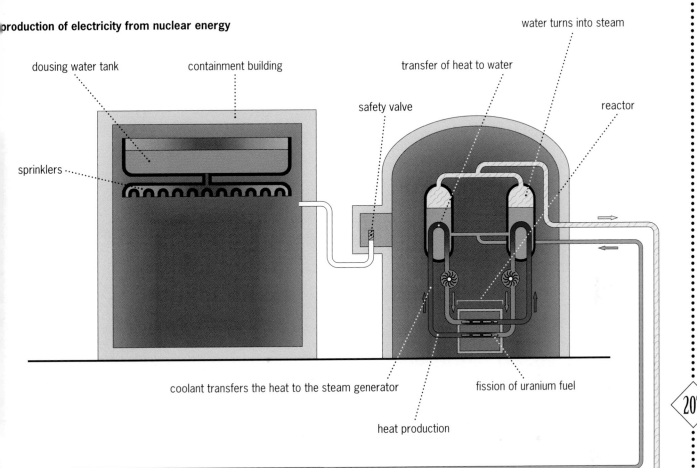

dousing water tank

containment building

water turns into steam

transfer of heat to water

safety valve

reactor

sprinklers

coolant transfers the heat to the steam generator

fission of uranium fuel

heat production

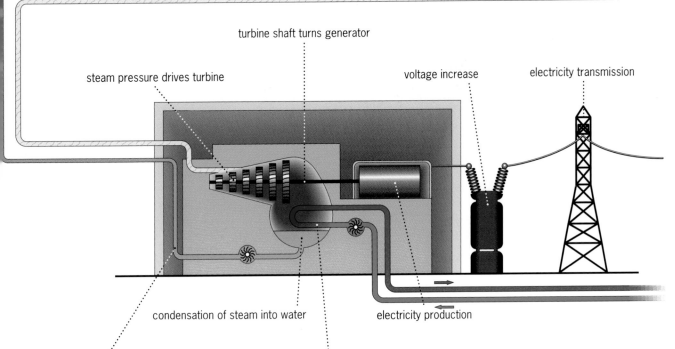

turbine shaft turns generator

steam pressure drives turbine

voltage increase

electricity transmission

condensation of steam into water

electricity production

water is pumped back into the steam generator

water cools the used steam

ENERGY

SOLAR ENERGY

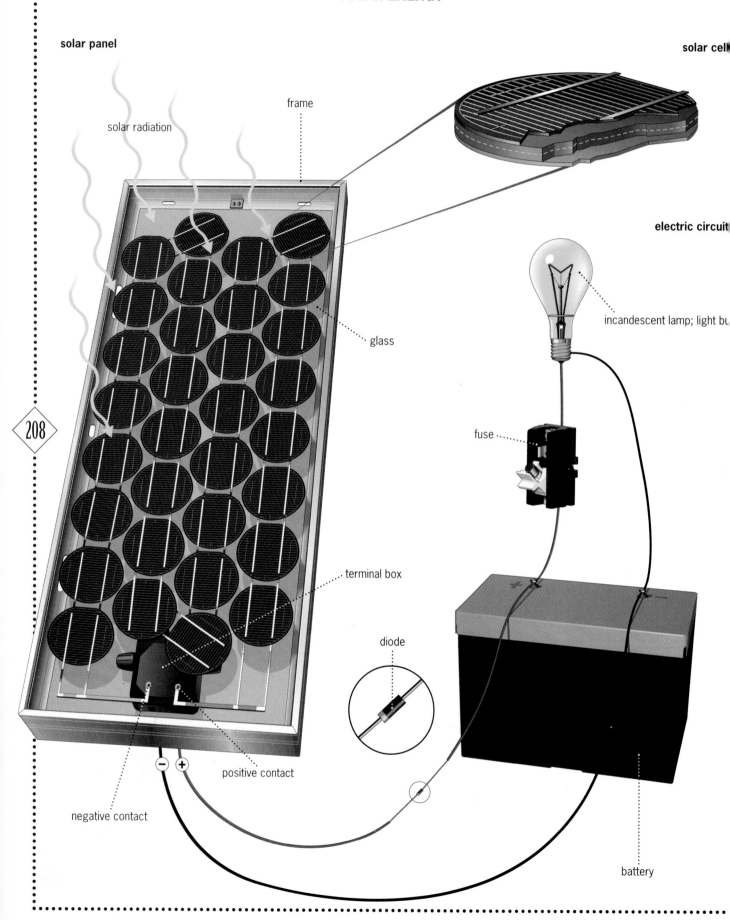

solar panel

solar cell

frame

solar radiation

electric circuit

glass

incandescent lamp; light bulb

fuse

terminal box

diode

positive contact

negative contact

battery

208

WIND ENERGY

horizontal-axis wind turbine

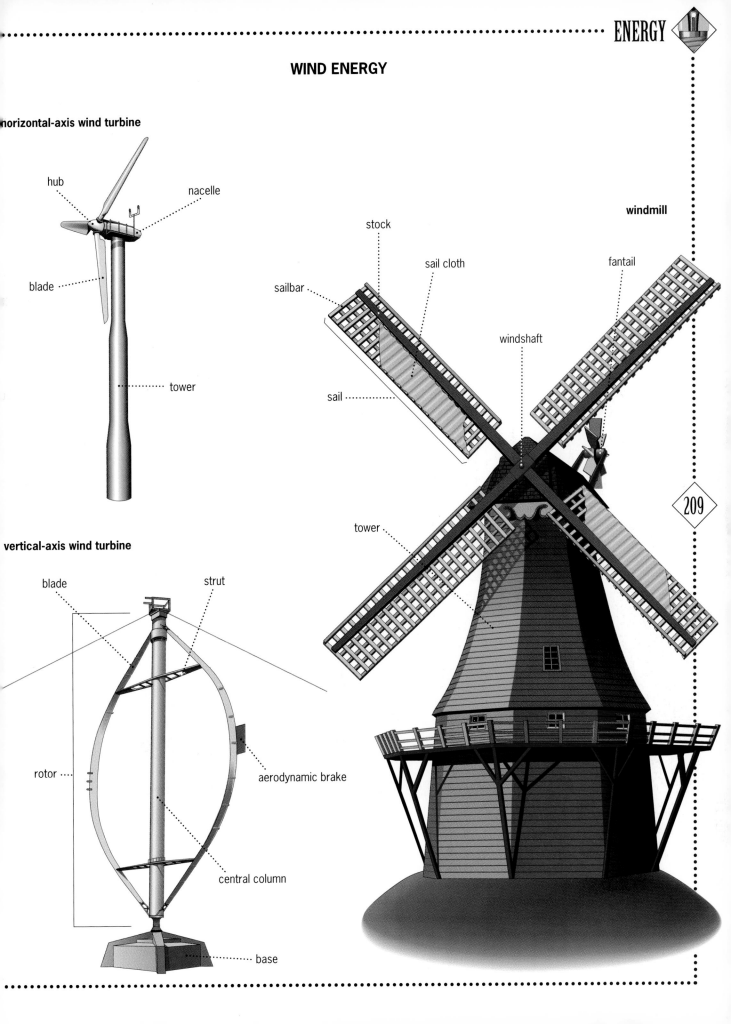

hub

nacelle

blade

tower

vertical-axis wind turbine

blade

strut

rotor

aerodynamic brake

central column

base

windmill

stock

sail cloth

sailbar

fantail

windshaft

sail

tower

FIRE PREVENTION

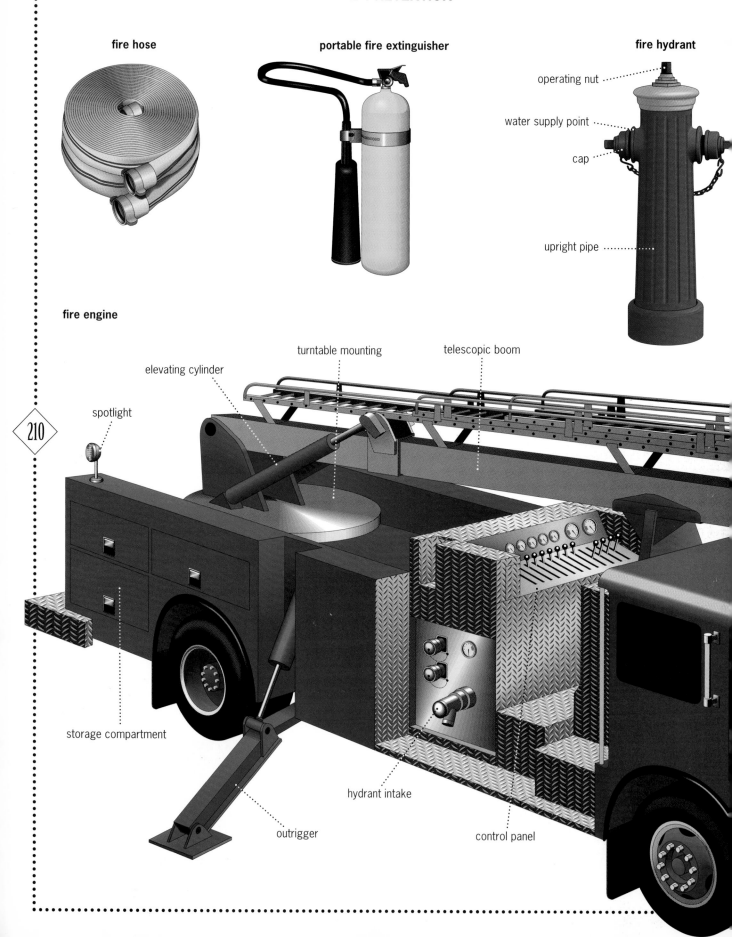

fire hose

portable fire extinguisher

fire hydrant

operating nut

water supply point

cap

upright pipe

fire engine

turntable mounting

telescopic boom

elevating cylinder

spotlight

storage compartment

hydrant intake

outrigger

control panel

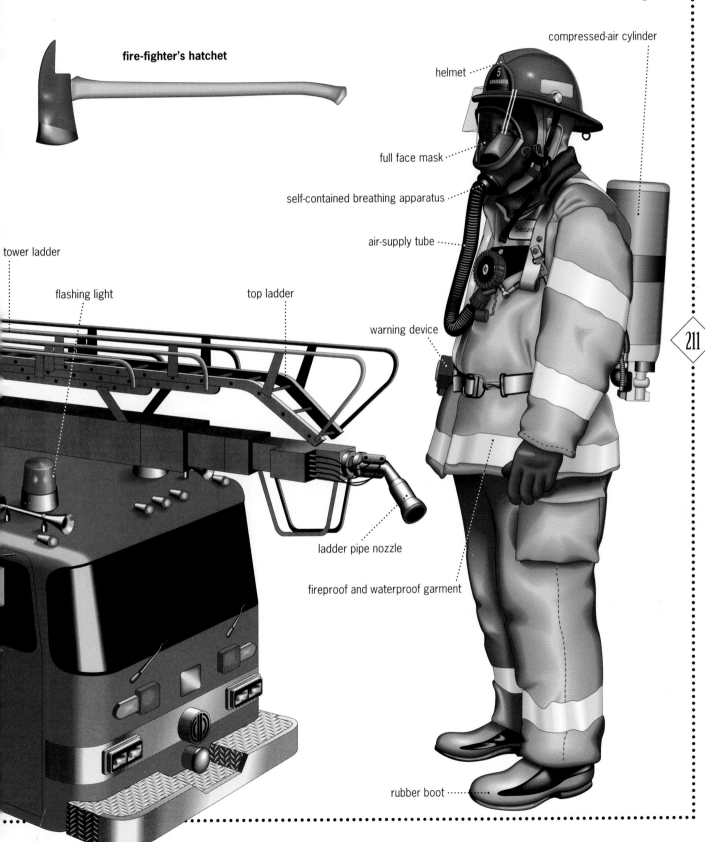

pike pole

fire-fighter's hatchet

fire-fighter

compressed-air cylinder

helmet

full face mask

self-contained breathing apparatus

air-supply tube

tower ladder

flashing light

top ladder

warning device

ladder pipe nozzle

fireproof and waterproof garment

rubber boot

211

HEAVY VEHICLES

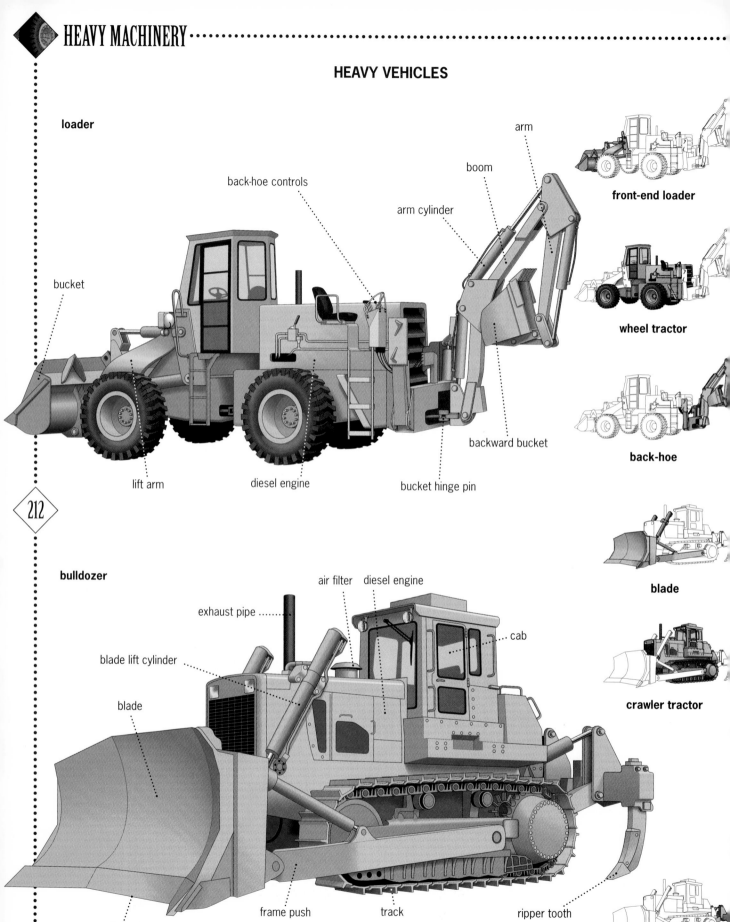

loader

arm

boom

back-hoe controls

arm cylinder

bucket

backward bucket

lift arm   diesel engine   bucket hinge pin

front-end loader

wheel tractor

back-hoe

212

bulldozer

air filter   diesel engine

exhaust pipe ....

blade lift cylinder

cab

blade

cutting edge   frame push   track   ripper tooth

blade

crawler tractor

ripper

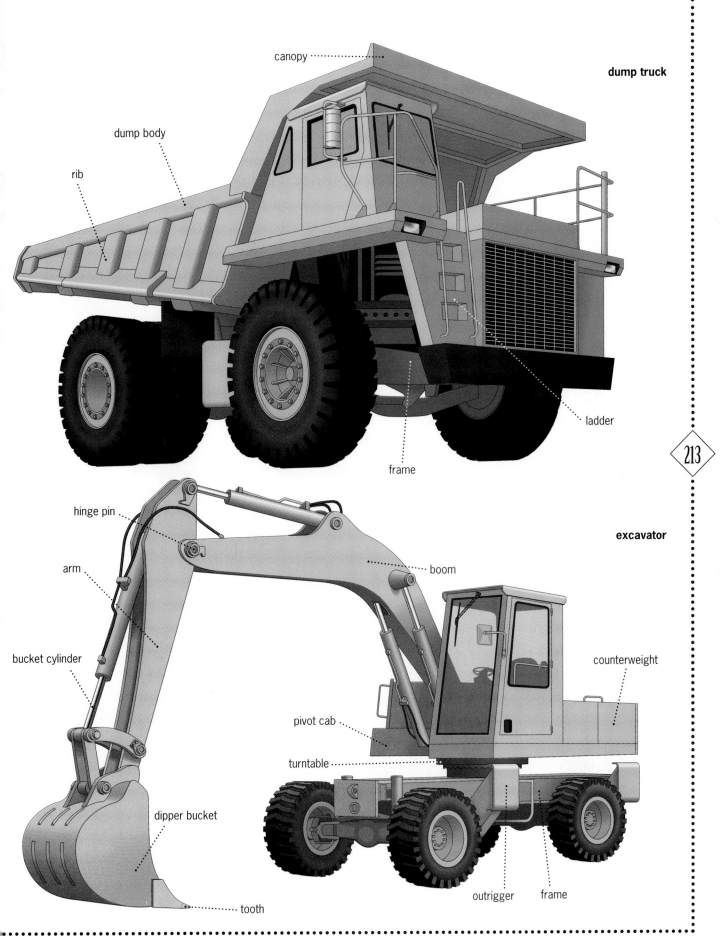

dump truck

canopy

dump body

rib

ladder

frame

excavator

hinge pin

arm

bucket cylinder

boom

counterweight

pivot cab

turntable

dipper bucket

tooth

outrigger

frame

HEAVY MACHINERY

tower crane

jib

trolley

crane runway

trolley pulley

operator's cab

hoisting rope

hoisting block

hook

street sweeper

collection body

central brush

watering tube

lateral brush

tower mast

projection device

snowblower

worm

DANGER

counterweight

214

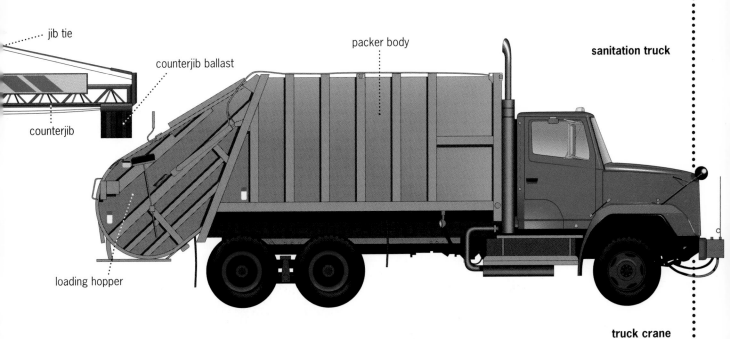

jib tie

counterjib ballast

counterjib

packer body

sanitation truck

loading hopper

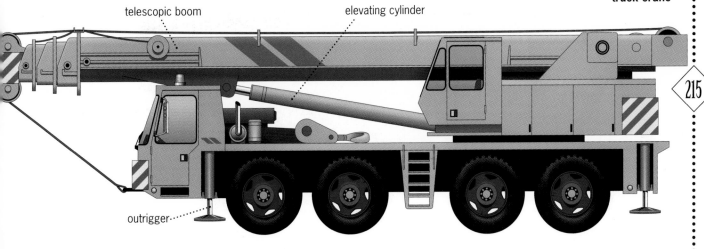

truck crane

telescopic boom

elevating cylinder

215

outrigger

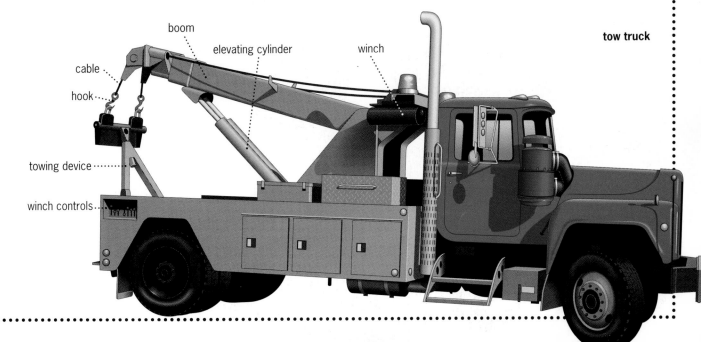

tow truck

boom

elevating cylinder

winch

cable

hook

towing device

winch controls

SYMBOLS

COMMON SYMBOLS

women's rest room

men's rest room

wheelchair access

hospital

telephone

no smoking

camping (tent)

camping prohibited

stop at intersection

SAFETY SYMBOLS

corrosive

electrical hazard

explosive

flammable

radioactive

poisonous

PROTECTION

eye protection

ear protection

head protection

hand protection

foot protection

respiratory system protection